THE COMMUNICATIVE BODY

Northwestern University
Studies in Phenomenology
and
Existential Philosophy

THE COMMUNICATIVE BODY

Studies in Communicative Philosophy, Politics, and Sociology

John O'Neill

Northwestern University Press   Evanston

1989

Northwestern University Press
Evanston, IL 60201

© 1989 by John O'Neill
All rights reserved. Published 1989
Printed in the United States of America

Library of Congress Cataloging-in-Publication Data

O'Neill, John, 1933-
　　The communicative body : studies in communicative
　philosophy, politics, and sociology / John O'Neill.
　　　　p. cm.
　　Includes index.
　　ISBN 0-8101-0801-1.—ISBN 0-8101-0802-X (pbk.)
　　1. Communication—Philosophy. 2. Sociology—Philosophy.
　3. Philosophical anthropology. I. Title.
　P90.O5 1989
　302.2'01—dc20   89-3436
　　　　　　　　　　　　　　　　　　　　　　　　　　　　　　CIP

This is Susan's book.

Contents

Acknowledgments

Some of the essays in this volume were revised from the following original publications and are used here with permission: "Phenomenology in the Natural Attitude," "The Structures of Behavior," "The Phenomenology of Perception," "Corporeality and Intersubjectivity," "Institution, Language, and Historicity," and "Between Montaigne and Machiavelli: The Life of Politics" from *Perception, Expression, and History: The Social Phenomenology of Maurice Merleau-Ponty* (Evanston, Ill.: Northwestern University Press, 1970); "Childhood and Embodiment" from A. Dreitzel, ed., *Recent Sociology No. 5* (New York: Macmillan, 1973); "The Specular Body: Merleau-Ponty and Lacan on Infant Self and Other" from *Synthese* 66 (1986); "The Prose of the World" from Maurice Merleau-Ponty, *The Prose of the World,* ed. Claude Lefort, trans. John O'Neill (Evanston, Ill.: Northwestern University Press, 1973); "Situation, Action, and Politics in Sartre and Merleau-Ponty" and "Can Phenomenology Be Critical?" from *Sociology as a Skin Trade* (London: Heinemann, 1972); "The Phenomenological Critique of Marxist Scientism" from *Canadian Journal of Social and Political Theory* 2:1 (Winter 1978); "*Introitus:* A Phenomenology of Approach," "The Place of Sociology in the Conversation of Mankind," "Communicative Sociology and Its Circumstance," "The Holy Watch: A Meditation upon Method in the Human Sciences," and "Concluding Sociological Prayer" from *Making Sense Together* (London: Heinemann, 1974).

ACKNOWLEDGMENTS

The following publishers have generously given permission to use extended quotations from copyrighted
works: from *A Death in the Family,* by James Agee. Copyright 1957 by the James Agee Trust. Reprinted by permission of Grosset & Dunlap and Peter Owen; from *The
New Science of Giambattista Vico—Revised Translation of the
Third Edition (1744),* by Thomas Goddard Bergin and Max
Harold Fisch. Copyright 1968 by Cornell University Press.
Reprinted by permission of the publisher; from *The Teachings of Don Juan: A Yaqui Way of Knowledge,* by Carlos Castaneda. Originally published by the University of
California Press. Reprinted by permission of the Regents
of the University of California; from *The Praise of Folly,* by
Erasmus, trans. Hoyt Hopewell Hudson. Copyright 1941
by Princeton University Press. Reprinted by permission
of the publisher; from *Let Us Now Praise Famous Men* by
Walker Evans and James Agee. Copyright 1960 by Walker
Evans; renewed 1969 by Mia Fritsch Agee. Reprinted by
permission of Houghton Mifflin Company and Peter
Owen; from "The Voice of Poetry in the Conversation of
Mankind," in *Rationalism in Politics,* by Michael Oakeshott.
Copyright 1962 by Michael Oakeshott. Reprinted by permission of Basic Books and Methuen & Co., Ltd.; from
The Duino Elegies, The Ninth Elegy, by Rainer Maria Rilke,
trans. J. B. Leishman and Stephen Spender. Copyright
1939 by W. W. Norton and Co. Reprinted by permission
of the publisher; from *The Making of Americans,* by Ger-
trude Stein. Reprinted by permission of Harcourt Brace
Jovanovich.

PART   1

COMMUNICATIVE PRAXIS

Preface

Communicative

Praxis

In this study I propose to set forth the very basic concepts of Merleau-Ponty's phenomenological analysis of the specifically human body, that is, that visceral body whose capacity for language and society is the foundation of all other institutions, whether of political economy, history, or science, or of philosophy, the arts, and psychoanalysis. I shall call this body the *communicative body*. I do so in order to convey the fundamental claim that we are born into a world of institutions of which the human body is the necessary organ, furnishing the bio-text upon which the principal social institutions inscribe themselves. This is possible because institutions, as we now see,[1] operate through discursive codes that inscribe the body's organs, senses, labor, and reproduction. Thus we can say that, on the one hand, we have the bodies we have because they have been inscribed by our mythologies, religions, philosophies, sciences, and ideologies. But, on the other hand, we can also say that we have our philosophies, mythologies, arts, and sciences because we have the body we have—namely, a communicative body. This is the great insight of Vico's *New Science* of our humanity. It is also the very heart of Freud's discovery of psychoanalysis. Merleau-Ponty's phenomenology has no such explicit links with

3

Vico as it has with Freud and Lacan. Yet it can be said
that Merleau-Ponty's concept of mind as an institution, which we shall develop later on, complements the
Viconian concept of human institution grounded as it is,
at first, in the generically human body and only later
ruled by the autonomy of rational mind. The recuperation of the first order of embodied communication is central to the task of phenomenological critique in Husserl,
Heidegger, and Merleau-Ponty. As such, it is considered
a necessary step in recovering the forgetfulness in the
presumption of rational mind to complete cultural autonomy. This is the presumption that divides the mind against
the body, science against art, adults against children, and
technical cultures against native cultures. It is a presumption that has always met with some resistance in the
humanities and arts, to which both science and religion
often provided a common front. In this respect, it might
be said that Marx and Freud are outstanding counter-
cultural figures inasmuch as they fought in one case to
deliver the human body from the pain of labor and in
the other to release the body of incommunicable pain so
that we might all express ourselves in the risen body of
the communicative community. The regulative principles
of such a human society have been formulated by Habermas, but he largely ignores the phenomenological tradition, despite his more recent attention to the problems
of the life-world threatened with colonization by the rational sciences. Although it is important not to attribute
more foresight to Merleau-Ponty than the issues in his
society allowed, I think it is worth stressing the unity of
his studies in phenomenology, politics, history, and language. In this way, Merleau-Ponty's thought provides us
with a standard for tackling some of the central issues
that concern us in the communicative theory and practice
of the human sciences. Above all, he offers us a model of
patient reflection undaunted by ambiguity and resistant
to the equal exercises of subjectivism and antihumanism
that have marked the decades since his death in 1961.

At several points in this study, in particular where I
compare Sartre and Lacan with Merleau-Ponty, I empha-
size the priority of consensus over conflict and I insist that
alienation must be grounded in a first intersubjectivity of

self and world given with the mother-body. This argument is developed at length and is not simply a naïve
insistence upon a metaphysics of presence. It is not metaphysical in any abstract or arbitrary sense because, as we
understand it from Merleau-Ponty, it is the human body
that is the metaphysical subject of the world—and thereby
of history and politics. It is this subject that is presupposed in the Hegelian and Lacanian dialectics of desire,
and it is because Sartre starts from an alienated body that
he has such trouble in constructing anything but a wholly
voluntarist politics that in turn subject an inert proletariat
to the will of the Party and its determined theorists. In
short, I am arguing for the inseparability of the will to
consensus and of the will to conflict within an overriding
coexistence of humanity given with our very birth, and
that is why I have also developed Merleau-Ponty's studies
of the infant body. The gist of this argument is nicely
expressed in the following remark by Merleau-Ponty:

My awareness of constructing an objective truth would never
provide me with anything more than an objective truth for
me, and my greatest attempt at impartiality would never
enable me to prevail over my subjectivity (as Descartes so well
expresses it by the hypothesis of the malignant demon), if I
had not, underlying my judgments, the primordial certainty
of being in contact with being itself, if before any voluntary
adoption of a position I were not already *situated* in an
intersubjective world, and if science too were not upheld by
this basic *doxa*. With the *cogito* begins that struggle between
consciousnesses, each by one of which, as Hegel says, seeks
the death of the other. For the struggle ever to begin, and for
each consciousness to be capable of suspecting the alien
presences which it negates, all must necessarily have some
common ground and be mindful of their peaceful coexistence in the world of childhood.[2]

I have therefore made some effort to develop the figures of generality, impersonality, and anonymity that articulate the human bond at the level of the arts and
sciences, including philosophy itself, so that these may be
kept in mind amid the current emphasis upon ideological
conflict, sexual difference, and rejection of any master
narrative in the human sciences. For there is a current

danger of losing sight of the original covenant whose realization is at times distant, especially since we must accept the paradox that we have no single authority in imposing its vision. It is for this reason, however, that we must project a *long* history of human history and maintain a constant vigilance against those powers and ideologies that claim to foreshorten it. It is such an enduring history of human history that in Part Two I have made the subject of what I have called *wild sociology*. Here I intend to defend the ordinary labor of commonsense knowledge and shared belief with which men and women have preserved, protected, and honored the human family. The civil beauty and historical endurance of this human institution have no doubt cost men and women and their children much suffering. At the same time, it has been their shelter and their memory. Today, the state and its social sciences aspire, in conjunction with those machineries that promise to do our living for us, to offer us an alternative civil matrix. This experiment, however, is not likely to succeed except where it can draw upon that great legacy bequeathed to each of us in the long history of the human family.[3] Nothing can turn back our determination to try the self's path. Yet our beginnings and our ends remain outside the self's orbit. Between these points we may still hope that our mythologies have not deserted us.

1

The
Communicative
Body

Human beings do not emit speech the way an electric bulb becomes incandescent. Rather, we have to think of speech as a form of conduct that is misconceived in idealist and empiricist accounts of it. The idealist account cannot make adequate sense of why it is that thought seeks completion in speech, why something is indistinct until we have found words for it, nor, above all, how we can begin to speak and write without yet knowing but in order to know what it is we mean to say. The same phenomena must be taken into account on the side of the listener who gathers our meaning from nowhere else than what we are embarked upon saying:

> In understanding others, the problem is always indeterminate because only the solution will bring the data retrospectively to light as convergent, only the central theme of philosophy, once understood, endows the philosopher's writings with the value of adequate signs. There is, then, a taking up of others' thought through speech, a reflection in others, an ability to think *according to others* which enriches our own thoughts. Here the meaning of words must finally be endured by the words themselves, their conceptual meaning must be formed by a kind of deduction from a *gestural meaning*, which is immanent in speech.[1]

Thus we feel our way into one another's thoughts, speech, and writing as we do into a foreign country whose life opens to us the more we are thrown into its local contexts, catching its style here and there, until we are able to launch ourselves as local characters in a café, or in a series of everyday interactions accomplishing what at first seemed impossible—namely, sense and intelligibility. All this is achieved once we no longer have to visualize the words we are looking for, once there is no longer a separable activity of searching the dictionary in our heads and from there composing sentences in accordance with the grammarians' laws. Rather, we throw ourselves into a linguistic context, finding our words as though we had a linguistic body that, like our first body, always knew viscerally what it needed to do in reaching, lifting, speaking, writing:

> I do not need to visualize external space and my own body in order to move within the other. It is enough that they exist for me, and that they form a certain field of action spread around me. In the same way I do not need to visualize the word in order to know and pronounce it. It is enough that I possess its articulatory and acoustic style as one of the modulations, one of the possible uses of my body.[2]

Therefore we do not add spoken language, so to speak, to the body's language, as though speech were a second language with greater affinities to our mind and only by necessity translated into sounds and script. We might, rather than speak as idealists or empiricists do, say that we have nothing in mind while speaking or writing. Only once we have said or written something can we discover, discuss, and modify our thought, usually with the aid of others present really or fictively. Writing and speaking, rather than being translations of thought, are more like music and drama, that is, performances consubstantial with their meaning, analyzable only after the play:

> The process of expression, when it is successful, does not merely leave for the reader and for the writer himself a kind of reminder, it brings the meaning into existence at the very heart of the text, it brings it to life in an organism of words, establishing it in the writer or the reader as a new sense organ, opening a new field or a new dimension into our experience.[3]

It is through our bodies that we communicate with the things and persons around us in a world that we do not first synthesize in the mind or only collect contingently through the senses. Our bodies are/ have from the very start a world that we articulate, so to speak, according to its sensory dimensions. Thus the spectacle of the world is properly there only for our body as the mirror of being. There can be no question, then, of reducing existence to embodiment or the latter to sexuality. Existence is not composed in any such way. What is fundamental is *the metaphysical structure of the body* that renders it an object for others and a subject for itself and makes it the ambiguous setting of mastery and servitude, desire and shame, autonomy and dependence. The metaphysical realm is therefore an opening in the world that is there first of all through the body rather than the mind. Our sexuality, then, is rather like a general dimension of this metaphysical body, a capacity for assuming specific sexual states and relationships. By the same token, our sexuality is always our own since it is inseparable from our own body; yet it is always something else since our own body is never totally within our conscious grasp:

> Why is our body, for us, the mirror of our being, unless it is a *natural self,* a current of given existence, with the result that we never know whether the forces which bear on us are its or ours—or with the result rather that they are never entirely its or ours.[4]

To inaugurate the concept of communication that derives from a phenomenology of bodily expression rather than from the mechanics of telecommunication, Merleau-Ponty invokes a myth of the original song of language in which nothing is conventional because its history from first to last is unthinkable according to any algorithm. Rather, speech is merely one of the irrational powers whereby the human body achieves expression: "to sing the world's praises and in the last resort to live it."[5] As such, speech effects a supervenient order of communication for which the human body appears always to have been articulated: "Speech is the surplus of our existence over our material being."[6] Of course, most of the time we dwell within the institution of a ready-made language whose original expressivity is no longer available to us. It falls to artists, poets, and musicians to awaken in themselves that originary speech that inaugurates human expression, and it is their efforts, rather than the dominant paradigm of the sciences of communication, that inspire Merleau-Ponty's phenomenology of expressive behavior.[7]

We begin by rejecting the model of a disembodied consciousness communicating in the mode of

1. transcendental autoaffection or the mind's conversation with itself prior to speech and writing (Derrida's critique of Husserlian phonocentrism[8])
2. the double black-box of two consciousnesses whose sole relation consists of the input-output of messages, or information without interpretation.

We rather conceive of the communication as an embodied, historical, and geographical relationship whose figures are the anthropomorphizing questions: who am I, who are you, what am I trying to say, what are you trying to say, do we understand each other? In short, the presence of an embodied consciousness to itself is from the beginning its copresence to a similarly embodied consciousness suspended in language whereby each explores its own horizon and overlap of spatial and temporal orientation in a world of things and persons, identities and purposes that are mine and thine.[9] Embodied consciousness cannot be oriented toward the unmediated presence of itself to itself, except in death. It is otherwise a familied, fraternal, discursive, and temporalized communicative activity both on the sensory and on the cognitive level. An embodied consciousness can only create a private life as a linguistic loop, so to speak, within its social life. Thus words may be used

a. to intend speaker's meaning; and similarly,
b. to indicate states of the speaker; or
c. to indicate the speakers' presumption of states in the *other* akin to (b), for example, earnestness or doubt;
d. as indexical and occasional expressions, for example, "I am happy here";
e. as objective expressions in an analytical language achieve the greatest abstraction from usages in (a)–(d).

The philosophically conceived transcendental consciousness only communicates with a (bracketed) world because it presumes upon its potency as a sophisticated-monologic speaker. Husserl confused

1. the truth of an expression given in intuitive evidence,
2. the meaning of an ("empty") expression given in a language, whether true or false.

Meaning is not repetitious because it can at any time be rendered present to a transcendental subject. Meaning is iterable because the linguistic signs, whose phonic immediacy Husserl confused with transcendental intuition, function in an anonymous semiotic system to represent inner and outside states, activities, and values of the world and persons.

We propose therefore to reverse the transcendental direction of the subject-object communication model and the traditional ontology that it presupposes, namely,

1. a sphere of consciousness: being-for-itself,
2. a sphere of objectivity: being-in-itself.

Thus Merleau-Ponty adopted the ontological postulate of the *primacy of perception,* that is, the naïve thesis that we inhabit the world through our body and that it is only through the languaged body that we achieve ideal generality or textuality. Our perceptual body can always vary its access to things and persons, just as at the level of the cultural body we can rethink an interpretation of another body's behavior. But in each case the corrigibility involved does not benefit from any universal perspective. Indeed, the latter presumption rests upon a notion of the disembodied eye, entrenched in optical culture. The critique of this assumption involves a reemphasis upon *sensory coenesthesia.* We must reembed vision in the seeing-seen body and rethink the domain of visibility, intersubjectivity, and language.

It may be useful to begin, as Merleau-Ponty does, with a look at Sartre's position on embodiment. Sartre divides embodiment into two essentially different orders of reality:

1. On the level of consciousness: "my-body-for-me"
2. On the level of objectivity: "my-body-for-others"

We can suspend the dualism of Sartre's *l'en-soi* and *le pour-soi* because every perception takes place in an atmosphere of generality and is presented to us anonymously. So that if I wanted to render precisely the perceptual experience, I ought to say that *one* perceives in me, and not that I perceive. Sensation can be anonymous only because it is incomplete—any sensation belongs to a certain *field.* To say that I have a visual field is to say that by reason of my position I have access to and an opening upon a system of beings, visible beings; that these are at the disposal of my gaze in virtue of a kind of primordial contact and through a gift of nature, with no effort made by me, from which it follows that *vision is prepersonal.* The sensory modes overlap unless I thematize them, as what precisely am I hearing, seeing, touching:

> Synaesthetic perception is the rule, and we are unaware of it only because scientific knowledge shifts the centre of gravity of

experience, so that we have unlearned how to see, hear, and generally speaking, feel, in order to deduce, from our bodily organization and the world as the physicist conceives it, what we are to see, hear and feel.[10]

The unity of the thing, its transcendent presence-absence, derives from the metaphysical unity of the *body image,* which is open and limitless. Thus perception grasps a first or antepredicative unity of the world whose physiognomy it in turn reverberates on the level of language and the concept where we articulate the world's intelligibility as an ideal community:

> We are not, then, reducing the significance of the word, or even of the percept, to a collection of "bodily sensations" but we are saying that the body, in so far as it has "behaviour problems", is that strange object which uses its parts as a general system of symbols for the world, and through which we can consequently "be at home in that world, understand it and find significance in it."[11]

Perception does not constitute the perceived; it is sunk in it and has to alter the preperceptual synthesis that my body has already rendered habitual and sedimented. What and how one sees derive from this *perceptual tradition;* the perceiving body secretes temporality (it's late, I'm getting tired, this is too heavy). Lived time, then, is continuously synthesized, whereas philosophical reflection always presupposes an unreflective, original past:

> The true *cogito* is not the intimate communing of thought with the thought of that thought; they met only on passing through the world. The consciousness of the world is not *based* on self-consciousness: they are strictly contemporary. There is a world for me because I am not unaware of myself; and I am not concealed from myself because I have a world.[12]

The perceptual synthesis is the same thing as the body's temporality, that is, the perceptual tradition in which its specific sensations arise, are present, and fade without any absolute beginning or end. The human senses present us with a coherent, unified experience because they are synthesized in the knowing body, where they immediately translate one another:

> My body is the fabric into which all objects are woven, and it is, at least in relation to the perceived world, the general instrument of my "comprehension."[13]

Even our sexual body is misconceived if we think of it as the subject of states of arousal excited within us from an outside body whose own sexuality is similarly set in motion. Nor are things improved if we think of sexuality in terms of experiences we project upon other bodies according to their "heterosexualizability" whose modalities erogenize the body in a gendered history of relations that range from flirtation to copulation, happiness, and sorrow:

> Erotic perception is not a *cogitatio* which aims at a *cogitatum;* through one body it aims at another body, and takes place in the world, not a consciousness . . . in so far as a man's sexual history provides a key to his life, it is because in his sexuality is projected his manner of being towards the world, that is, towards time and other men.[14]

Thus we should not simply explain the anorectic's rejection of food as due to oral fixation. Rather, in order to reject the relation that opposes a young girl's desire to see her young man, a daughter must refuse her mother's conversation and food because only then can she excommunicate herself. She thereby protests a forbidden relation by rejecting the very communicative grounds of her being. From the mother's side, we might rather speak of an oral fixation since she wishes her daughter to live on this level without communicating her sexuality in accordance with her own life. In all this the anorectic theater is not played out in the mind, nor on the body, but at another level, where our anonymous life opens to or refuses the rest of our living:

> Loss of voice as a situation may be compared to sleep: I lie down in bed, on my left-side, with my knees drawn up; I close my eyes and breathe slowly putting my plans out of my mind. But the power of my will or consciousness stops there. As the faithful, in the Dionysian mysteries, invoke the god by miming scenes from his life, I call up the visitation of sleep by imitating the breathing and posture of the sleeper. The god is actually there when the faithful can no longer distinguish themselves from the part they are playing, when their body and their consciousness cease to bring in, as an obstacle, their particular opacity, and when they are totally fused in the myth. There is a moment when sleep "comes", settling on this imitation of itself which I have been offering to it, and I succeed in becoming what I was trying to be: an unseeing and almost unthinking mass, riveted to a point in space and in the world henceforth only through the anonymous alertness of the senses. It is true that this last link makes waking a possibility:

> through these half-open doors things will return or the sleeper will
> come back into the world. In the same way the patient who has
> broken with co-existence can still perceive the sensible integument
> of other people, and abstractly conceive the future by means, for
> instance, of a calendar. In this sense the sleeper is never completely
> isolated within himself, never totally a sleeper, and the patient is
> never totally cut off from the intersubjective world, never totally ill.
> But what, in the sleeper and the patient, makes possible a return to
> the real world, and are still only impersonal functions, sense organs
> and language.[15]

Our body is the very ground of our presence and withdrawal from
the world, but never so absolutely that I am in the world like a stone
or removed from it like a dead man. My body cannot not project for
itself its sensory world, its living sense for itself and for things and
others around me:

> In this way the body expresses total existence, not because it is an
> external accompaniment to that existence, but because existence
> comes into its own in the body. This incarnate significance is the
> central phenomenon of which body and mind, sign and significance
> are abstract moments.[16]

My body is never in the world for me as objects are; it can never be
absent as they can. Yet it is not present to me as are my thoughts, as
a continuous flow of consciousness. How is it in between? My body
is the setting and instrument of my world, like my eyes, which I never
see but through which I see everything else and have the same visibility as anything or anyone else. I do not have another body with
which I explore my own body. Rather my *own body (corps propre)* is
such that all other bodies can be there for me and for themselves:

> In order that my window may impose on me a point of view of the
> church, it is necessary in the first place that my body should impose
> upon me one of the world; and the first necessity can be merely
> physical only in virtue of the fact that the second is meta-
> physical. . . .[17]

Thus neither my visual nor my tactile body is ever seen or touched
by me as a physical object without remainder. Rather, my body is that
whereby there are visibility and tactility as variations within a field of
primordial presence, the original structure of my own body, my basic
habit:

> Thus the permanence of one's own body, if only classical psychology has analyzed it, might have led it to the body no longer conceived as an object of the world, but as our means of communication with it, to the world no longer conceived as a collection of determinate objects, but as the horizon latent in all of our experience and itself ever-present and anterior to every determining thought.[18]

Objective science abstracts from the embodied genealogy of being that is the proper object of our concern. The psychology of perception, sensory experience, and judgment thereby constructed turns upon its presumption of

a. the ideal constancy of the object,
b. the absolute externality of the subject.

The critique of the constancy hypothesis (see Chapter 3) shows that what the science of perception reveals is more the perception of science itself as a historical and socially organized mode of inquiry than the first science of the lived body of which it is forgetful.[19]

It is this *communicative body* that we must fully explore if we are to understand how we make sense together. Thus in the touching-touched experience of one hand to the other there opens up "a kind of reflection," an affectivity that is the flesh of the world and nowhere else and nowise other than ourselves. All this is reduced to nothing in classical psychology, or else it is attributed to the refractoriness of the contents of consciousness that leave unaffected the physical body and its eventual reduction to the laws of consciousness. The disembodied standpoint of psychologist may well, of course, discover the regularities he seeks in *experimental bodies.* But this is possible precisely because these bodies are abstracted by a methodology suited to them but hopelessly inadequate to the exploration of the experience of the lived embodied subject for whom the unity of soul and body is a presumption in the discovery of his world and not another fact found in it:

> To be a consciousness or rather *to be an experience* is to hold inner communication with the world, the body and other people, to be with them instead of being beside them.[20]

We need to underwrite the official history of truth as philosophers have conceived it with an "organic history" that accounts for the real historicity of truth. To do so, we have to rediscover the spiritual interior of the lived body, to show that the human body is a psychophysical body whose aesthesiology makes it conformable to the world of things and persons in the same fashion as it is itself a *communis sensorum*. This is not discoverable outside language. All the same, language is preceded and always surrounded by those silent bodies of things and persons whose destiny of becoming speech we are trying to describe:

> The taking possession of the world of silence, such as the description of the human body effects it, is no longer this world of silence, it is the world articulated, elevated to the *Wesen*, spoken— the description of the perceptual λόγος is a usage of λόγος προφορικός.[21]

We are trying to rearticulate seeing, speaking, and thinking before they are organized around the mind and body or subject-object dualism:

> If we could rediscover within the exercise of seeing and speaking some of the living references that assign them such a destiny in language, perhaps they would teach us how to form our new instruments, and first of all to understand our research, our interrogation, themselves.[22]

The communicative body is the hinge of our world; it establishes an identity-within-difference that overrides the subject-object dualism of transcendental phenomenology. To understand this, we must return to the analysis of sense experience and its vital reference to the heavy mass of our body. We have to rediscover the basis for those intelligible clusters of meaning that form like the intentional tissue of our life without any ideal model before them, and yet without any merely contingent or strictly causal connection beneath them.

2

The Body
as a Work
of Art

A philosophy becomes transcendental, or radical, not by
taking its place in absolute consciousness without mentioning
the ways by which this is revealed, but by considering itself
as a problem; not by postulating in knowledge rendered
totally explicit, but by recognizing as the fundamental
problem this *presumption* on reason's part.[1]

The aim of Merleau-Ponty's *Phenomenology of Perception* is to de-
construct the aesthetics of logocentrism on the two fronts of
idealism and empiricism considered as disambiguating strategies
that in the end must be brought back to the ambiguity of perception and its proper phenomenology. Rather than follow the path
to this conclusion now (we shall take it up later), we shall move directly
to the analysis in the essays *Eye and Mind* and *The Visible and the Invisible*.
Here we encounter the problem in its uncanny form expressed in
the painter's remark that, when painting the forest, he felt that it was
he who was seen by the trees rather than he who was the agent of
vision. Now, nothing is gained from this reversal of vision if we try to
understand the vision of the trees on the same model as the painter's
own vision. This is because the thing in question is precisely the
painter's vision. Rather, it is the logocentric presumption underlying
his vision that the painter puts in question by interrogating the visibility of the trees from their side, from the side of their mutual being-
in-the-world of their mutual visibility-vision.

We need to move to the level of an elemental being in which
the distinctions among things, bodies, and persons are suspended in

the indivision of sensible being that I am and in which everything else senses itself—to a wild being or flesh of the world where the following apply:

1. The empirical self and body are not immediately given objects.
2. I can never say "I" absolutely.
3. Every act of reflection is based on the ground and the proposition of a prepersonal consciousness.
4. The sensible has not only a motor and vital significance, but is nothing other than a certain way of being in the world (as in this year's colors, or evening wear) suggested to us from some point in space, and seized and acted upon by our body, provided that it is capable of doing so, *so that sensation is literally a form of communion.*[2]
5. Sensations have a *sacramental value.* Thus I do not observe things except as one observes a custom, making its observance, repetition, and observation thereby a momentary and local law.
6. The blue sky before "thinks itself 'within me'" (Valéry); not the astronomer's sky, but the sky that offers me "the theatre of a certain living pulsation adopted by my body," like a winter sky, or an evening sunset.

In vision we are at grips with the things we speak of as though they were only at the ends of our vision or touch. At the same time, we are not totally possessed or swallowed up by them, since it is in us that they are visible, tangible, audible, expressible. Thus things are, on their side, not quite identical with themselves, and we, from our side, are not quite empty, open to any and all impressions. The world is not naked before our look because our gaze envelops it and seems to clothe it with our flesh and so too unveils its visibility:

> whence vision is question and response.... The openness through flesh: the two leaves of my body and the leaves of the visible world.... It is between these intercalated leaves that there is visibility.... My body model of the things and the things model of my body: the body bound to the world through all its parts, up against it all this means: the world, the flesh not as fact or sum of facts, but as the locus of an inscription of truth: the false crossed out, not nullified.[3]

Vision espouses its objects, envelops and marries them, like two bodies in one flesh. This is because we encounter things like persons whom we meet, finding retrospectively that what we call "love at first sight" turns out to have been a storyable "déjà vu," and in the course of our lives and relationships we had been looking for this love, already knowing her long before we ever saw, heard, or touched her. It is this body before the seen, heard, and touched body; beneath those bodies, our flesh, that drifted toward that first encounter that is prepared in us as a bride prepares for her wedding. Thus in perceiving, speaking, touching, listening to one another, our senses are married to one another, and each to each in understanding and in love. It is in some such way that the insides of the body cross over into the body's outside and are doubled in drawing out the insides of things—so that we may speak of this chiasma as the *body's inspiration,* breathing in and breathing out the world and other bodies of its own kind.

Between myself and the perceived world there is a certain density of things and my body that permits the two to ramify in one another, to be accessible in and through the midst of one another. Here we are not speaking of any anthropomorphism; it is not any projective effort of the human body. Rather, the mystery of the body's communion is a variant of the mystery of how it is that Being separates from itself. Thus we have to dwell upon how it is that the hand that can be touched and the eye that can be seen like any other thing in the world can nevertheless reverse this touch and vision, opening up the field of communicative Being. We want a way of understanding this kinship between the body and the world that makes them members of the same flesh and family. Thus the body is not in the world any more than one is in a family; the body is familied through and through, just as there are no families outside their embodied members.[4] The relationship, in short, cannot.be spatialized. Each member is a valence of the other so that the family from my point of view and I from the point of view of the family, although separate, are shot through with one another; and if the first view corresponds to our primary narcissism the second corresponds to a secondary narcissism. Each is the "element" of the other. We always see ourselves when we see our family. But, by the same token, we are always seen, resonated, and seduced by our family's view of us. And it is this we call flesh and communion, that in the end we have one body and one world, because we are inhabited by an anonymous sensibility that originates in no one of us and never closes entirely around any single thing or expression:

> for the first time, the body no longer couples itself up with the world, it clasps another body, applying [itself to it] carefully with its whole extension, forming tirelessly with its hands the strange statue which in its turn gives everything it receives; the body is lost outside

of the world and its goals, fascinated by the unique occupation of floating in Being with another life, of making itself the outside of its inside. And henceforth movement, touch, vision, applying themselves to the other and to themselves, return toward their source and, in the patient and silent labor of desire, begin the paradox of expression.[5]

Our birth, then, is not a point of origin but advenes upon a long interior history of the body that prepares it for the probable if not inevitable history of the sensory folding back of life upon itself in the opening fields of movement, vision, touch, and voice. Thus we know that we are human bodies because the world is conformable with our senses and with others' senses, even though our experience never completely overlaps with that of others and does not completely absorb the things at the ends of our senses but opens our living into those sensory fields through which we discover ourselves. We must conceive the relation between thought and our senses as a provisional separation, an invagination or folding back of the seen/seeing, the touching/touched, or as a transfiguration of the body's natural light, the voice of things, and the place where the flesh turns to word.

In order to speak and understand, I respond to clusters of meaning whose signs I could not possibly analyze anymore than a woman who adjusts her body or dress from a vague sense of being a body looked at, modulating her corporeal scheme and its world without formulating either—doing so imperceptibly, so to speak. And, indeed, these movements, though silent, do in fact begin to say something, to outline a meaning, an idea of the flesh. The latter is not above its objects but a difference between them on a certain level, that is, the carnal or wild being where I am inserted into the world and espouse its sensible ways. I thereby become pregnant in the double sense of responding in a typical and fecund way to the world's requirements of what is good for the body's senses. Thus the world and my flesh intertwine in an inscription that transposes the phenomenal and objective bodies but as configurations of a single being in the world integrated nowhere else:

> With life, natural perception (with the savage mind) is perpetually given to us the wherewithal to set up the universe of immanence— And yet, this universe tends of itself to become autonomous, realizes of itself a repression of transcendence—*The key is in this idea that perception qua wild perception is of itself, imperception, tends of itself to see itself as an act and to forget itself as latent intentionality, as being at——*[6]

Because we are embodied beings, our thoughts and senses are not our own activities, absolutely speaking, because we are already in the world as a world from which all our sensory activities, speech, and thought derive, but around a heartbeat that precedes them. Our mind is unthinkable except around its body: "There is a body of the mind, and a mind of the body and a chiasm between them."[7] The mind's body is not the objective body, not the body thought of the mind, but the phenomenal body, the field that reverses everything in it as sensible, as content or dimensionality of my being-in-the-world. The mind's body is a scheme of difference, of the doubling of the world's insides and outsides, of activity and passivity. It is nature, flesh, mother, preindividual and prepassive, as well as preproductive: "A philosophy of the flesh is the condition without which psychoanalysis remains anthropology."[8] Thus we have not to think of the Freudian archaeology of the body in terms of the positive stages of orality, anality, and genitality. Rather, these are differentiations of the founding ontological difference of our being that is flesh. And the task is not to explain behavior in terms of the causalities of psychoanalysis but to understand how we continuously invest in ourselves in our own reflected being,[9] living off our own reflections, that we are, so to speak, the mirror of being.

Although I would warn against any anachronistic attribution of postmodernity to Merleau-Ponty, I think it is fair to say that his meditations on structuralism go beyond that paradigm, while marking its achievements.[10] Merleau-Ponty's poststructuralism, if you will, lies on the side of his concept of the flesh of the world: the lived-body whose structures of practical relevance necessarily sediment into the body's habits and cultural gestures. The latter are indeed describable in terms of those binary codes that structuralists and deconstructionists make the object of their analysis. But what emerges from the conflict of these two interpretations can only be imagined if we try to interpret Merleau-Ponty's last meditations on the body's cathexis of being through which we live, so to speak, in our "element," that is, prior to the division between subject and object, inside and outside. Thus the color yellow is rather a universe than a skin of things, a mirror of transcendence without intentionality except in a body like ours, painting or glad, where it becomes transposable in thought and speech. The flesh of the world is that elemental being of ours that can be articulated into every other body, perception, and relation of ours. Its "in-division" funds every other division and difference in our world and as such is an inexhaustible explosion of Being, "the eternal body," or chiasm, as Merleau-Ponty calls it:

the idea of *chiasm*, that is: every relation with being is
simultaneously a taking and a being taken, the hold is held, it is
inscribed and inscribed in the same being that it takes hold of. . . .
    No *absolute* difference, therefore, between philosophy or the
transcendental and the empirical (it is better to say: the ontological
and the ontic)—No absolutely pure philosophical word.[11]

We might say that Merleau-Ponty's principle of difference—or flesh—
is the great mother body that generates every play of identity and
difference in the receptacle of Being (*Chora*), calling back all identities, theologies, and symbolic registers in order to disperse them in
new radiations of meaning and desire in the universal flesh of the
world. There is, so to speak, a conaturality of the world and ourselves,
like the overlap between the mother body and the infant body, which
dispossesses the narcissism of each one so that their relationship is
prior to the synergy between them. These two bodies are the element
of each other, and the body between them exceeds what can be found
in their biology, chemistry, and psychology. It is this carnal excess that
goes into language, art, mythology, and psychoanalysis through which
we explore ourselves as a universe upon which we have no extrater-
ritorial stance and that is entered only through the opening in Being
articulated with our birth.[12]

3

Phenomenology in the Natural Attitude

I n this chapter I will comment largely on the preface to *Phenomenology of Perception* (pp. vii–xxi). The phenomenological approach to the problems of perception and reflection seeks to avoid the antinomies that embroil idealism and realism. "The whole question is ultimately one of understanding what, in ourselves and in the world, is the relation between *significance* and *absence of signification*."[1] However, the results of a phenomenological critique are not to be gained except as a recovery of meaning from its alienation in philosophical idealism and realism considered as essential moments in the history of the Western spirit. There is no phenomenological result apart from the experience through which it comes about, in which it remains essentially open to its own history and the intersubjectivity of interpretation and critique.

"Phenomenology is accessible only through a phenomenological method."[2] Thus Merleau-Ponty lays upon any commentator the most stringent requirement for the comprehension of a philosophy that is self-consciously the recuperation of the history of philosophy and, therefore, as necessary to what it presupposes as it is impossible without what went before it and seemed always to presage it. To some it may seem that to pose the problem of interpretation in this manner is to intrude unnecessarily the style of Hegelian phenomenology whose dialectical certainties are entirely foreign to Husserl's "unfinished" phenomenology. It would be foolish, indeed, for the sake of a superficial expression, to introduce problems of comparative exegesis that might carry us far from our central theme, which is, as Merleau-Ponty expresses it, the problem of the relation among meaning, presence, and absence. What we have in mind is that in both Hegel and Husserl there is a dialectical relation between a presentification of meaning that is realized before (*für*) consciousness and the participation of consciousness in this process as its proper intentionality, essential to its full manifestation. That is to say, consciousness in the natural attitude is already an anticipation of consciousness-in-and-for-itself; its forgetfulness of itself is already the path by which it may come to self-recognition. But this means that a phenomenological reduction cannot pretend to suspend the existence or facticity that is presupposed by the negativity of consciousness nor can it recover any level prior to language and intersubjectivity as the presupposition of the dialectic of the self-recognition of consciousness.

It is not the intention, nor is it within the competency of this writer, to develop a phenomenology of phenomenology. What is attempted here is to follow a phase in the critical reconstruction of the history of phenomenology to be found in the highly original interpretation and inspiration that result from Merleau-Ponty's relation to Husserlian phenomenology. Such a procedure is justified not so much by the considerable knowledge of Husserliana that Merleau-Ponty possessed, for we are not interested primarily in documentation,[3] but by the light that it hopes to throw upon the *motivation* or style of the phenomenological reduction.

In Husserl's own confrontation with the problematic of the phenomenological reduction, Merleau-Ponty discerned a progressive integration of the eidetic and transcendental reductions as negative and positive moments in a reflection that withdraws us from the natural attitude only in order to reveal to us the project toward the world that we are. Thus the motive of the reduction is to restore us in wonder before a world that understands us in the same way that we understand the world.

> All the misunderstandings with his [Husserl's] interpreters, with the existentialist "dissidents" and finally with himself, have arisen from the fact that in order to see the world and grasp it as paradoxical, we must break with our familiar acceptance of it and, also, from the fact that from this break we can learn nothing but the unmotivated upsurge of the world. The most important lesson which the reduction teaches us is the impossibility of a complete reduction.[4]

There would be no motivation for the phenomenological reduction if we were absolute mind. The problem of motivation exists because, on the contrary, we are in the world and the process of reflection is carried out in a temporal flux in which we dwell and in which we perceive that the world is there already latent with our own future. Hence the motive for the phenomenological reduction is archaeological, a quest for our origins suspended in wonder at what it always knew was there to be found. There is an inversion at the heart of our teleology: the knowledge of last things awaits us from the very beginning.

In the preface to *Phenomenology of Perception*, we find Merleau-Ponty's raising the question, What is phenomenology?, still unanswered more than fifty years after Husserl's first works. But the lack of a definition and the absence of a phenomenological system are no reproach to phenomenology. Rather they are characteristic of its style as a reflection upon our openness toward the world as a solicitation prior to all categorization and predication. Thus Merleau-Ponty's account of the nature of phenomenology is, so to speak, a report in progress, both in its initial formulation and in the later reconsiderations that supplement it. Phenomenology is a philosophy that embraces antinomies. It is an eidetic analysis. Yet it considers the comprehension of man and the world impossible from any other basis than the facticity of existence. It is a transcendental philosophy that "puts out of play" the existence of the world as we hold to it in the natural attitude. But it does so only to recuperate the correlativity of the world and the intentionalities that bind us to it. Thus it proposes phenomenological descriptions of space, time, and the world as "lived experiences," while also professing to be a "rigorous science." And, as though to turn back upon his own starting point, Husserl in his later works speaks of a "genetic phenomenology," whereas he had professed to describe experience as it is, apart from the causal analysis of the natural and social sciences.

It is striking that Merleau-Ponty gives no prominence to the notion of intentionality in his presentation of phenomenology.[5] Too often considered the principal discovery of phenomenology, the concept of intentionality can in fact only be understood through the reduction. But the "problematic of reduction" is one that never ceased to concern Husserl. For this reason Merleau-Ponty is insistent that any attempt to develop phenomenology that takes the reduction as given is premature.[6] What must absorb our interest is precisely Husserl's emphasis upon the tension between the natural attitude and the results of phenomenological reflection. "C'est l'experience muette en-

core qu'il s'agit d'amener à l'expression pure de son propre sens."
Such a definition of the task of phenomenology renders it almost
impossible. How shall we bring brute experience to yield its meaning?
How shall we bring the silence of things into the discourse (*la parole*)
of philosophy? Thus understood, phenomenology is founded upon
a conflict and tension rather than upon a preestablished harmony.

Every reduction is necessarily both transcendental and eidetic.
That is to say, we are not able to submit the stream of our perceptions
to philosophical reflection without withdrawing from the flux of lived
experience and the world that we naturally posit. In philosophical
reflection we are obliged to pass from the *fact* of existence (*Dasein*) to
the *nature* (*Wesen*) or articulation of the world upon which our existence opens. Thus there can never be any coincidence between reflection and the stream of perception. For it is precisely the task of
reflection to disengage things and the world from the perception of
the world by subjecting them to a systematic variation that reveals
"intelligible clusters" that nevertheless retain an impenetrable aspect.
Thus, from the very fact that every reduction is initially eidetic, it
follows that it can never yield an adequation of thought and experience, since there always remains a separation between experience and
the eidos, a separation required, indeed, by philosophical reflection.
It may even be questioned whether it is ever possible to adopt the
standpoint of pure transcendental consciousness. For we cannot avoid
reflection upon the source of the resistance that lived experience offers to reflection. It is not enough simply to acknowledge this resistance as a nameless adversity. It is an experience outside the experience
of transcendental consciousness that has its own truth and value, of
which we must provide an account.

The sense that Merleau-Ponty drew from these difficulties in
the reduction lies in the direction of what we have decided to describe
as a *phenomenology in the natural attitude*. By this we mean a phenomenology in which the reduction is employed as a means rather than
an end in order to reveal within the facticity of our existence a pro-
togenesis of the world and reflection. "Husserl's essences are destined
to bring back all the living relationships of experience, as the fisherman's net draws up from the depths of the ocean quivering fish
and seaweed."[7] Merleau-Ponty's conception of phenomenology is
rooted in a philosophy of life and nature that he was still working on
in *The Visible and the Invisible* when he died. The phenomenological
method, guided by Husserl's prescription of a return to the "things
themselves," is a method of description that excludes equally the procedures of scientific explanation and analytical reflection. "To return

to things themselves is to return to that world which precedes knowledge, of which knowledge always *speaks,* and in relation to which every scientific schematization is an abstract and derivative sign-language as is geography in relation to the countryside in which we have learnt beforehand what a forest, a prairie or a river is."[8] At the same time, this move is not a retreat into the unsituated remoteness of a consciousness that lays down the laws of experience while enjoying its own immunity. Phenomenological reflection is not a retreat from the world toward a basis in the transcendental unity of consciousness; it separates the intentional lines between us and the world in order to uncover the umbilical cord that ties us to the world.

> Husserl's transcendental is not Kant's and Husserl accuses Kant's philosophy of being "worldly," because it *makes use* of our relation to the world, which is the motive force of the transcendental deduction, and makes the world immanent in the subject, instead of *being filled with wonder* at it and conceiving the subject as a process of transcendence towards the world.[9]

Nevertheless, for a very long time Husserl's presentation of the reduction remains couched in terms of a return to a transcendental consciousness before which the world is a transparent element. We shall have to take up the critical developments involved here. Their consideration will serve us as the transition to the second phase of Merleau-Ponty's interpretation of Husserl's turning toward a phenomenology in the natural attitude.

We consider now an example of what Merleau-Ponty regarded as a genuine phenomenological reduction involved in the critique of the constancy hypothesis. In the language of the psychology of perception we find the notions of sensation and attention that are not confirmed by the experience of perception but are introduced as hypotheses in favor of the prejudice of an objective, determinate world. Red is not a sensation or an element of consciousness, but a property of the object, a red cheek or a red sky, and has a meaning that only becomes determinate in the lived world, in what mothers perceive, or shepherds.

> There are two ways of being mistaken about quality: one is to make it into an element of consciousness, when in fact it is an object *for* consciousness, to treat it as an incommunicable impression, whereas it always has a meaning; the other is to think that this meaning and this object, at the level of quality, are fully developed and

determinate. The second error, like the first, springs from our prejudice about the world.[10]

For example, the two straight lines in Muller-Lyer's optical illusion are of neither equal nor unequal length.

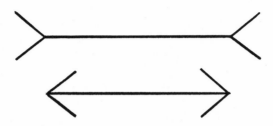

This is a problem that belongs in the construction of an objective world that can tell us nothing about the *field of vision*. In the visual field we do not see the two lines in a realm that permits comparison; we experience the lines as each having its own universe. To introduce the notion of attention in order to save the "analytic perception" of the two main lines in the figure as the case of "normal perception" is merely to presuppose rather than to establish the constancy hypothesis. The analytic method forces the phenomenal universe into categories that only make sense in the discourse of science. In the objective "reality" of science two equal lines should always appear equal in perception—indeed, this constitutes the "normal case." What in fact occurs for perception in Muller-Lyer's illusion is that one of the lines ceases to be equal to the other without thereby becoming "unequal": it becomes "different." By its nature, perception naturally admits the ambiguous and the shifting and is shaped by its context. For perception, an isolated line and the same line taken in a figure cease to be the "same" line, and it is only "second nature" to perceive the lines as identical. "The theory of sensation, which builds up all knowledge out of determinate qualities, offers us objects purged of all ambiguity, pure and absolute, the ideal rather than the real themes of knowledge: in short, it is compatible only with the lately developed superstructure of consciousness."[11]

The theory of sensation admits only a nominalist account of meaning through contiguity and association. Formalism, instead of explaining the structure of perception in terms of association, attempts to reconstruct it through the notion of "judgment" as *what sensation lacks to make perception possible.* Perception is reduced to an interpretation of signs furnished through the senses in accordance with physiological stimuli. But since the least sensible phenomenon involves an excess over the physical impression, every sense experience involves judgment and we lose sight of the function of judgment as the constitution of truth, without getting any closer to the experience of meaning in the sensible prior to all prediction. If every perception involves judgment, then we cannot distinguish true and false judgments formally but are obliged to have recourse to a purely conjectural layer of objective impressions to be translated, correctly or incorrectly, in the operation of judgment. But, of course, it is precisely the original compossibility of veridical and illusory perception that remains to be explained. Authentic reflection must explain how there comes to be a meaning in the sensible figure; it must describe the perceptual syntax that is the matrix of truth and illusion.

> Empiricism cannot see that we need to know what we are looking for, otherwise we would not be looking for it, and intellectualism fails to see that we need to be ignorant of what we are looking for, or equally again we should not be searching. They are in agreement in that neither attaches due importance to that circumscribed ignorance, that still "empty" but already determinate intention which *is* attention itself.[12]

It is through our incarnation that we operate a correlation of perception and the world, a circumscription of ignorance in the terrain between silence and lucidity that implies a new theory of natural reflection and a *tacit cogito.* We know that at first children distinguish colored objects only in a general way from colorless objects. Thereafter, colored objects are further distinguished in terms of "warm" and "cold" colors, and finally detailed color discriminations are acquired. The empiricist prejudice of determinacy requires that we say the child sees a color *where it is* but has not yet learned to associate a name with it, rather than recognize that color discrimination is a secondary formation that presupposes an original acquisition of the color-quality as a structure of consciousness. The first act of perception is to acquire for itself a *field* in which the movements of the exploratory organ become possible. The moon when seen through a cardboard tube looks no bigger on the horizon than at the zenith. But we have no reason to believe that the sixpenny moon is the one we see on the horizon unaided by instruments whose results reflect nothing more than the principles of their own construction. "When I look quite freely and naturally, the various parts of the field interact and *motivate* this enormous moon on the horizon, this measureless size which nevertheless is a size."[13] Similarly, there is no reason to ignore the role of our marginal perception of the intervening objects between us and an object in the distance upon which we fix our eye. For when these intervening objects are screened there appears a shrinkage in the apparent distance, and when we remove the screen we see distance generated, as it were, by the intervening objects. "This is the silent language whereby perception communicates with us: interposed objects, in the natural context, "mean" a greater distance. It is not, however, a question of a connection recognized by objective logic, the logic of constituted truth: for there is *no reason* why a steeple should appear to me to be smaller and farther away when I am better able to see in detail the slopes and fields between me and it. There is no reason, but there is a *motive*."[14] The mode of existence that objects come to have for perceptual consciousness requires a mode of description other than causal analysis and reconstruction.

> On the other hand, the phenomenological notion of *motivation* is one of those "fluid" concepts which have to be formed if we want to get back to phenomena. One phenomena releases another, not by means of some objective cause, like those which link together natural events, but by the meaning which it holds out—there is an underlying reason for a thing which guides the flow of phenomena without being explicitly laid down in any of them, *a sort of operative reason*.[15]

There is a natural perception, a nonthetic mode of consciousness that is not yet in possession of fully determinate objects or of any explicit logic, but that is nevertheless conformed to the style of the world as its own immanent logic. It was in order to get at this level of protoreflection that it was necessary to subject the concepts of empiricist and formal psychology to a phenomenological reduction. We see that the attempt of classical psychology to reconstruct veridical perception involves a secondary reconstruction that remains in the natural attitude, for the reason that it still presupposes the *originating* experience of perception as the appropriation of *significations* that are the condition of the values assumed by determinate perceptions. We need to distinguish the notions of structure and significance.[16] The gestalt or structure of the circle is engendered according to a rule of understanding. The significance of a circle is its physiognomy as a modulation of consciousness and its world. The former is constructed in accordance with a norm, the latter is *a birth of a norm*, the conformation of the external and the internal and not the projection of the internal upon the external. What makes phenomenology a phenomenology is that it is not confined to seeking the conditions of the possibility of being but is a genealogy of being, that is, "a study of the *advent* of being into consciousness, instead of presuming its possibility given in advance."[17] We see now that what distinguishes the phenomenological concept of intentionality from the Kantian relation to a possible object is that the unity of the phenomenal world is experienced as already there for the incarnate subject whose nature is spontaneously conformed to the world as its behavioral field.

> It is a question of recognizing consciousness itself as a project of the world, meant for the world which it neither embraces nor possesses, but towards which it is perpetually directed—and the world as this preobjective individual whose imperious unity decrees what knowledge shall take as its goal. This is why Husserl distinguishes between *intentionality of act,* which is that of our judgments and of those occasions when we voluntarily take up a position—the only intentionality discussed in the *Critique of Pure Reason*—and *operative intentionality (fungierende intentionalität),* or that which produces the natural and antepredicative unity of the world and our life, being apparent in our desires, our evaluations and in the landscape we see, more clearly than in objective knowledge, and furnishing the text which our knowledge tries to translate into precise language. Our relationship to the world, as it is untiringly enunciated within us, is not a thing which can be any further clarified by analysis; philosophy can only place it once more before our eyes and present it for our ratification.[18]

4

The Structures
of Behavior

Merleau-Ponty's analysis of the structures of behavior proceeds by means of a critical confrontation of the realism of traditional psychology and physiology with a psychology of form whose implicit naturalism is likewise rejected.[1] The Gestalt critique of the constancy hypothesis,[2] if properly interpreted, means that the sensible configuration of an object is not a datum of immediate experience; what is immediate is the meaning or structure of the object correlative with the "articulation and melodic unity of my behavior." The meaning of an object is revealed as a possibility that is only actualized as being-in-the-world when inserted into a certain conduct that distributes functional values according to the demands of the total configuration.

The aim of physiological psychology is to describe a topography without norms or intentionality, as in the classical theory of reflex behavior. However, once one attempts to make the notions of stimulus, receptor, and reflex arc more precise, this aspiration of reflex theory recedes and is salvageable only by appeal to mechanisms of inhibition and control.[3] For example, an increasing and continuous stimulation of the concha in the ear of a cat does not produce responses according to a continuous diffusion of excitation through preestablished, continuous motor circuits, as would be expected according to classical reflex theory.[4] The reactions of the cat are in sequence: movements of the neck and front ipsilateral paw, movements of the back ipsilateral paw, contractions of the muscles of the tail and the torso, movements of the contralateral back paw, and movements of the front contralateral paw. The significance of the elaboration of the response is that it is distributed according to the vital movements of the animal rather than according to the anatomical distribution of the motor impulses. In other words, everything happens so as to maintain the upright position of the animal, or "to release a gesture endowed with biological meaning." In a curious way, the case of "experimental neurosis" induced in one of Pavlov's dogs through repeated experiments forces upon the theory of conditioned reflexes the recognition of a pathological behavior induced through the restriction of a biologically meaningful environment for the animal.[5] To summarize the first order of behavioral structure, we may say that *physiology cannot be conceptualized without biology.*

In his treatment of the central sector of the nervous system and the classical theory of localizations, Merleau-Ponty frames his discussion in terms of Buytendijk's question whether, in dealing with nerve phenomena, we are dealing in reality "with functions of the structure or with functional structures."[6] The implications of this approach emerge in the study of pathological behavior, where what is impaired is not so much the content of behavior but rather its structural functions, what Gelb and Goldstein[7] refer to as the "categorial attitude," or Head's[8] power of "symbolic expression." For example, a patient may be able to "name" (pseudonaming, that is, a simple association of a word with an object) a "bread knife," an "apple parer," a "pencil sharpener," and "knife and fork" whenever a knife is present with the associated objects but be quite unable to name the "knife" in a categorial sense, that is to say, to assume an abstract attitude toward it. Now, as Goldstein points out, this loss of the abstract term is a general behavior change: "To have sounds *in an abstract meaning as symbols for ideas means the same concerning language as to have the possibility of approaching the world in general in abstract attitude.*"[9] Furthermore, the patient's substitution of concrete speech behavior cannot be simply identified as a symptom of an impaired speech function without knowledge of the total situation in which the patient's reactions occur. The suppression of the abstract attitude toward the knife might, in the case described, involve behavior designed to handle anxiety about that instrument, which would then indicate the real status—that is, the functional structure—of the speech behavior.

The nervous system distributes spatial, chromatic, and motor values in a system of transformations that demands that the physiological processes involved be understood by starting from "phenomenal givens." The point of view of conditioned-reflex theory is to consider these systematic transformations as a sum of local transformations, localizable in each point of the cortex by the conditioning effect of the stimulus. But in the case where I put on my coat, thrusting my left arm into the right sleeve that faces me as I go to put it on, there occurs a transformation of spatial indices that, far from depending upon the retinal stimulus as such, depends upon a constellation of both proprioceptive and exteroceptive stimuli. Thus the apparent position of my coat and its virtual variations involved in the course of putting it on must be a function of two variables: the afferent ocular excitations and the ensemble of excitations that represent the current position of my body in the cerebral cortex, changes in the spatial field being a function of my body schema. "Each perceived position has a meaning only as integrated into a framework of space which includes not only a sensible sector, actually perceived, but also a 'virtual space' of which the sensible sector is only a momentary aspect."[10] The structure of behavior involved in putting on my coat involves an integration of two distinct constitutive layers, the physiological process of grasping concrete space in the visual field, and the normal perceptual behavior that integrates concrete space into a virtual space. To summarize the second order of behavioral structure, we may say that *physiology cannot be conceptualized without psychology.*

On the basis of his critique of the reductionism and elementarism of behavioral theory, Merleau-Ponty proposes to classify behavior according to a continuum whose upper and lower limits are defined by the submergence of the structure of behavior in content, at the lowest level, to where structure emerges at the highest level as the proper theme of activity. One might then distinguish three levels of behavior—"syncretic forms," "amovable forms," and "symbolic forms"—present in varying degrees in all animal and human behavior. In the simplest syncretic forms of behavior the responses of the organism are, so to speak, total for a specific vital situation rather than drawn from a variable repertoire that would involve the use of *signals* not determined by the organism's instinctual equipment. It is in the amovable forms, or higher animal behavior, that reactions are structured in accordance with the perception of space-time relationships. This is not merely a question of perception by means of de facto contiguities of space and time, as is shown by Koehler's chicken experiments, but involves responses as a relation between relations (Sign-Gestalt).[11] But in the case of animals, space-time and means-end relationships are not purely abstract significations that can regulate behavior as at the human level. Koehler's chimpanzee, when presented with fruit separated from it by the vertical sides of a box, is unable to move the fruit toward the open end of the box in order to get at it, despite the fact that it will make a detour to retrieve fruit thrown outside a window. For the chimpanzee the goal (fruit) is the fixed point and his body is the mobile point. He is unable to exchange these functions so as to make his body the fixed point and the fruit a movable object. "What is really lacking in the animal is the symbolic behavior which it would have to possess in order to find an invariant in the external object, under the diversity of its aspects, comparable to the immediately given invariant of the body proper and in order to treat, reciprocally, its own body as an object among objects."[12] The chimpanzee lacks the symbolic behavior through which the thing-structure becomes possible.

In animal behavior signs remain signals dependent upon empirical associations and never become symbols of true signs in which the representation of the signified is not a relation of correspondence but of expression and orientation toward the virtual. The expression of significations is thematic, as, for example, in the case of the organist who can play a passage without being able to designate separately each key that corresponds to a note. The correlations of visual stimuli and motor excitations are achieved only as transition points in an ensemble of signification that is not a function of the associated visual and motor structures but the reason for their integration. We do not say that the behavior of playing the organ *has* a signification: it *is* itself signification. The organist does not play in objective space but in an expressive space. "In reality his movements during rehearsal are consecratory gestures: they draw effective vectors, discover emotional sources, and create a space of expressiveness as the movements of the augur delimit the templum."[13]

Human behavior, which is essentially symbolic behavior, unfolds through structures or gestures that are not in objective space and time, like physical objects, nor in a purely internal dimension of consciousness, which would be foreign to the world. Merleau-Ponty's analysis and integration of the structures of behavior avoid the dualism of objectivism and subjectivism through a conceptualization of the body-organism as a mode of being-in-the world or belonging in the world through its openness to the solicitation of the world. "The world, inasmuch as it harbors living beings, ceases to be a material plenum consisting of juxtaposed parts; it opens up at the place where behavior appears."[14]

The conceptualization of behavior requires the category of Form in order to differentiate the structures of quantity, order, and value or signification as the relatively dominant characteristics of matter, life, and mind and at the same time relativize the participation of these structures in a hierarchy of forms. Form is not itself an element in the world but a limit toward which biophysical and psychobiological structures tend. In other words, the analysis of form is not a question of the composition of real structures but of the perception of wholes. In a given environment each organism exhibits a preferred mode of behavior that is not the simple sum or function of its milieu and its internal organization but is determined by its general attitude to the world.[15] Through the notion of signification, or coordination by meaning, it is possible to take into account the fact that the organism modifies its milieu in accordance with the internal norms of its activity, while avoiding any notion of vitalism or the constitutive activity of the norm upon structure. The organism is a *phenomenal body* in the Kantian sense of a unity of signification in which environment and response are polarities in the same structure of behavior.

5

The Phenomenology of Perception

T he theory of the body image is, implicitly, a theory of perception." The phenomenal body is the matrix of human existence. It is the center around which the world is given as a correlate of its activities. Through the phenomenal body we are open to a world of objects as polarities of bodily action. The phenomenal body is a modality of being-in-the-world that is privileged because it is the Archimedean point of action and neither a passive agency of sensory perception nor an obstacle to idealist knowledge. Ordinarily, in the sense that philosophical psychology is implicitly dualist, consciousness is defined as the possession of an object of thought or as transparence to itself and action is defined as a series of events external to each other; consciousness and action are juxtaposed or set in a relation of speculative hierarchy. "Whether consciousness be continuous duration or a center of judgments, in either case this pure activity is without structure, without nature. Correlatively, perception and action taken in that which is specific to them, that is, as the knowledge and modification of reality, are rejected from consciousness." It is the task of a phenomenological description of perception to reveal the structures of knowledge and action in which consciousness is engaged by virtue of its incarnation or embodiment through which it experiences the solicitation of the world and its own activity upon its surroundings (*Umwelt*).

The "I am" is, as Alphonse de Waelhens puts it, a rhetorical affirmation of my belonging to the realm of being, not that I situate myself among objects in a way analogous to the juxtapositions that obtain between things, for I cannot speak of these physical relations as external to me without instituting a relation of exteriority between myself and my body. Such indeed is the epistemological model of physical science. The latter suppresses the immediacy of the mind-body relation and constructs an abstract epistemological subject whose sole function is to survey a field of physical objects and relations. A phenomenological psychology rejects the subject-object dualism because it retrieves an ontological and epistemological unity prior to the disjunctions of natural science. The status of my body is privileged. I can never be detached from it, not even in the attitude of objectivity. "To say that it is always near me, always there for me, is to say that it is never really in front of me, that I cannot array it before my eyes, that it remains marginal to all my perceptions, that it is *with* me."[1] My body is the vantage point from which I perceive all possible objects. It is my body that is the vehicle of my perception and movement in the world. In neither case are the spatiality and the motility of the body geometric or discrete. The body is the schema of my world; it is the source of an abstract movement or projection that "carves out within that plenum of the world in which concrete movement takes place a zone of reflection and subjectivity: it superimposes upon physical space a potential or human space."[2]

Thus, to take an illustration from Merleau-Ponty, for the player on the field the football field is not an "object" but a field of forces, vectors, and openings that call for "moves" in accordance with the play. The player is not a consciousness surveying the field as a datum; the field is present only as "the immanent term of his practical intentions," and the lines of force in it are continuously restructured with his moves in the course of the game: "the player becomes one with it and feels the direction of the 'goal,' for example, just as immediately as the vertical and horizontal planes of his own body."[3] The player "knows" where the goal is in a manner that is "lived" rather than known, that is to say, in the order of "naturizing thought which internally subtends the characteristic structure of objects."[4]

In order to characterize the openness of objects to perceptual consciousness and the structures of signification that distinguish them from appearances, Merleau-Ponty proposes to call the objects of perception "phenomena." Consequently, insofar as philosophy is an inventory of consciousness as the milieu of the universe, philosophy becomes a phenomenology whose mark is an inescapable existential index. The objects of perception are not close entities whose structural laws are known to us a priori, but "open, inexhaustible systems which we recognize through a certain style of development." The phenomenon of perspective reveals a synthesis of immanence and transcendence that contains the ambiguity of perception. For the perceived thing exists only insofar as I perceive it, and yet its being is never exhausted by the view I have of it. It is this simultaneous presence and absence that is required for "something" to be perceived at all. The sequence of perspectives that we have of a cube is not a logical transition synthesized by a geometrical hypothesis, but "a kind of practical synthesis"—what Husserl called a "synthesis of identification" in which I anticipate the unseen side of the lamp because I can manipulate it. "One phenomenon releases another, not by means of some objective efficient cause, like those which link together natural events, but by the meaning which it holds out—there is an underlying reason for a thing which guides the flow of phenomena without being explicitly laid down in any one of them, *a sort of operative reason.*"[5]

We understand the world and the objects it presents to us in a kind of symbiosis in which the object's color or tactile quality solicits our being and presents it with a question whose answer is discovered in following the perspectives of the object through in accordance with a symbolism that links each of the sensory qualities of the object. The vehicle of these symbolic interrelations between things or aspects of things is our body, upon which the world exerts a magnetic attraction: "the whole of nature is the setting of our own life, or our interlocutor in a sort of dialogue." To possess a body that is capable of intersensory synergy is to possess a universal setting or schema for all possible styles or typical structures in the natural world, not in accordance with the invariable formula of a *facies totius universi* but as a temporal synthesis of horizons implicit in intentionality. "For us the perceptual synthesis is a temporal synthesis, and subjectivity, at the level of perception, is nothing but temporality, and that is what enables us to leave to the subject of perception his opacity and historicity."[6] The unity of the object is foreshadowed by its qualities just as the object itself is the outline of the world and the unity of the world invokes the unity of the cogito.

The *cogito* of which Merleau-Ponty speaks is not the *spoken cogito,* or the one that is the subject of discourse and essential truth, but a *tacit cogito,* that is, "myself experienced by myself."[7] This subjectivity does not constitute its world, for it has only a precarious grasp upon a world in which it finds itself "like that of the infant at its first breath, or of the man about to drown and who is impelled towards life." This tacit subjectivity only becomes a cogito through its articulation in speech and the perceptual exploration and symbolization of the total logic of the world presupposed by the tacit cogito. The logic of the world and subjectivity is neither sequent nor synthetic. It is a "living cohesion" in which I belong to myself while belonging to the world. Pascal's remark that in one way we understand the world and in another it understands us presents the possibility of avoiding the antitheses of idealism and realism if we understand that these are one and the same understandings. I understand the world because there is for me near and far, foreground and horizon, and hence a landscape in which things can appear and acquire significance. And this is because my subjectivity is in the world through the body that is the original source of perspective and the possibility of situations. For a disembodied spirit or transcendental subjectivity there can be no perspective, and, far from everything's appearing explicitly to such a consciousness, everything would cease to be, for such a world would be uninhabited. Thus there is no contradiction between Pascal's two modes of understanding. The only possibility is a complementary relationship between "the omnipresence of consciousness and its involvement in a field of presence."

6

Corporeality
and
Intersubjectivity

I t is a characteristic of the progression of Merleau-Ponty's thought
that his conclusions represent fresh starting points. Thus the concluding evaluation of the contribution of phenomenology is beset
with new problems that we need not take up in a second-order
reflection upon the phenomenon of the phenomenon. "Probably the
chief gain from phenomenology is to have united extreme subjectivism and extreme objectivism in its notion of the world or rationality. . . . To say that there exists rationality is to say that perspectives
blend, perceptions confirm each other, a meaning emerges."[1] The
world is never given to us as a flat surface over which we cast our
speculative glance. Our world is given to us in the hollows between
things, as the field of our exploratory senses that polarize objects as
the immanent ends of our intentions, in the paths where our experience and that of others intersect and blend together. "Rationality is
not a *problem*." Our everyday experience witnesses to the network of
relationships between us and things and between ourselves and other
people that we literally are as incarnate subjects. We may say that,
though not a problem, rationality of the phenomenon of a common
world is a mystery, but it is a mystery solved through our corporality,
which is our intersubjectivity no less than our subjectivity.

Nevertheless, phenomenology experiences temptations in the
course of bringing its precious cargo to port, and to reach home it

must hug the contours of the land rather than sail by the stars. For a long time phenomenology remains obsessed by a transcendental unity that is the impartial law of the spectacle of the world in myself and others. The transcendental ego is the norm that makes possible a common world but remains blind to its own ontogenesis, the contingency of its inherence in a particular subject who never has more than a partial comprehension of a world not of his making. Nor can there be any recognition of the problem of intersubjectivity where Peter and Paul exist solely as values of a consciousness that confronts the world as its immanent universal. Phenomenology recognizes that the *alter ego* is a paradox. Whereas the *cogito* defines *me* as the thought that I have of myself, and that I am alone in having, then it is never I that the other sees when he sees me, unless I am the exterior that I present to others.

> For the "other" to be more than an empty word, it is necessary that my existence should never be reduced to my bare awareness of existing, but that it should take in also the awareness that *one* may have of it, and thus include my incarnation in some nature and the possibility, at least, of a historical situation. The *Cogito* must reveal me in a situation, and it is on this condition alone that transcendental subjectivity can, as Husserl puts it, *be* an intersubjectivity.[2]

The final condition of phenomenology is a "return" to a philosophy of nature,[3] always present in Husserl's troubled reflection upon the phenomenological reduction, and the unbroken circle of Merleau-Ponty's own thought from the *Structure of Behavior* to *The Visible and the Invisible*. In *Ideen* I, 50, there is a progression in which the intentional relation between consciousness and nature is transformed into the contingency of nature relative to absolute consciousness that emerges from the natural attitude by operating (*Vollziehen*), ideally, a suspension of any empirical order given to it. Thus the reduction of the natural attitude merges with the transcendental constitution. Nevertheless, Merleau-Ponty argues that the direction of phenomenology, by the time of *Ideen* II, is not that of the philosophy of mind.[4] The distinction between a pure subject and pure things (*blosse Sachen*), the disinterested knower who grasps things simply as things, is rendered problematic in the search for a more fundamental relation to being that relativizes the "theoretical attitude." The transcendence of the natural world is not simply the antithesis of its transcendental immanence in "reduced" consciousness. The ontological milieu that our natural life intends is not a theoretical attitude; far less is it a natural "attitude," which we might refuse to entertain.[5]

But this is what is maintained in the view of mind and nature held by the philosophical reflection that underlies scientific *naturalism*.

> The natural attitude really becomes an attitude—a tissue of judicatory and propositional acts—only when it becomes a naturalist thesis. The natural attitude itself emerges unscathed from the complaints which can be made about naturalism, because it is "prior to all thesis," because it is the mystery of a *Weltthesis* prior to all theses. It is, Husserl says in another connection, the mystery of a primordial faith and a fundamental and original opinion (*Urglaube, Urdoxa*) which are thus not even in principle translatable in terms of clear and distinct knowledge, and which—more ancient than any "attitude" or "point of view"—give us not a representation of the world but the world itself.[6]

The relationship between the transcendental and natural attitudes is better described as circular rather than sequential or parallel. *There is a preparation for phenomenology in the natural attitude,* a "pretheoretical constitution" that is natural to incarnate consciousness. At the same time, the transcendental attitude poses itself as a question for itself, in an infinite meditation upon the relation between reflection and that which resists reflection,

> and the ultimate task of phenomenology as philosophy of consciousness is to understand its relationship to non-phenomenology. What resists phenomenology within us—natural being, the "barbarous" source Schelling spoke of—cannot remain outside of phenomenology and should have its place within it. The philosopher bears with him his shadow which is not simply the material absence of light from the future.[7]

The philosopher is not a disembodied consciousness contemplating objects that exist only in the light of mind. The philosopher is an embodied consciousness open to objects through the same light and shadow cast by his own body. The world is given to us primordially not in the cogito, but in the incarnate subject (*Subjektleib*) as a *possum* (I am able to). It is through the body that we discover a "subject-object" relationship that is the definitive articulation of an "irrelative" in perceptual experience that is the "statutory basis" (*Rechtsgrund*) of all the constructions of the understanding. Through my body I experience a spiritualization of matter and a materialization of spirit, the enigma of sensible matter given to itself through a "sort of reflection" (*eine Art von Reflexion*). When I touch my right hand with my left I experience the right hand as a physical thing that almost simultaneously begins to reverse the process, *es wird leib, es empfindet* (*Ideen* II, 145). Here we can no longer understand intentionality as the "idea" of the coincidence of the subject and object; intentionality lies in the *reversibility* of the objective and phenomenal body, that is, in the "flesh of the world." My body is the zero point at which there opens up a world and others, separated from me by an *aesthetic distance* that I am sure of crossing with a glance, but that I can never totally embrace.[8]

Nevertheless there remains a problem of *solipsism*. The generality of the body remains the other side of an inalienable consciousness present to itself even in the act of self-sacrifice. How are we to find *elsewhere* in the perceptual field such a presence of self to self. The problem of intersubjectivity is here identical with the problem of transcendental subjectivity in general, namely, "*how the presence to myself* (Urpräsenz) *which establishes my own limits and conditions every alien presence is at the same time depresentation* (Entgegenwartigung) *and throws me outside myself.*"[9] And in this case reflection must as in all other cases reveal something of its object in an unreflective experience of the other, or we should not be able to present to ourselves the problem of solipsism. It is in the tissue of sensible being that the other person is given to me as I am given to myself—the prereflexive cogito is not a struggle to the death but a coexistence of consciousnesses. Thus when I shake another person's hand there occurs a similar reversibility of the touching-touched: I experience a different sensibility (*Empfindbarkeit*), another perceiving body prior to the secondary constructions of soul and personality. Nor is this a process of *introjection*. It is not simply an "I think *that* he thinks" in which the cogito would still fail to escape from itself.

> Man can create the alter ego which "thought" cannot create, because he is outside himself in the world and because one ekstasis is compossible with other ekstases. And that possibility is fulfilled in perception as vinculum of brute being and a body. The whole riddle of *Einfuhlung* lies in its initial, "esthesiological" phase; and it is solved there because it is a perception. He who "posits" the other man is a perceiving subject, the other person's body is a perceived thing, and the other person himself is "posited" as "perceiving." It is never a matter of anything but co-perception. I see that this man over there sees, as I touch my left hand while it is touching my right.[10]

Thus we see that we are no longer forced to develop the phenomenological reduction and its existential condition or facticity as alternatives; for the intentional correlative of the world is not the transcendental Ego but intersubjectivity. The Husserlian reflection is both an analytics of essences and an analytics of existences. Husserl's conception of Nature is one of a world of objects fundamentally present to sensible being and ideally to a community of sensible beings. There is no longer any question of a direct ontology or constitution, but only of an incomplete reduction that reveals the *Weltthesis.* "La Nature est cette chance offerte à la corporeité et à l'intersubjectivité." But this is only possible because our corporeality possesses a power of self-forgetfulness (*Selbstvergessenheit*)[11] that is the source of the transition from the latent to the theoretical constitution, which in turn is only a test of our primordial bond with the world and others. Originally an attempt to conquer the world as the mind's creature, the constitution becomes the revelation of the world as the earth and native abode of rationality. The facticity of the world and our incarnation is the lesson of patience; and the phenomenological description is ultimately a meditation "as painstaking as the works of Balzac, Proust, Valéry or Cézanne—by reason of the same kind of attentiveness and wonder, the same demand for awareness, the same will to seize the meaning of the world or of history as that meaning comes into being."[12]

7

Childhood and
Embodiment

Any theory of child socialization is implicitly a theory of the construction of social reality, if not of a particular historical social order.[1] In this chapter I propose to give an account of the phenomenological approach to the basic presuppositions of child socialization. I shall restrict my account to the writings of Maurice Merleau-Ponty, who, although widely known as a philosopher and political theorist, remains to be known for the lectures on child psychology that he gave for many years at the Sorbonne.[2] For reasons of economy it is not possible to follow the whole of Merleau-Ponty's interpretation and critical evaluation of the literature concerning the physiological, intellectual, moral, and cultural development of the child with which he familiarized himself, not to mention his close reading of psychoanalytical and American anthropological research. Much of the literature is in any case now all too familiar to workers in child psychology, although Merleau-Ponty's close reading and phenomenological critique of Piaget's work[3] might be given special mention because of its continuing interest.

Merleau-Ponty's analysis of the child's relation to others, his family, and the world around him may serve as introduction to the whole of Merleau-Ponty's phenomenology of perception, expression, and the sociohistorical world of human institutions.[4] At all events, the topic and its phenomenological horizons are inseparable and can only be managed in a short space by focusing upon the very fundamental presuppositions of the phenomenon of the child's orientation to the world and others around him through the mediations of the body, language, perception, and reflection. The phenomenological concern with these basic structures of child development involves an implicit concern with the way in which they may be prejudged by the assumptions of unreflexive research.

The starting point in any study of child psychology and socialization must be the child's relation to the adult world, its social relations, and its linguistic, perceptual, and logical categories. By insisting on this point, Merleau-Ponty dismisses any notion of a psychology of the child, the sick person, the man, the woman, or the primitive as an enclosed nature. Indeed, there is a *complementary feature* of the child-adult relationship, namely, the reverse adult-child relationship. This obliges us in the methodology of child studies to design research procedures that are sensitive to the two-way and even asymmetric relation between the child's orientation to the adult world and the adult world's interests in fostering, enforcing, and moralizing upon its own interests and hopes in the child world. We cannot here look down the path toward the "politics of experience" that this first methodological observation opens up.[5] It must suffice to remark that it points to a cultural dilemma that is generic to human relations and thus makes it impossible to conceive of child psychology and psychoanalysis outside specific cultural frameworks.

Another general conclusion that we may elicit from the interactional nature of the object of child studies refers to a phenomenon that is common to the object of all social studies. The natural scientist for most purposes is concerned only with the observer's experience, however mediated by his instruments, of the object under study. Even if we take into account the problems of interference referred to by the Heisenberg uncertainty principle, the problem here is merely that the scientist must allow for changes in the behavior of experimental objects due to the interference effects of his own methods of study. But although this problem produces a greater similarity between the natural and social sciences than was imagined earlier, it leaves unchanged an essential difference between them: namely, where the object of science is a human relationship or set of human relationships, a custom, or an institution, the "ordering" of the relationship is not merely a scientific construct. It is first of all a pretheoretical construct that is the unarticulated "commonsense" knowledge of others as "relatives" who experience dependable needs and wants expressed through the "relevances" of the human body, time, and place.

The burden of Merleau-Ponty's methodological critique of research methods in studies of child perception, language, and morals
is that they proceed without the benefit of any reflection upon the
way their methods already prejudge the nature of the phenomena
they are intended to elicit. In the first place we must rid ourselves of
a "dogmatic rationalism" that consists in studying the child's world
from above and thereby construing the child's efforts as prelogical or
magical behavior that must be sloughed off as a condition of entry
into the objective, realist world of adults. Such a prejudice overlooks
the way in which child and adult behavior are solidary, with anticipations from the side of the child and regressions on the side of the
adult that make their conduct no more separable than health and
sickness. Indeed, the real task of a genuine psychology must be to
discover the basis of *communication* between children and adults, between the unconscious and consciousness, between the sick and the
sane.[6]

"We must conceive the child neither as an absolute 'other' nor
just 'the same' as ourselves, but as polymorphous."[7] This remark may
serve as a guiding principle in following Merleau-Ponty's subtle interweaving of the processes of structure and development in the child's
relation to others. The notion of *development* is, of course, central to
the psychology of the child; it is, however, a complex notion since it
implies neither an absolute continuity between childhood and adult-
hood nor any complete discontinuity without phases or transitions.
It is here that we need to avoid the twin reductions of the phenomena
of development that Merleau-Ponty labels "mechanist" and "idealist"
exemplified, respectively, by the learning theory approach originated
by Pavlov and the cognitive approach of Piaget. Here we are on explicitly philosophical ground because the continuity between childhood and adult life raises the question of how it is in principle that
individual and intersubjective life are possible.

Mechanist, reflex, or learning theory accounts of child development involve us in the difficulty that their causal explanations fail
to cover the phenomena of adult initiative, creativity, and responsibility. Reflex theory reduces conduct to a structure of conditioned
reflexes built into increasingly complex patterns whose principle of
organization is always conceived as an environmental stimulus to which
the responses of adaptation occur without internal elaboration. Reflex
theory attempts to explain conduct in terms of physiological process
without norms or intentionality. But even at its own level reflex theory
is not sure of its foundations.[8] Once one attempts to make the notions
of stimulus, receptor, and reflex more precise, reflex theory becomes

riddled with question-begging hypotheses about mechanisms of inhibition and control, acquired drives, and the like. The case of "experimental neurosis" in one of Pavlov's dogs involved in repeated experiments reveals that the consequences of the restriction of a biologically meaningful environment in order to induce conditioned reflexes results in pathological behavior.[9] By the same token, the acquisition of human habits is not a strictly determined reflex but the acquisition of a capability for inventing solutions to situations that are only *abstractly* similar and never identical with the original "learning situation." What is involved in the formation of human habits is the acquisition of a "categorical attitude"[10] or a power of "symbolic expression,"[11] and it is only in pathological conduct that atomistic and associationist explanations appear plausible.

While rejecting naturalistic reductions of child development, Merleau-Ponty is equally critical of idealist or cognitive accounts of the phenomena of perception, intelligence, and sensory-motor behavior. The basic fault in cognitive approaches to the child's relation to the world and others is that they sacrifice the immediate, *visceral knowledge* of self, others, and the world that we possess without ever having apprenticed ourselves to the "rules" of perception, language, and movement. This preconceptual knowledge is neither subjective nor objective and requires a conception of *symbolic form* that rests upon neither a realist nor an idealist epistemology but instead seeks what is complementary in them. Because the philosophical presuppositions of psychology are implicitly dualistic, consciousness is usually described as the transparent possession of an object of thought, in distinction from perceptual and motor acts, which are described as a series of events external to each other. Thought and behavior are juxtaposed or else set in a speculative hierarchy. Against these alternatives, Merleau-Ponty proposes to classify behavior according to a continuum whose upper and lower limits are defined by the submergence of the structure of behavior in content, at the lowest level, that is, "synenetic forms," and, at the highest level, the emergence of structure as the proper theme of activity, that is, "symbolic forms."

The conceptualization of behavior requires the category of Form in order to differentiate the structures of quantity, order, and value or signification as the dominant characteristics, respectively, of matter, life, and mind and at the same time to relativize the participation of these structures in a hierarchy of forms of behavior. Form is itself not an element in the world but a limit toward which biophysical and psychobiological structures tend. In a given environment each organism exhibits a preferred mode of behavior that is not the simple aim or function of its milieu and its internal organization but is structured by its general attitude to the world. In other words, the analysis of form is not a matter of the composition of real structures but the perception of wholes. Human behavior, which is essentially symbolic behavior, unfolds through structures or gestures that are not in objective space and time, like physical objects, nor in a purely internal dimension of consciousness unsituated with respect to historical time and place.

Merleau-Ponty calls the objects of perception "phenomena" in order to characterize their openness to perceptual consciousness to which they are not given a priori but as "open, inexhaustible systems which we recognize through a certain style of development." The matrix of all human activity is the *phenomenal body* that is the schema of our world, or the source of a vertical or human space in which we project our feelings, moods, and values. Because the human body is a "community of senses" and not a bundle of contingently related impression, it functions as the universal setting or schema for all possible styles or typical structures of the world. These, however, are not given to us with the invariable formula of a *facius totius universi* but through the temporal synthesis of horizons implicit in intentionality. "For us the perceptual synthesis is a temporal synthesis, and subjectivity, at the level of perception, is nothing but temporality, and that is what enables us to leave to the subject of perception his opacity and historicity."[12] The cognitive approaches to child development overlook the *tacit* subjectivity that does not constitute its world a priori nor entirely a posteriori but develops through a "living cohesion" in which the embodied self experiences itself while belonging to this world and others, clinging to them for its content.

Thus in his analysis of the child's perception of causal relations[13] Merleau-Ponty argues that it is not a matter of a simple ordering of external data but of an "informing" (*Gestaltung*) of the child's experience of external events through an operation that is properly neither a logical nor a predicative activity. Similarly, in the case of the child's imagination,[14] it proves impossible to give any objective sense of the notion of *image* even as photograph, mimicry, or picture, apart from an "affective projection." Imagination is therefore not a purely intellectual operation but is better understood as an operation beneath the cognitive relation of subject and object. The "imaginary" and the "real" are two *forms of conduct* that are not antithetical but rest upon a common ambiguity that occasionally allows the imaginary to substitute for the real. The child lives in the hybrid world of the real and the imaginary that the adult keeps apart for most purposes or is otherwise careful of any transgression wherein he catches his own conscience. Again, in the analysis of the child's drawing,[15] it is also improper to treat the child's efforts as abortive attempts to develop "adult," or rather perspectual, drawing, which is itself a historical development in art dominated by the laws of classical geometric perspective. The child's drawing is not a simple imitation of what he sees any more than of what he does not see through lack of detailed "attention." The child's drawings are expressive of his relations to the things and people in this world. They develop and change along with his experience with the objects, animals, puppets, and persons around him, including his own experience of his body, its inside and outside.[16] "The child's drawing is *contact* with the visible world and with others. This tactile relation with the world and with man appears long before the looking attitude, the posture of indifferent contemplation between the spectator and the spectacle which is realized in adult drawing."[17]

It is above all in the child's acquisition of language that we observe the complex interrelation of cognition and affectivity that can only be made thematic in later phases of development by presupposing the massive inarticulable background of the world into which we import our categories, distinctions, and relations. Language and intelligence presuppose one another without priority, and their development rests rather upon the ability of the child to assimilate his linguistic environment as an open system of expression and conduct, comparable to his acquisition of all his other habits. Again, for reasons of economy we cannot deal with the broad range of the phenomenology of language.[18] Instead, we must focus attention upon Merleau-Ponty's interpretation of the social contexts of the acquisition of language.[19]

> It is a commonplace that the child's acquisition of language is also correlated with his relation to his mother. Children who have been suddenly and forcibly separated from their mothers always show signs of a linguistic regression. At bottom, it is not only the word "mama" that is the child's first; it is the entire language which is, so to speak, maternal.
>
> The acquisition of language might be a phenomenon of the same kind as the relation to the mother. Just as the maternal relation is (as the psychoanalysts say) a relation of *identification,* in which the subject projects on his mother what he himself experiences and assimilates the attitudes of his mother, so one could say that the acquisition of language is itself a phenomenon of identification. To

learn to speak is to learn to play a series of *roles,* to assume a series of conducts or linguistic gestures.[20]

This hypothesis on the development of language in relation to the child's familial roles is illustrated in terms of analysis of the expression of child jealousy.[21] Upon the birth of a new baby the younger of two children displays jealousy, behavioral regression (carrying himself as though he were the baby), and language regression. There, phenomena represent an initial response to the threatened structure of the child's temporal and social world of the "latest born" child. The emotional response of jealousy expresses the child's attachment to a hitherto eternal present. A little later the child begins to identify with his older brother, adopting the latter's earlier attitudes toward himself as the "youngest." The chance circumstance of the visit of another child bigger than his older brother relativizes once and for all the "absolute eldest" and the child's jealousy recedes. At the same time as these "sociometric" experiences are acquired the child's linguistic experience of temporal structure also expands. "He considered the present to be absolute. Now, on the contrary, one can say that from the moment when he consents to be no longer the latest born, to become in relation to the new baby what his elder brother had until then been in relation to him, he replaces the attitude of 'my place has been taken' with another whose schema might be somewhat like this: 'I *have been* the youngest, but I *am* the youngest no longer, and I *will become* the biggest.' One sees that there is a solidarity between the acquisition of this temporal structure, which gives a meaning to the corresponding linguistic instruments, and the situation of jealousy that is overcome."[22]

The child's resolution of his jealousy permits us to make some general remarks upon the relation of the cognitive and affective elements in the child's conception of the world and others around him that will then permit us to deal finally with the fundamental problem of the possibility of social relations of any kind.[23] In overcoming his jealousy we might, as Piaget would say, speak of the child's having solved the egocentric problem by learning to decenter himself and to relativize his notions by thinking in terms of reciprocity. But these are clearly not purely intellectual operations; rather, what is called *intelligence* here really designates the mode of intersubjectivity achieved by the child. The intellectual and linguistic elaboration of our experience of the world always rests upon the "deep structures" of our affective experience of the interpersonal world against which we elaborate only later our modes of inductive and deductive thinking.

The perception of other people and the intersubjective world are problematical only for adults. The child lives in a world which he unhesitatingly believes accessible to all around him. He has no awareness of himself or of others as private subjectivities, nor does he suspect that all of us, himself included, are limited to one certain point of view of the world. That is why he subjects neither his thoughts, in which he believes as they present themselves, without attempting to link them to each other, nor our words, to any sort of criticism. He has no knowledge of points of view. For him men are empty heads turned towards one single, self-evident world where everything takes place, even dreams, which are, he thinks, in his room, and even thinking, since it is not distinct from words. Others are for him so many gazes which inspect things, and have an almost material existence, so much so that the child wonders how these gazes avoid being broken as they meet. At about twelve years old, says Piaget, the child achieves the *cogito* and reaches the truths of rationalism. At this stage, it is held, he discovers himself both as a point of view on the world and also as called upon to transcend that point of view, and to construct an objectivity at the level of judgement. Piaget brings the child to a mature outlook as if the thoughts of the adult were self-sufficient and disposed of all contradictions. But, in reality, it must be the case that the child's outlook is in some way vindicated against the adult's and against Piaget, and that the unsophisticated thinking of our earliest years remains as an indispensible acquisition underlying that of maturity, if there is to be for the adult one single intersubjective world. My awareness of constructing an objective truth would never provide me with anything more than an objective truth for me, and my greatest attempt at impartiality would never enable me to prevail over my subjectivity (as Descartes so well expresses it by the hypothesis of the malignant demon), if I had not, underlying my judgements, the primordial certainty of being in contact with being itself, if, before any voluntary *adoption of a position* I were not already *situated* in an intersubjective world, and if science too were not upheld by this basic δοξα. With the *cogito* begins that struggle between consciousnesses, each of which, as Hegel says, seeks the death of the other. For the struggle ever to begin, and for each consciousness to be capable of suspecting the alien presences which it negates, all must necessarily have some common ground and be mindful of their peaceful co-existence in the world of childhood.[24]

Classical psychology, however, renders the intersubjective world that is the presupposition of all socialization entirely problematic. This arises from the assumption that the psyche is *what is given to only one person,* intrinsically mine and radically inaccessible to others who are similarly possessed of their own experiences. The same assumption is also made with regard to the body, namely, that it is as *individual* as the psyche and knowable by me only through the mass of sensations it gives me. So conceived, the problem of the experience of others presents itself as a system with four terms: (1) myself, my "psyche"; (2) the image I have of my body by means of the sense of touch or cenesthesia, that is, the "introceptive image" of my own body; (3) the body of the other as seen by me, that is, that "visual body"; (4) the hypothetical "psyche" of the other, his feeling of his own existence that I must reconstitute by means of (3) the "visual body."[25]

The difficulties intrinsic to the operation of this schema are apparent from what it assumes in the analysis of the child's response to the other's smile.[26] The child responds very early to facial expressions and, of course, verbal expressions of dos and don'ts without being able either to compare his "motor smile" with the "visible smile" of the other or to correlate just what it is that he is doing that meets with approval or disapproval. Rather than engage in point for point comparisons the child can only respond to global situations and attitudes, in other words, to his surroundings, as motivation or conduct. This means that we must reject the individualist and solipsistic conceptions intrinsic to the dual worlds of the mind and body as conceived in classical psychology and its philosophical tradition.[27] We can no longer conceive of the psyche as a series of enclosed "states of consciousness" inaccessible to anyone but myself. Consciousness is turned toward the world; it is a mode of conduct toward things and persons[28] that in turn reveal themselves to me through their style and manner of dealing with the world. By the same token we must revise our conception of the body as an agglomeration of senses that are mine and that are only to be guessed at in the case of others. My awareness of body is the activity of a postural or corporeal schema that is the lived experience of a cenesthesia or play between my various senses and the senses of others visible in their comportment.

> Thus in today's psychology we have one system with two terms (my behaviour and the other's behaviour) which functions as a whole. To the extent that I can elaborate and extend my *corporeal schema*, to the extent that I acquire a better organized experience of my own body, to that very extent will my consciousness of my own body cease being a chaos in which I am submerged and lend itself to a transfer to others. And since at the same time the other who is to be perceived is himself not a "psyche" closed in on himself but rather a *conduct*, a system of behaviour that aims at the world, he offers himself to my motor intentions and to that "intentional

transgression" (Husserl) by which I animate and pervade him. Husserl said that the perception of others is like a "phenomenon of coupling" [*accouplement*]. The term is anything but a metaphor. In perceiving the other, my body and his are coupled, resulting in a sort of action which pairs them [*action à deux*]. This conduct which I am able only to see, I live somehow from a distance. I make it mine; I recover [*reprendre*] it or comprehend it. Reciprocally I know that the gestures I make myself can be the objects of another's intention. It is this transfer of intentions to my own, my alienation of the other and his alienation of me, that makes possible the perception of others.[29]

Here we can only point to the complementarity between the role of the corporeal schema and the work of social actors in elaborating the field of impressions and visual data inadvertently and deliberately presented to him as the motives and expectations of social interaction or the typification of personal and institutional conduct, as analyzed by Mead, Goffman, and Schütz.[30] Likewise, without any further comment upon the relation between transcendental phenomenology and mundane intersubjectivity,[31] we must now conclude with an analysis of the formation of the child's corporeal schema in the early stages of socialization.

The problem is to account for how it is that we become aware of the distinction between our own body and the other's body while acquiring the ability to transfer our intentions to the facial and linguistic expressions of the other as the prima facie basis of their further elaboration and making our own gestures similarly available to the other's intentions and expectations.[32] We may distinguish three principal stages in this process, at each point commenting upon the conceptual revisions that are implicit in their structure and development during the first three years of the child's life.

The first phase is that of *precommunication* in which the child does not experience himself as a single individual set over against all others. The first *me* is still a latent or vertical possibility within our experience of an anonymous or collective existence. What is sometimes called egocentrism at this stage refers not to an experience of self-other contrast but precisely to the experience of a *me* that dwells as easily in others as in itself and is in fact no more aware of itself than it is of others. For this reason, however, the child's *me* can be extremely demanding and volatile. But the phenomena of the child's appearing to be wilfully different from situation to situation, playing several roles with himself, and even attributing his experiences to others ("transitivism") mislead us into attributing them to the child's egocentrism. But these phenomena are actually symptomatic of the as yet unacquired structure of his own perspective as an *I* and that of others in which every *you* is also an *I* and neither he nor they an undifferentiated *me* without limits of time and space. The full development of this structure of experience has as its "correlate" the development of lingustic competence with the system of pronouns that in turn elaborates an interpersonal order through this very perspective.

The second phase that we distinguish intervenes in the development of the first phase from precommunication to the acquisition of personal perspective and its implicit competence with orderly social life gained by the child's second year or so. This is the stage of the child's awareness of his *own body (corps propre)* and the *specular image (l'image speculaire).*[33] At this stage the development of consciousness toward what is called intelligence proceeds by means of an expanded awareness of the child's own body through the acquisition of its specular image that in turn involves a general mode of conduct beyond the episodic event of seeing his body image in a mirror. Moreover, the mastery of this specular image is more difficult for the child to achieve than the distinction between his father, say, and his father's image in the mirror—even though he still allows the image a quasi reality similar to that we feel in the presence of portraits, however much we "know better." But in the case of his own specular image the child can make no visual comparison to establish the difference between the experience of his body seen in the mirror and his body of which he can only see the hands, feet, or other parts but that is otherwise a totality of which he has only a lived experience. Yet the child has now to understand that although he is his own body and not its image in the mirror, his own body is nevertheless visible to others like its mirror image.

Since Merleau-Ponty is not concerned to make an absolute distinction among the three phases of early child development, we may mention the overlap between the second and third phase here, that is, the "crisis at three years." This phase is marked by the child's refusal to allow his body and thoughts to fall under any perspective or interpretation than his own. He wants his own way and this he works out by stubbornly requiring the resistance of others to his own negativity. Through everything the child refuses—his parents, their words, and their food—there arises the structure of oedipal relations in which again the child's world and his conception of social reality are reducible neither to cognitive nor to solely affective factors.

The interpretation of the development of the specular image again involves taking a position on the reduction of cognitive and affective behavior. Merleau-Ponty rejects the view that the specular image involves a cognitive process in which the relation between reality and image, the body here and its image or shadow over there, is established once and for all. The specular image involves a new form of conduct, a shift from the lived body to the visible body, the object of social attention, projection, and mimesis. The body is now a form of conduct, of an identification with others that is never quite stabilized but is the basis of the child's joys and sorrows, his jealousies and tender loyalties that are the experiences of growing up among others: the possiblity of a super ego.

> Thus one sees that the phenomenon of the specular image is given by psychoanalysts the importance it really has in the life of the child. It is the acquisition not only of a new content but of a new function as well: the narcissistic function. Narcissus was the mythical being who, after looking at his image in the mirror of water, was drawn as if by vertigo to rejoin his own image in the mirror of water. At the same time that the image of oneself makes possible the knowledge of oneself, it makes possible a sort of alienation. I am no longer what I felt myself, immediately, to be; I am that image of myself that is offered by the mirror. To use Dr. Lacan's terms, I am "captured, caught up" by my spatial image. Thereupon I leave the reality of my lived *me* in order to refer myself constantly to the ideal, fictitious, or imaginary *me*, of which the specular image is the first outline. In this sense I am torn from myself, and the image in the mirror prepares me for another still more serious alienation, which will be alienation by others. For others have only an exterior image of me, which is analogous to the one seen in the mirror. Consequently others will tear me away from my immediate inwardness much more surely than will the mirror. "The specular image is the 'symbolic matrix,'" says Lacan, "where the I springs up in primordial form before objectifying itself in the dialectic of identification with the other."[34]

The acquisition of the specular image introduces the child into the drama of social life, the struggle with the other, ruled by desire and recognition, even to death. It lies outside the scope of this essay to pursue these themes in terms of the conjuncture between Hegelian phenomenology and Lacanian psychoanalysis.[35] But this is certainly a direction in which we might pursue the dialectic between personal and public life that we repeat in the spectacle of the *body politic* and the struggle between the "organization" of authority and the delinquencies of love's body.[36]

8

The Specular Body:
Merleau-Ponty
and Lacan
on Infant Self
and Other

It would appear to be an ordinary academic task to compare the views of Lacan and Merleau-Ponty on the mirror image. Both writers are intrinsically interesting; their views are original and worth the difficulties one might experience in trying to understand them. Having said this, however, it is necessary to caution against the hope that one can introduce anything like a common terminology to rule the exercise of comparison and evaluation. Nothing of the sort exists for studies in child psychology, psychoanalysis, or phenomenology. We are, therefore, obliged to "misread"[1] our authors as responsibly as we can. There seems to be no general usage in the literature for the concept of body image or of the uses of the mirror image. Seymour Fisher[2] and Fisher and Cleveland[3] virtually ignore phenomenological and psychoanalytical usage in their vast series of quantitative psychological studies. Fisher, Gorman,[4] and Shontz[5] make reference to Schilder,[6] as does Merleau-Ponty.[7] But neither Merleau-Ponty nor Lacan finds any important place in the literature. The phenomenological and psychoanalytical interpretation of the body image and the mirror stage, although itself not ignorant of experimental literature, seems to fall outside contemporary experimental psychology. Lacan's *stade du miroir*[8] involves a revised psychoanalytical reading of psychological and biological data concerning the infant period from six to eighteen months. Of course, at the time Freud was hardly available to French readers, and so we must realize that to a large extent we are dealing with Lacan's retrospective revisionism. But in view of the multiple discourses involved, and the casual practices of cross-reference, nothing is to be gained from trying to coordinate concepts and theory. This is, to be sure, a venerable academic exercise,[9] but it misses the life of science. In practice, each theorist is likely to try to win over everyone to his distinctive discourse rather than try to subordinate himself to a lingua franca. Beyond that, the normal scientists will generally stay behind their chosen leader, defending, patching, and repairing his usage.

1.

Merleau-Ponty's treatment of the mirror image[10] consists of an extensive commentary on the work of Wallon.[11] In the course of his critical evaluation of Wallon, he draws upon Lacan's views. The question we have to decide is whether the Lacanian view of the body image at the mirror stage is really as compatible with Merleau-Ponty's phenomenology of the infant's corporeal schema as he himself takes it to be. In short, as Dillon[12] has observed, we need to be careful with the "visual bias" in the specular image, and we shall have to see whether in fact it faults Merleau-Ponty's better understanding of the mother-infant bond. A similar caution has been raised by Henri Ey, who considers the infant's intersubjective experience of embodiment prior to the visual moment of self-knowledge at the mirror:

> On one level what has so often been repeated to us is true, that the self and the "body image" become confused with one another. Though this is certainly not true for the self which has unfolded in its history, it is true for the "I" appearing in its prehistory. This body among other objects is mine. It is in effect the proto-experience of the subject in its own space. It is as a spatial modality of a spatial property that the self perceives itself as an object in its first self-consciousness. This is the reason for the importance of the "mirror stage." It would doubtlessly be naive to pretend that in order for the self to become conscious for itself it would be enough for it to "see itself" or to perceive itself in the reflected image of its

body. This is true precisely because the self cannot see itself unless it knows itself. We should instead understand the necessity of the reflection of the self upon itself as the absolute of a fundamental structure: that of the relationship of the self to others. To see oneself appear "as other" which is the self, the mirror image of which sends back its image to myself, is the objectification of the self, or as is often said, as its "alienation". The self appears as a person opposite oneself, in the eclipsing of the subject, in its "fading" (Lacan's term), and, as it were, in its disappearance. The self is grounded in and through this negation of its absolute.[13]

According to Lacan, the acquisition of subjectivity is achieved only at the level of language, or in the symbolic order. This stage is reached on the basis of two prior moments: (1) *the mirror phase* and (2) through the relationships experienced as the *castration complex*. The first stage of "I" constitution occurs in the infant's confrontation with his mirror image, or with the experience of a unified body image that is both present and absent. In its wholeness, however, the unified body image projects for the infant an ideal of integrity that his own bodily experience of taste, smell, and motor relations toward things has yet to achieve. To this imaginary wholeness the infant adopts a narcissistic attitude, caught up in the split between self-presence and self-absence.

Lacan treats the infant's grasp of his total body form in the mirror image as an event that is entirely premature and as the prefiguration, so to speak, of an alienated destination:

> The *mirror stage* is a drama whose internal thrust is precipitated from insufficiency to anticipation—and which manufactures for the subject, caught up in the lure of spatial identification, the succession of fantasies that extends from a fragmented body-image to a form of its totality that I shall call orthopaedic—and, lastly, to the assumption of an armour of an alienating identity, which will mark with its rigid structure the subject's entire mental development. Thus, to break out of the circle of the *Innenwelt* into the *Umwelt* generates the inexhaustible quadrature of the ego's verification.[14]

Thus the mirror image, as Lacan interprets it, constitutes a prospective-retrospective complex of identity and separation that prefigures all later separations, from weaning to castration. The ego is constituted in imaginary servitude for which the love of others is always an intrusion upon the madness of the self project. It is beyond the scope of this argument to trace Lacan's account of the oedipal triangulation of the infant's desire for his mother as the primordial real object and

his father as an imaginary ideal self. Thus in-the-name-of-the father
the mother weans her infant on to desire, that is, the discovery of
absence, or lack ruled by law. A point of controversy is whether we
consider the infant to be a "body in bits and pieces" (*corps morcelé*)
prior to the mirror stage. On this interpretation, the *event* of the
mirror image offers to the broken body an ideal of integration and
harmony, an ideal self, *Idealich*. I shall argue instead that the mother's
face is the original reflecting mirror of what in the eyes of her infant
she sees as the bond that, because it is not yet ready for separation,
is unquestioned.[15] The "Madonna" thereby constitutes a presence that
can become an absence, a plenitude that can be symbolized in the
separation and embrace of the other in the endless negativity or play
(*jeu*) of Discourse.

2.

It must be remembered that the *Phenomenology of Perception* argues
that both the body and the mind are structures of experience in their
own right. In particular, then, the mind, so far from making sense of
the body, itself trades upon a preconceptual carnal knowledge of
worldly relations within which self, things, and others are articulated
in a mode of "reciprocity," for which "intelligence" is only another
name. The body is our fundamental yet contingent (that is, mortal
and pathological) relation to the world that funds symbolic consciousness, habit, and reflexivity.[16] Man's senses and intelligence are ways
of being in the world rather than outside it, however much of this is
suggested by idealist and empiricist accounts. According to Merleau-
Ponty, all individuality and every specific sociality presuppose an
anonymous intersubjectivity that is the ground of our figural relations
with things and persons in-and-as-our-world. This lived-world is ours
through the lived-body; it rests on a perceptual faith that is prior to
conceptual articulation. It is our primordial presence to a human
milieu that inaugurates all other specific relations, experiences, and
temporal expressions of our being-in-the-world. This lived-world is
prior to the known-world and is coevally populated with others who
as kindred bodies share the same lived-world as I do. This is our
perceptual faith and not at all a contingent achievement of reasoned
argument, despite the conceits of the Cartesian ego or of the Kantian
imperative.

The articulation of the infant's world likewise presupposes this funding of anonymous intersubjectivity. We shall otherwise misconstrue the infant's developmental stages as a continuous fall from intersubjectivity, or else as a yearning for a future incorporation as fantastic as its first loss. Before a mirror, the infant believes both that he is in the mirror and that he sees himself therein from where he stands. Thus he has not yet constructed a mirror image distinct from himself; he dwells in an *interworld* in which he has not yet articulated either his own egological perspective or yet a sociological orientation toward the other in his propriety. Yet it is only from this ground of anonymous intersubjectivity—not yet ego, not yet alter—that he can experience the generics of a bodily and personal self in a world similarly incorporated. At the same time, this primordial intersubjectivity grounds all later perception, desire, identity, and alterity in the faith that the individual can be valorized for himself by another who in turn shares similar expectation of mutual recognition.

The structure of identity, according to Merleau-Ponty, is a *psychophysical posture* that arises within the field of intersubjectivity, within the familial field, disposing the infant toward self-knowledge and social understanding. The structure of comportment that will generate identity and sociality is not a field of drives and instincts. It is rather a mode of experiencing biopsychic and sociopsychic relations charged with individualizing and familizing significance, that is, with situationally specific desires, loves, hates, and fears projected by the infant upon the social body. Thus the infant body and psyche are reciprocal modes of existence and not at all instrumental functions whose integration or hierarchization would require a further function. Each is given in the primordial intersubjectivity of anonymous being, of the life one has before the life one thinks, feels, and lives with specific others.

Merleau-Ponty is concerned to modify the cognitivist approach to the mirror image and the infant's approach to space, self, and other relations. From this standpoint, and given the basic assumption of psychology that the psyche is accessible only to its owner, the problem of intersubjective experience involves the following quadrature:

> The problem of the experience of others poses itself, as it were, in a system of four terms: (1) myself, my "psyche"; (2) the image I have of my body by means of the sense of touch or of cenesthesia, which, to be brief, we shall call the "introceptive image" of my own body; (3) the body of the other as seen by me, which we shall call the "visual body"; and (4) a fourth (hypothetical) term which I must

reconstitute and guess at—the "psyche" of the other, the other's feeling of his own existence, to the extent that I can imagine or suppose it across the appearances of the other through his visual body.[17]

The cognitive troubles of this approach are evident. The monodological psyche, once assumed, is embroiled in an exhausting guessing game with regard to the relation between inside and outside experiences of the other projected on the basis of his own trust in his own correlations of inside-outside experience. But in practice the infant short-circuits this game of correspondences with a global body overlap, as when the infant responds to a smiling face with his own smile. Here no judgment is involved, no point-to-point correspondence, since the infant cannot see his own face, except in the eyes of his mother. What he "sees" there is not a reflection so much as a gesture that provokes a gesture "within" or from him. This means, however, that the infant's body is not solidary with its own sensations. Its sensations are rather gestures that flow from a "postural" or "*corporeal schema*," the ability to respond to the situated conduct of others with the very conduct elicited *in situ* and as the embodied sense of interaction.

The infant's corporeal consciousness is at first fragmentary and fixated on parts of the body (feet, mouth, and hands), in himself, and in others. As yet, the infant self is latent and submerged in an overlap with the maternal body: *une vie à deux*. The necessary separation of the infant and maternal bodies may be conceived from the very start as a precipitation of self and not-self in every motor and sensory behavior, involving social mediations and possibly a critical moment such as the mirror stage. The latter, in turn, may be seen as critical to a series of later maturational crises, in particular those of weaning and castration. In every case, there is surely a neurophysiological infrastructure, and Merleau-Ponty refers to the function of myelinization in connecting the introceptive and extroceptive body functions.

After a very close reading of Wallon's account of the specular image, Merleau-Ponty concludes that the problem it poses from the cognitive bias of the adult—namely, how to reduce the mirror image to a mere reflection—should be distinguished from the child's acquisition of a self image that remains of interest throughout his life. In other words, the mirror image is transvalued into a corporeal conduct in which reality and appearance are occasioned distinctions. Thus the specular image functions to raise the visual body into a sociopsychological space in which the infant continues to explore self and other relations. In psychoanalytic terms, the specular image is the basis for a superego. Sociologically, the looking-glass self is the basis for life among others.[18] The mirror image, then, prefigures the jubilation of the child's narcissistic self as well as the sorrows and pain of life among others to whom the infant has access only through the lack recognized in him by others. As Merleau-Ponty expresses it in a gloss on Lacan:

> From this moment on, the child is also drawn from his immediate reality: the specular image has a de-realizing function in the sense that it turns the child away from what he effectively is, in order to orient him toward what he sees and imagines himself to be. Finally, this alienation of the immediate *me*, its "confiscation" for the benefit of the *me* that is visible in the mirror already outlines what will be the "confiscation" of the subject by the others who look at him.[19]

3.

The process of identification involves a double structuration of identifying something or someone and identifying one's self in the same course of interaction. Thus *identification* may be said to include a double process of *introjection*, bringing another into the self, and *projection*, bringing the self into another. The mother-infant relation is the primordial relation of identification in this double sense. It is, however, a genetic relation from conception, to embryo, to infant and later child years, if not throughout one's life. It is perhaps best to speak of a relation of *projective preidentification* in recalling the infant's most early experience of the mother's womb, face, voice, and hands, and of *introjective preidentification* in the feeding experience at the breast. This, too, is the stage at which the infant's musculature and coordination are relatively undeveloped and he is submerged in visceral and emotional experiences of the human world. It should not be overlooked that with respect to the issue of the emergence of ego identification as the necessary boundary implied by the mechanisms of projection and introjection, Freud appears to have had in mind a *body-ego*, a cutaneous surface upon which the subject can explore insides and outsides, part and whole, pleasure and pain. Thus, according to Laplanche and Pontalis, Freud derived the ego from a double source:

> On the one hand, the ego is the surface of the psychical apparatus, gradually differentiated in and from that apparatus, a specialized organ continuous with it; on the other hand, it is the projection of metaphor of the body's surface, a metaphor in which the various perceptual systems have a role to play.[20]

With each passing month, the infant's motor and perceptual comportment achieves increasing articulation and thereby engages a claim upon identity and character whose linguistic and socially organized achievement at this stage is closely bound to the pronominal and oedipal systems. In other words, the infant embarks upon an *anthropomorphosis* that involves mutually articulated levels of structuration that are

1. motor-perceptual
2. psychosocial
3. linguistic-conceptual

However, the phenomenological interpretation of these levels is radically different from what we find in textbook psychology and psychoanalysis. At the motor-perceptual level, we are not dealing with mechanical drives, pushes, and pulls, nor with instincts. Rather, we are in the presence of a physical *posture* that is capable of empathizing immediately and nonverbally with the other's postural attitude, as though each were a physical sketch of the other. Thus mutual co-orientation is struck intuitively in-and-as the setting of any further articulation of copresence. It involves a preknowledge that is prior to explicitly imitative behavior that is a later phase of infant intersubjectivity. Even in the latter case, what is involved is a psychomuscular response, rather like that of a conductor whose bodily movements reproduce the orchestra's efforts without imitating them. Literal imitation of persons constitutes a hostile social gesture, a potential degradation rather than communion. At this level, introjection involves a mutual coordination of bodies, a postural agreement that underwrites being-together, upon which talk, thought, and other conducts can be articulated. Understood in this way, introjection is the other side of a projective comportment in which we bring our own posture within another's pastural schema in order to articulate further communion.[21] Taken together, these introjective and projective postures cast us in a psychomuscular, or motor-perceptual, field of the corporeal presence of ourselves to others and of the self to itself. Thus there can be nothing inert or inexpressive about the lived-body, not even in sleep. The existence of another human being is *reciprocal* with my own existence.

It is this norm of reciprocity that is further articulated at the psychosocial and linguistic-conceptual levels of anthropogenesis. Here language and the oedipal myth are the primordial sociolinguistic structurations of identity. The postural identification we have described lies at the basis of later child and adult dramaturgical identification with other human senses, emotions, and events into which he can be drawn conaturally, as it were. Here, again, the neutral observer standpoint of the sciences trades upon a postural involvement that is preconceptual but nevertheless funds all participant and quasi-neutral observation. Thus we relive human dramas, identify with their personages, not because we know the lines but because corporeally we are the text in which life's lines are inscribed from earliest infancy.[22] In this sense, we live our lives through others before ourselves and only with difficulty, as Montaigne observes, do we learn to preserve for ourselves a "backstage."

4.

Dillon has argued that Merleau-Ponty mistimes the correlation of self and other recognition at the mirror stage. The infant cannot handle the recognition that he is an object for others at the same time as he struggles with the recognition of himself as an object for himself. This is because he has not yet freed himself from syncretic sociability. But to do so, Dillon argues, requires much more than a visual experience. This is because the phenomenal body is a synesthetic whole of affective and conative behavior sensitive to the rejecting, weaning, and punishing behavior of others. It is from these experiences rather than the mirror image as such that the infant learns self and other relations as alienative modes of being-in-the-world.

It is not easy to decide this argument on purely textual grounds. I think, therefore, that it may be pertinent to introduce further data upon the infant-mother relationship in order to contextualize the experiences attributed to the specular image. Thus Winnicott has argued for an intermediate developmental stage between the infant's inability and increasing ability to distinguish "not-me" objects. This occurs in the first few months as the infant moves from fist-to-mouth exploration onto some favored object, blanket, or teddy bear. He calls the shift from oral eroticism to object relations and the attendant babbling "transitional phenomena." Although the teddy bear or favorite blanket is clearly a partial object (the mother's breast), it is just as important that it is not the breast. Hence the symbolic value of the transitional object demonstrates that the infant is already exploring similarity and difference, and so moving from magical control to reality testing.[23] The mother's cooperation in this transition is absolutely vital. In Winnicott's terms, the "good-enough" mother must lead her baby into abandoning the magical omnipotence with which she at first conspired. Precisely because she has sustained the infant's early illusion, she can then successfully "disillusion" the infant in the transition to reality testing. In other words, weaning can only be successful if the question it eventually resolves is not posed from the very start: that is, what is the thing in the outside world that might match my inside world?

> The transitional object and the transitional phenomena start each human being off with what will always be important for them, i.e., a neutral area of experience which will not be challenged. *Of the transitional object it can be said that it is a matter of agreement between us and the baby that we will never ask the question: "Did you conceive of this or was it presented to you from without?" The important point is that no decision on this point is to be expected. The question is not to be formulated.*[24]

It is this provision that enables the infant to deal with the loss of omnipotence. Through the transitional object the infant creates an objective environment. The good-enough mother at first allows the infant to experience a sense of *being,* that is, the lack of any need to question the boundary between the breast and the infant. Thereafter, the drive satisfactions within the infant and the mother's independence, alternative commitments, and need to be elsewhere involve the infant in coming to terms with the boundary between inside and outside worlds and the exploration of object relations and uses. This is achieved in what Winnicott calls a *"potential space,"* the place where we come to live and play:

> I refer to the hypothetical area that exists (but cannot exist) between the baby and the object (mother or part of mother) during the phase of the repudiation of the object as not-me, that is, at the end of being merged in with the object.
> From a state of being merged in with the mother the baby is at a stage of separating out the mother from the self, and the mother is lowering the degree of her adaptation to the baby's needs (both because of her own recovery from a high degree of identification with her baby and because of her perception of the baby's new need, the need for her to be a separate phenomenon).[25]

Bettelheim[26] also stresses the infant's experiences at the breast as the basic source of trust in self and other persons. In the mutual give-and-take between infant and mother each educates the other in the articulation of the fundamental human bond. The mutuality of the infant and nursing mother sets the stage for all later intersubjective relations. It establishes the "potential space" in which the infant creatively explores the transition to world of not-me, of things and others, the world in which the infant self separated from its mother will learn what it can do on its own.

As I see it, prior to the games of *Fort! Da!*[27] and the great oedipal drama, the mother and infant bodies work between them to construct a potential space in which the events of identity and separation can be further articulated within the domains of language and the family. This space is celebrated in every Madonna and Child. It is recreated in the faces of every mother and infant mirroring each other, and by each of us in a lifelong personal reflection. The infant becomes more human, we might say, when it begins to be able to *provoke* desire rather than be subject to it. But this means that the infant begins to master the alternation of presence and absence in the light of his relations to his immediate family in which he first experiences the self and not-self. That is to say, as we have seen, that the mother-infant couple is the ground for the foregrounding-backgrounding of presence and absence vocalized in the infant's game of *Fort! Da!* Freud's observations can, I think, be repeated in the game of peek-a-boo. The infant's delight in hiding increases with every confession of the father that he can't find those toes sticking out from behind the curtains or that he can't hear the shrieks of laughter when he fails to see the little thing hidden before his eyes. The pleasure of peek-a-boo reaches a crescendo when the infant begins to fear that he may have hidden himself too well—and be lost! At this point, the infant finds himself for his daddy: I'm here, daddy, I'm here! One can think of other infant experiences with the mediation of object and person relationships. For example, the same circuit of desire and recognition is involved in the infant's first steps toward the parent, trusting to be caught in a fall, or trusting to be caught when tossed by the parent, who thereby restores the risked body. By the very same token, by his body, the infant has learned to integrate his fear of disintegration in the social relations that continuously proffer sustenance and separation. I am suggesting, then, that we ought to think of the *stade du miroir* as a series of experiences that articulate the self-other circuit before language and before oedipal society. This is compatible with Lacan's own usage:

> The jubilant assumption of his specular image by the child at his *infans* stage, still sunk in his motor incapacity and nursing

dependence, would seem to exhibit in an exemplary situation the symbolic matrix in which the I is precipitated in a primordial form, before it is objectified in the dialectic of identification with the other, and before language restores to it, in the universal, its function as a subject.[28]

5.

I think it is important for a phenomenological analysis not to fall into a narrow psychosexual schematization of the body image. We need to consider the body image as a synthesis of physiological and psychological organization heavily mediated by family relations. In its early months the infant's bodily experiences of food, hunger, warmth, cold, pleasure, pain, and gravitational swings are beyond his control. Simultaneously, he has to explore this world, to solicit support in it and continuous reassurance of love and care. His whole body communicates with the mother, who is the most immediate source and register of his experiments with her and his probes into the outer world. At the same time, the infant explores his mother's body as well as his own and must also acquire a sense of the consistency, size, weight, and texture of all of the bodies that make up his environment. Security and gratification alternate with fear and displeasure in the course of these bodily probes. Adult attitudes will be vital in the mediation of the infant's bodily inquiry, heightening and reassuring its positive experiences, rescuing and removing from painful encounters. Of course, the parent may also be an ambivalent participant, discouraging and disappointing the infantile inquiry. All this registers in the infant's posture and movements associated with the face, mouth, eyes, fingers, toes, and body arching. Thus the infant's search for security is not to be equated with passivity. On the contrary, security underwrites the infant's mobility, grasping, rhythm, gurgling, and play. These in turn will underwrite his efforts to achieve upright posture, to walk, and to climb, despite falls. The infant who begins with a strong attachment to his mother, seeking, grasping, and clinging, will simultaneously explore the distance between himself and his mother, continuously widening the circle of her watchful care until he can enter and leave it without fear. Considered in this fashion, then, there is a constant interplay among the infant's achievement of psychosomatic integration, security, and social separation.

For these reasons, Schilder argues that the infant fears for its *whole* body, for its insides, its orifices, and its outsides—and not just for its sexual organs. Thus in the psychoanalytic literature the notion of the castration complex has been widened to include any separation experience, such as birth and weaning (the child's experience of divorce?). Schilder's view, however, is that the integrity of the body image remains central to infant development:

> It is perfectly true that there is something in common in all infringements on the integrity of the body, but the body is more than just an annex to the sex parts. It has a definite value in itself, and it is arbitrary to view the integrity of the body merely as an aspect to the integrity of the sex parts. . . . I prefer to speak about the wish for the integrity of the body and the fear of being dismembered.[29]

Empirical studies of the infant's response to the mirror image report a variety of self-conscious behavior from embarrassment to coyness, delight, and suspicion. It appears then, that the mirror stage should be regarded as a continuous and multilevel experience, rather than as a climactic moment. Thus we might distinguish in the mirror-experience the (1) beginning of awareness of oneself, (2) awareness of oneself as distinct from others, (3) awareness of oneself as seen by others, (4) affective self-consciousness allied to shame and social embarrassment.[30] These experiences are related to kinesthetic and sensory feelings in the infant body during its first year of life. In the second year, the infant-self-conscious seems to acquire a representation level that permits it (1) to treat its own body as an object, (2) to struggle toward upright posture and locomotion, and (3) to direct its attention toward its own genitals. Thus the infant body, its orifices and erogeneous zones, becomes the focus of self-consciousness and its social counterpart in shame and embarrassment.

Infantile narcissism, therefore, cannot be restricted to the passive mirror image; the infant's delight there merely foreshadows his later joy in walking and climbing, even with its pitfalls. Thus Erikson[31] has developed a theory of pregenital body zones and stages infested with infantile libido that enhances the oral, anal, and limb movements. Each of these zones at a specific stage is the site of a changing pattern of mutual regulation between the infant and mother. Erikson first identifies an oral-respiratory-sensory stage in which the incorporative mode is dominant, including spitting up and nuzzling. This is not a passive stage. Rather, the infant, in learning to get someone to meet his needs, learns also to become a giver. In the next stage, with the appearance of teeth, the infant can bite on, off, and through things, as well as take, grasp, and hold on to things. At this stage, the infant's sense of trust and mistrust is tested; he may have teething problems, and weaning is imminent. The potential troubles of intake and release, therefore, are heightened around the anal zone inasmuch as the familial concern with retention and elimination is highly focused, at least in Western society. Finally (or as far as we shall go here), once the infant can sit squarely and achieve some locomotion, he is even more able to test his relations to things and others and thereby to himself. At each level, stress can be relieved or relived through regression to thumbsucking, crying, tantrums, and teddy bears.

From Melanie Klein[32] we also learn that the processes of introjection and projection involve a continuous exchange of unconscious fantasies that enrich the infant's inner world and improve his relations with the external world. A specific mechanism engaged in this exchange is the process of "splitting" whereby the dependent infant separates the good aspects of its mother from the bad or damaging aspects of its dependency upon her presence, breast, milk, smile. The bad aspects, absence, withholding, irritability, are then managed through projective identification. They are located in another person with whom the infant then identifies in order to protect the good mother from himself. What is fundamental in these processes is that they are set in the flesh, so to speak, of the mother-infant body. Their goodness and badness, their successes and failures are then translated into traces at each higher level of biopsychological self-awareness and relationship. The vital role of the mother's body is that its presence to the infant be "good enough," as Winnicott says, not to raise prematurely the question of separation from the mother. Thereafter, she may initiate the infant into its own search for separation, without thereby prolonging the trauma of birth.

I also think we should set aside the notion of passivity of the infant in its relation to the mother as part of the retrospective myth of plenitude. Even in the womb the embryo is active and the activity increases until the crescendo of birth. Thereafter, of course, the infant responds to auditory and tactile stimuli, as well as to taste and smell. Visual stimuli increase, and the infant's body becomes at once the source of interior sensations and a perceptual object, at least partially, as a finger or toe. At this stage, then, sensation and perception are relativized, as we subjectivize experience and the external world. If anything, the value of the infant's milieu will be determined by its bodily sensations rather than perceptions of external reality, and its contact with the latter will also be mediated by those larger human bodies that solicit, interpret, and requite the infant's wants. At this stage, infant libido remains with the body but will develop beyond this primitive narcissistic level as the oral, anal, and genital levels of experience are organized and, so to speak, familized. Thus the libidinal body is psychologically and sociologically organized to shift preoedipal infantile sexuality into a secondary narcissism founded upon a family mediated ego ideal.

The infant's response to others as potentially helpful or harmful is *quasi-postural.* By the same token, it is not a constructed or conceptual attitude. It is a corporeal response to a lived social situation. Moreover, the infant is responsive to this social milieu more directly than to his physical milieu.[33] Indeed, he seeks access to the latter through his social world long before he learns to interact directly with his physical world. In this "parasitic" stage, psychological reality pervades the infant's body so that it seems to resonate pure pleasure and pain in its successes and failures with others and their mediation of the things he seeks. Indeed, the infant appears to be a natural social psychologist, moving the adult world around him, delighting and disappointing it according to the infant's register of smiles and cries. It is to free themselves from this helpless tyrant that parents begin to impute motive, reason, cause, and insight to the infant in their exchanges with him. In this way, they are able to draw the infant into a contract from which they can responsibly withdraw. Thus the prephysical and presocial world of the infant is gradually articulated into the two domains of the world of objects and the world of persons. The hinge, so to speak, of this double articulation of the physical and social world is the infant's *own body.*

The infant does not have a social world by means of a detour through his own world, although this may be true of the child once he has acquired language as part of the competent articulation of his relations to others and his own interests. To the infant the social world is, so to speak, *physiognomic.* His own corporeal world resonates the sounds, smells, smiles, caresses, warmth, coldness, and hurts with which he is surrounded. But the infant does not project upon his mediators the responses evoked in himself before the spectacle he enjoys or dislikes. The infant's egocentrism at this stage is a bodily circuit rather than an intellectual circuit of reflexivity or *Verstehen.* Yet the expressivity of the infant's postural response, the way it seeks to prolong or to reject an approach, already conscripts the other as a witness, an accomplice, or a nuisance in the infant's world. Before language, the infant's body seems already to be a *text of pleasure and pain*[34] with which its parents are obsessed, reading in every sound, in each stir, smile, or tear, their own fates. Thus each new generation of parents willingly enthralls itself to the royal pantomine of its children.

Institution, Language, and Historicity

We may now be in a position to interpret Merleau-Ponty's suggestion that we conceive consciousness as *institution* rather than constitution.[1] We need to understand how consciousness is given to itself neither all at once nor at the expense of others but in a field of presence and coexistence that situates consciousness and truth as a sedimentation and a search. The notion of consciousness as "institution" restores subjectivity and objectivity to the matrix in which conduct is generated as a recovery of being that is simultaneously self-discovery.

> Thus what we understand by the concept of institution are those events in experience which endow it with durable dimensions, in relation to which a whole series of other experiences will acquire meaning, will form an intelligible series or a history—or again those events which sediment in me a meaning, not just as a survival or residue, but as the invitation to sequel, the necessity of a future.[2]

The temporal ekstasis of the instituting consciousness is the acquisiton and renovation of a style of being through its openness to expression and conduct. This is to say that consciousness is never a real adequation of the self to itself, but rather an intentional unity whose infrastructure is temporality or historicity precisely because it is only in subjectivity that there is found that possibility of not-being which delineates past and future, whereas the plenum is too solidary for there to be temporality.[3] The significance of time comes from what we are and what objects can be for us. Subject and object are, in other words, "two abstract 'moments' of a unique structure which is presence." It is in the field of presence that there is consciousness of what has passed and what is to come, and this field lies in the hollow of the for-itself, the revelation of the self to the self. We are present to a world that is carried forward along vectors of intentionality that trace out the style of the world to come. The present, in the strict sense of a "now," is not posited by us. "I do not so much perceive objects as reckon with an environment; I seek support in my tools, and I am at my task rather than confronting it." The present is the privileged zone in which being and consciousness coincide, not in the sense that our being is reducible to the knowledge we have of it—for perception reveals only our primitive alliance with the world—but in the sense that consciousness is nothing but belonging to the world and thereby to ourselves as ecstatic beings. The discovery of the self is not an atemporal act, but rather, we must think of subjectivity as temporality, the search for a meaning that can never be absolutely totalized. It is not, of course, that our gestures and thoughts never succeed in expressing our intentions, nor that it is impossible to detect meaning in historical events. It is rather that in the creative act or expression there is no meaning that precedes it and that it simply translates. Its meaning is discovered in the act of expression as the style of the world revealed through the vehicle of the artist, the statesman, or the speaking subject, all of whom discover their own meaning as a correlative of the expressive gesture.

The *institution* of self-consciousness, no less than the institution of ideas, truth, and culture, is founded upon a series of exchanges between subjectivity and situation in which the polarities of means and ends and question and answer are continuously established and renewed. The model of such exchanges is to be found in the relation of consciousness to language and speech and may also serve as an introduction to other cultural institutions, including history and the social sciences themselves as symbolic institutions. This suggestion is the result of abandoning the attempt to construct an eidetic of all possible symbolic structures as the correlative of a universal and timeless constituting consciousness as first conceived by Husserl and that raised its own difficulties with regard to intersubjectivity, rationality, and philosophy itself.[4]

Starting from the later writings of Husserl and from Saussure's work in linguistics,[5] a conception of the relation of language to consciousness emerges in which, so far from being an external instrument of thought, language appears as the embodiment of thought without which thought would achieve neither ideal existence nor intersubjective value. Language is not simply a mnemonic device that thought employs in order to facilitate its expression but might discard for wings of its own. We express our thought by bringing it to inhabit the spoken word (*la parole*): we know what we have in mind (*vouloir dire*) or what we mean once we know how to say it, by a kind of permutation of the intentional object and its embodiment in an expressive gesture. The incarnation of thought in the word (*la parole, logos*) actualizes the transcendental affinities of thought and being in a process of the recovery of a truth that can never be absolutely totalized.

> It is like a wedge that we sink into the present, a landmark which testifies that at this moment something has happened for which being was always waiting or intending to say from the very beginning, and which will never cease, if not to be true, at least to be significant and to arouse our thinking resources to the need for drawing from it truths more comprehensive than itself.[6]

Since perception never reveals to us a totality and our perspectives fall upon a world that encloses them, our expression of the world in language, thought, and art can never be the prose reproduction of a preestablished nature. We express the world through the poetics of our own being-in-the-world, beginning with the first act of perception that carves into being the perspectives of form and ground whereby the world has an architecture or foundation. In the gesture of pointing our body opens up a world whose schema it bears within itself and through which it possesses the world, as it were, at a distance. All other cultural gestures are continuous with the first gesture of human behavior in opening up a world that expresses meaning by an indirection that takes root in us as the fruit of human labor and is never a completed task.

The ontological bearing of language may be clarified if we draw a distinction between *language* as an objective structure studied by linguistics and *speech,* which is the use-value language acquires when it is turned toward expression. It is not because they are the sign-correlates of mental significations that words succeed in conveying thought. Rather than interpose themselves between us and what we mean to say, words signify only through the texture of our discourse that at any given moment is nothing more than a "*determinate gap* to be filled in by words."[7] Our "thoughts" find expression through a sensible articulation of which we are capable without prior reflection because we are, as Valéry says, the "animal of words."[8] In speech there occurs a reversal of language that has us and language that we make ours through a series of "coherent deformations" (Malraux) that anchor new meaning for ourselves and our listeners. The manner in which this is achieved involves an institution of meaning in which both speaker and listener, writer and reader, share in the same expressive operation of the recuperation and innovation of a style of language. We start by reading an author, leaning at first upon the common associations of his words until, gradually, they begin to flow in us and to open us to an original sound that is the writer's voice borrowing from us an understanding that until then we did not know was ours to offer. "I say that I *know an idea* when the capacity to organize around it discourses which make sense has been instituted in me; and this capacity itself does not depend upon my alleged possession and face to face contemplation of it, but upon my having acquired a certain style of thinking."[9] Once we have acquired the author's style of thinking, our lives interweave in a presence that is the anticipation (*Vorhabe*) in the words of the whole of the author's intention and its simultaneous recovery (*Nachvollzug*) that continues the understanding. "A personal and interpersonal tradition will have been founded."[10]

We always mean to say something. That is the original promise conveyed in the human gaze, gesture, and language and solicited by the world itself. The task of expression is simultaneously a self-improvisation in which we borrow from the world, others, and our own past efforts. The act of expression is not a solitary exercise in initiation, but the acquisition of a tradition that is the ability to recover an interrogation opened in the past and to inscribe it in a living style of expression that it always called for in its truth. Each act of expression remains an exemplary type, inaugurates a world, and outlines a future that is not the simple sacrifice of the past, but the sedimentation of all presents in our own—

> and just as our body, insofar as it *lives* and makes itself gesture, sustains itself only through its effort to be in the world, holds itself upright because its inclination is towards the top and because its perceptual fields draw it towards that risky position, and could not possibly receive this power from a separate spirit; so that history of painting, which runs from one work to another, rests upon itself and is borne only by the caryatid of our efforts, which converge by the sole fact that they are efforts to express.[11]

The object of the historical and social sciences is, properly speaking, neither an object nor an act of contemplation but a verification (*reprise*) that each individual undertakes according to his situation in an attempt, which must be continually reviewed, to unearth sedimented structures of meaning, in a language or a culture. These structures, however, can never be fully brought to life for the reason that they are buried in our own primordial archaeology as an "operant or latent intentionality like that which is the soul of time, more ancient than the intentionality of human acts."[12] A social anthropology that is founded upon a phenomenological description of perceptual consciousness is simultaneously a metaphysical consciousness grounded in the paradox that the life of the individual is also a universal life, not as a biological or species identity but in the community of perception, dialogue, and tradition. The appeal of a cultural object, such as a painting, that makes it possible to speak of a universal Art, or history of art, can only be grasped if we recognize "*un ordre original de l'avènement,*" which is the nature of human expression to inaugurate a value supervenient to the level of fact and open to all other modes of expression insofar as they are similar designations of an order of significance that is continuous from the first gesture to the wall paintings.

Thus if we were to model history after art and language we might recover the true sense of the concept of history as expression, truth, and intersubjectivity.

> The linguistic relations among men should help us understand the more general order of symbolic relations and of institutions, which assure the exchange not only of thoughts, but of all types of values, the coexistence of men within a culture and, beyond it, within a single history. Interpreted in terms of symbolism . . . history is no more external to us than language.[13]

We should have to distinguish two sorts of historicity that have their origin in the two conceptions of consciousness as constitution and consciousness as institution. Constituting consciousness contemplates the history of art in the dead synthesis of the museum whose rooms present any style of art from an external perspective totally alien to the actual genesis of that style. The other historicity that is presupposed by the museum lies in the artist's institution of his own style from one work to another guided by the same fundamental problem of the world to be painted or described that outlines the history of art and the interest the artist has in always starting again. The museum ossifies this living historicity of a work in process into a series of dead-end works of art that reveal nothing of the matrix of acquisition and search in which the artist cannot say what comes from himself, what from others, nor what is added or taken away from the question that demanded his response.

Merleau-Ponty remarks how well Husserl's term *Stiftung,* foundation or establishment, captures the fecundity of cultural creations by which they endure into our present and open a field of inquiry to which they are continuously relevant. "It is thus that the world as soon as he has seen it, his first attempts at painting, and the whole past of painting, all deliver up a *tradition* to the painter—*that is,* Husserl remarks, *the power to forget origins* and to give to the past not a survival, which is the hypocritical form of forgetfulness, but new life, which is the noble form of memory."[14] It is the same fecundity that explains the unity of geometry as an intentional history of intellectual tradition.[15] The ideal unity of geometry and its historical development derive from the same source in individual acts of production and reproduction in which the historicity *of* geometry is as essential to its *history (Geschichte)* as is the linguisitic tradition that individual geometricians inherit and through which they contribute to the infinite ideal of pure geometry. Through language and writing what was only an ideal meaning in the mind of an individual achieves an objective and public status and enters a community of thinkers that is the presupposition of truth. Thus we have another instance of that circuit of reflection in which what was first recognized as neither local nor temporal "according to the meaning of its being" comes to rest upon the locality and temporality of speech that belongs neither to the objective world nor to the world of ideas.

> Ideal existence is based upon the document, not, of course, as a physical object, or even as the vehicle of one-to-one significations assigned to it by the language in which it is written, but upon the document insofar as, again by an "intentional transgression," it solicits and brings together all lives in pursuit of knowledge—and as such establishes and reestablishes a "Logos" of the cultural world.[16]

What emerges from these examples is that the universality and truth aimed at by theoretical consciousness is not an intrinsic property of the idea. It is an acquisition continuously established and reestablished in a community and tradition of science called for and responded to by individuals in specific historical situations. Understood in this way, history is the call of one thought to another, because each individual's work or action is created across the path of self and others toward a *public* that it elicits rather than serves.[17] That is to say, history is the field that individual effort requires in order to become one with the community it seeks to build so that where it is successful its invention appears always to have been necessary. Individual action then is the invention of history because it is shaped in a present that previously was not just a void waiting to be determined by the word or deed, but a tissue of calling and response that is the life of no one and everyone. Every one of life's actions, insofar as it invokes its truth, lives in the expectation of a historical inscription, a judgment not of its intention or consequences but of its fecundity, which is the relevance of its "story" to the present.

> True history thus gets its life entirely from us. It is in our present that it gets the force to refer everything else to the present. The other whom I respect gets his life from me as I get mine from him. A philosophy of history does not take away any of my rights or initiatives. It simply adds to my obligations as a solitary person the obligation to understand situations other than my own and to create a path between my life and that of others, that is, to express myself.[18]

The phenomenology of language and speech yields a basic intuition that liberates history from the false alternatives of materialism and idealism. The institution of language, which makes man and all other institutions possible, proceeds through an ever-open series of exchanges between the assumption of past linguistic acquisitions and the advent of expression that encounters the indirection of the world. In the act of speech the individual achieves an autonomy, an authentic style that at the same time is the declaration of his membership in a continuing linguistic community whose traditions are sedimented in his natural being. This presence of the individual in the institution and of the institution in the individual is particularly clear in the case of linguistic innovations. The need to speak and to be understood leads to new inflections and discriminations in which living speech rearticulates the possibilities of language and finds its innovations incorporated in the sense and history of its language.

Language provides us with more than an analogy for the understanding of the processes of structure and genesis in other social institutions.[19] Just as a language is a system of signs whose values are interdependent or diacritical, so every institution is a symbolic system in which the individual incorporates himself and through which his actions acquire a typical style. The reciprocal relation between the means of expression and the desire for expression is matched by the institutional distinction between the means of production and the social forces of history. There is a dynamic similarity, too, inasmuch as the internal rearrangements of the elements of the linguistic system are the result of neither purely intellectual nor purely molecular changes, but occur through existential modifications in the same community that is polarized by the desire to establish an intersubjective basis of human action and expression.

Once we have located all institutions, politics, religion, kinship, and technology, in their proper cultural or symbolic space,[20] it becomes possible to inquire into the relationships between them and the meaning that persists through them. The method of such a study has been outlined in Max Weber's phenomenology of the "affinity" of the institutions of religion and economics within the matrix defined by the historical *choices* of the Calvinist ethic and the "rationalization" of capitalism. Weber's notion of an "affinity of choices" (*Wahlwerwandtschaft*) is the intuition of a certain intelligible transition between the Calvinist transformation of nature to the glory of God and the "rationalization" of labor in capitalist enterprise. Calvinist consciousness oscillates between boundless guilt and utter vindication, just as capitalism is haunted by scarcity and glut. In each case, the flight into materialism results in a total loss of transcendence, vindicated as demystification that is also disenchantment (*Entzauberung*). It becomes possible to understand the solidarity of the orders of economics, politics, and religion as a value-additive rather than causal phenomenon once we treat the economic order itself as a choice of social and physical relations. It is then possible, given other preconditions, to see the capitalist system outlined in the Calvinist ethic and the Protestant Reformation in the program of capitalist rationalizations. The course of history also illuminates the nature of these fundamental choices. "What we assume in order to understand history is that freedom understands the uses of freedom."[21] The Calvinist juxtaposition of the finite and the infinite, at the same time blocking access to the other world, organized an obsession with this world. Although we have no reasons for saying that history will relieve this uneasiness, we can struggle to renew the demands of transcendence abolished in the capitalist world that only reveals that the question of transcendence has been poorly posed rather than eliminated.

Finally, it is unnecessary to reject either Marxian or Freudian explanations of history as fallacious reductions of a phenomenologically richer reality since neither is tied to causal language. Historical materialism consists as much in translating economics into a historical matrix as in bringing economics into history. This is because the Marxian conception of economics is not a closed system of objective facts, but a living cohesion of the material and social forces of production that is simultaneously an institutional and psychological formation. Historical materialism takes into account the objective framework of individual action in order to activate the latent structures of human relationships that generate the norms of collective existence. Such an interpretation is not an attempt to spiritualize history in a Hegelian fashion. Economic life is *already* transcendent in a confused way just as transcendence in human terms is already the demand for *a certain* type of economy. "Precisely because economics is not a closed world, and because all motivations intermingle at the core of history, the external becomes internal, and the internal external, and no constituent of our existence can ever be outrun."[22] Through language we first encounter that system of exchanges between consciousness and the world in which meaning is established and renewed in a permutation of the given and the possible that offers a paradigm of all cultural institutions, for it is the matrix of the acquisition and renewal of the tradition of humanity in each of us. Language, like other cultural institutions, is often regarded as a tool or an instrument of thought. But then language is a tool that accomplishes far more and is far less logical than we might like it to be. It is full of ambiguity and in general far too luxuriant for the taste of positivist philosophers. As a tool, language seems to use us as much as we use it, and in this it is more like the rest of our general culture, which we cannot use without inhabiting it. Ultimately, language, like culture, defeats any attempt to conceive it as a system capable of revealing the genesis of its own meaning. This is because we *are* the language we are talking about. That is to say, we are the material truth of language through our body, which is a natural language. It is through our body that we can speak of the world because the world in turn speaks to us through the body.

Since human perception falls upon a world in which we are enclosed, our expression of the world in language and art can never be a simple introduction to the prose of the world apart from its poetry. We express the world through the poetics of our being-in-the-world, beginning with the first act of perception that brings into being the perspective of form and ground through which the invisible and ineffable speaks and becomes visible in us. All other cultural gestures are continuous with the first institution of human labor, speech, and art through which the world takes root in us. In this sense, we may consider talk, reading, writing, and love as institutions, that is to say, polarizations of the established and the new.

Once we have acquired the author's style of thinking, our lives interweave in a presence that is the anticipation of the whole of the author's intention and its simultaneous recovery that continues the understanding. In talking and listening to one another we make an accommodation through language and the body in which we grow older together. We encroach upon one another and borrow from each other's time, words, and looks what we are looking for in ourselves. In this way our mind and self may be thought of as institutions that we inhabit with others in a system of presences that includes Socrates, Montaigne, or Sartre just as much as our friends in the room.

> When I speak or understand, I experience that presence of others in myself or of myself in others which is the stumbling-block of the theory of intersubjectivity, I experience that presence of what is represented which is the stumbling-block of the theory of time, and I finally understand what is meant by Husserl's enigmatic statement, "Transcendental subjectivity is intersubjectivity." To the extent that what I say has meaning, I am a different "other" for myself when I am speaking; and to the extent that I understand, I no longer know who is speaking and who is listening.[23]

Through language I discover myself and others, in talking, listening, reading, and writing. It is language that makes possible that aesthetic distance between myself and the world through which I can speak about the world and the world in turn can speak through me. Our thoughts and purposes are embodied in bodily gestures that in the act of expression structure themselves toward habit and spontaneity, and thus we make our world.[24] Finally, what we may learn from Merleau-Ponty's approach to the phenomenology of language is that expression is always an act of self-improvisation in which we borrow from the world, from others, and from our own past efforts. Language is the child in us that speaks of the world in order to know who he or she is.

10

The Prose of
the World

Phenomenology is remarkable for its introductions not only of itself but also of the world to which it returns us. Here we need a beginning that will catch[1] or fetch out a sense of Merleau-Ponty's conception of the relation between language and the world[2] and simultaneously convey this preoccupation as an expression of the crisis in philosophy in the same manner that Husserl considered that concern to be an authentic introduction to phenomenology. Such a beginning seems necessary because I see in Merleau-Ponty's work, from beginning to end, a critique of the two principal techniques of reason, namely, the analytic method of experimental science and the structuralist method of the human sciences through which the tradition of rationalism dominated the world by removing the responsible subject of human history. The success of Western science and its industrial organization is, as Weber and Marx showed, the result of an asceticism at the roots of the positivist mode of rationality. The methodological and technical success of Western science rests, as Husserl observes, upon a *residual concept* of reason that excludes any treatment of the *problem of reason.*[3] But these observations form part of the self-criticism of the ideal of phenomenology as a rigorous science begun by Husserl himself and, as I believe, adopted as the working principle of Merleau-Ponty's own phenomenology.

The problematic of *The Prose of the World*[4] was outlined in Merleau-Ponty's interpretation of the main features of Husserlian phe-

nomenology, for example, in his remarks on the notions of essence
and eidetic reduction:

> Every reduction, says Husserl, as well as being transcendental is
> necessarily eidetic. That means that we cannot subject our
> perception of the world to philosophy's scrutiny without ceasing to
> be identified with that act of positing the world, with that interest in
> it which delimits us, without drawing back from our commitment
> which is itself thus made to appear as a spectacle, without passing
> from the *fact* of our existence to its *nature,* from the Dasein to the
> Wesen. But it is clear that the essence is here not the end, but a
> means, that our effective involvement in the world is precisely what
> has to be understood and made amenable to conceptualization, for
> it is what polarizes all our conceptual particularizations. . . .
> Whatever the subtle changes of meaning which have ultimately
> brought us, as a linguistic acquisition, the word and concept of
> consciousness, we enjoy direct access to what it designates. For we
> have the experience of ourselves, of that consciousness which we
> are, and it is on the basis of this experience that all linguistic
> connotations are assessed, and precisely through it that language
> comes to have any meaning at all for us. "It is that as yet dumb
> experience . . . which we are concerned to lead to the pure
> expression of its own meaning." Husserl's essences are destined to
> bring back all the living relationships of experience, as the
> fisherman's net draws up from the depths of the ocean quivering
> fish and seaweed.[5]

Merleau-Ponty's formulation of the return to phenomena is
not intended to do away with language as such but to recover from
its particular vocabularies the genesis of the world and its appearance,
that is, the inspiration of poetry or of any creative act. Indeed, so far
from being destructive of philosophical language and its intentionality, Merleau-Ponty's appeal to the prelinguistic world is an effort to
free philosophical thinking from the habits of method and to recon-
nect it with the teleology of reason.

> Through this broadened notion of intentionality,
> phenomenological "comprehension" is distinguished from
> traditional "intellection," which is confined to "true and immutable
> natures," and so phenomenology can become a phenomenology of
> origins. Whether we are concerned with a thing perceived, a
> historical event or a doctrine, to "understand" is to take in the total
> intention—not only what these things are for representation (the
> "properties" of the thing perceived, the mass of "historical facts,"

the "ideas" introduced by the doctrine)—but the unique mode of
existing expressed in the properties of the pebble, the glass or the
piece of wax, in all the events of a revolution, in all the thoughts of
a philosopher. It is a matter, in the case of each civilization, of
finding the Idea in the Hegelian sense, that is, not a law of the
physico-mathematical type, discoverable by objective thought, but
that formula which sums up some unique manner of behaviour
towards others, towards Nature, time and death: a certain way of
patterning the world which the historian should be capable of
seizing upon and making his own. These are the *dimensions* of
history.[6]

These remarks of Merleau-Ponty are clearly programmatic,
but there are many senses in which this may be understood. I wish
to choose the direction of his concluding remarks upon phenomenological method as a way of moving further along the path that
Merleau-Ponty himself opened into the tradition of reason in the
human world.

Probably the chief gain from the phenomenology is to have
united extreme subjectivism and extreme objectivism in its notion of
the world or of rationality. Rationality is precisely measured by the
experiences in which it is disclosed. To say that there exists
rationality is to say that perspectives blend, perceptions confirm
each other, a meaning emerges. But it should not be set in a realm
apart, transposed into absolute Spirit, or into a world in the realist
sense. The phenomenological world is not pure being, but the sense
which is revealed where the paths of my various experiences
intersect, and also where my own and other people's intersect and
engage each other like gears. It is thus inseparable from subjectivity
and intersubjectivity, which find their unity when I either take up
my past experiences in those of the present, or other people's in my
own.[7]

The relation between speaking and the structure of language
raises the question of the dependence of the word on its divine anchorage, on ourselves, and on the variety of human history and culture. The responsibility of speech marks the autonomy of philosophical
reflection amid sophistry and rhetoric. But our own care with language belongs to the responsibility we have to ourselves and to the
nature of things. This, however, is not an invocation of a science of
language in its present sense or, in particular, its subordination of
commonsense everyday language. It is an invocation of the common
labor of turning common sense into good sense. That is, it is an

idealization of the community of truth rather than the packaging of being into competing domains of knowledge ruled by definitions and operations.

There are, of course, as many philosophies as there are philosophies of language. It has thus seemed to many that language is the scandal of philosophy, that a rigorous philosophy can be achieved only through the adoption of a "mathematical" language. The republic of knowledge is in this way made the construct of a rule of method that would provide future natives with greater clarity of judgment than philosophers of the past. This Cartesian dream of a universal language is at the same time, therefore, a prescription for social order, since clarity of mind eliminates the vexatiousness of theological and political controversy, not to mention the vanity of poets. The standards of science and technology translate the ideals of philosophical enlightenment and community into the everyday practices of public knowledge, health, and security. Plain language becomes the order of the day. Metaphysics and feudal privilege are swept into the trash of history. The new society is uniform and its icon is a "well-made language," the sublimation of civic order and technical optimism.

The pathos of philosophical speech is romantic and historicist. It rejects the universalism of scientific language in search of human expression and its power to articulate through the structures of divinity, stone, and commerce. A philosophy of speech is properly a philosophy of initiative, of style and gratuity, accomplished against the limits of received language. Speech is the invocation of our own being in concert with others. This is so even when our speech is disordered or mere chatter. The commonality of language and being is the prepredicative source of all predicative orders or domains of being and togetherness, as well as of alienation and falsehood. The efficacy of speech may present itself to us as the workings of an external order, of magic and institution, of divine fiat or plain sense. But these are equally the responses of speech in which nature, language, and society are addressed as the other of dialogue. We never escape the antinomy of expression and communication, because meaning is neither a collective representation nor a solitary accomplishment. The options of madness and officialese are the result of the suppression of the complementary orders of speech and communication. The expropriation of meaning is as pervasive in modern times as the alienation of labor. Its cause cannot without contradiction be attributed to language, art, and work. For each of these is the irremediable means of complaint and reform. What is expropriated is the standard by which we have anything in common, as Augustine suggests:

> When both of us see what you say is true, when we both see what I say is true—where do we see it, I ask you? Certainly, it is not in you that I see it, it is not in me that you see it. Both of us see it in immutable Truth, which is beyond our minds. (Augustine *Confessions* XII 35)

All agreements of fact are thus agreements in principle, that is, agreements of value that ground rules of logic and the common verbal and artistic currency. The crisis of communication is a crisis of transcendental values. Thus the modern concern with love, friendship, and communication is a concern about the fate of consciousness, of our being with being, that is, the hospitality of being.

The poet's experience with language and the artist's relation to tradition and style always appealed to Merleau-Ponty as the ground for the relation between expression and communication. Here we are tempted to speak of mastery and technique and to overlook the fact that these are only so many ways of being-in-the-world through our senses, through perception, language, and art. The science of language, as well as the history of philosophy and the history of art and science, begin with an autonomous object of study. But the life of philosophy, science, and the arts acquires its autonomy only through the subscription of living thinkers and artists whose encounter with tradition and its solicitation of their responses require that their own lives be the material and setting of the artifacts they create. The acquisition of speech, of thought, and of style is not a trick of skill, of technique, or of method.

The Prose of the World presupposes and illustrates Merleau-Ponty's conceptions of intersubjectivity and rationality and the fundamentals of his philosophy of perception and embodiment. The phenomenological approach to language is ultimately an introduction to the ontology of the world. It is a reflection upon our being-in-the-world through embodiment, which is the mysterious action of a presence that can be elsewhere. The philosophical puzzles of how we are in the world (ontology) or of how the world can be in us (epistemology), which have dictated quite particular analyses of the logic of language and thought, are transcended in the phenomenological conception of embodiment as a corporeal intentionality, a mode of knowledge, and an expression form.

I reach for my pen when I am ready to write, without consciously thematizing the pen as something with which to write or the distance between myself and where the pen lies. My hand is already looking for something with which to write and, as it were, scans the desk for a pen or pencil that is there "somewhere," where it usually is or where I have just put it down, so that it too seems to guide my hand in its search. But I can look for the pen only because in some sense I have my hand on it. If writing were painful to me or if I were sensible of having to write to someone for whom I did not care or I had only bad news, I could "put off" writing because I did not "feel" like writing. My pen there on the desk would not invite me to pick it up except with a painful reminder of my relations with someone else. Thus the structure of the experience of writing is there in my fingers, in the pen, and in my relations to the person to whom I am writing. It is neither a structure that I "represent" to myself—which would not take into account the knowledge in my fingers—nor is it a simple "reflex" stimulated by my pen—which would overlook my relations to the person to whom I am writing. The structure of writing is an "ensemble" in which the elements function only together and whose expressive value for me plays upon my relation to myself and others.

In the same way, speech is a capacity I acquire for communication. It arises not just from the expressive values of the words when joined with due respect for logic and syntax but also from my experience of the world, other persons, and the language I inhabit. Linguistics as a science of language treats language as a natural object, and logic treats it as an entirely artificial object. The linguistic conception of language presents language as a universe from which man is absent and with him the consequences of time and the disclosure of nature in magic, myth, and poetry. In logic man's power over language, which is ignored in linguistics, is raised above magic and poetry to the creation of a *mathesis universalis* that sloughs off all historical languages and purifies the word once and for all. The linguistic conception of the relation of language to meaning breaks down for the very reason that a language tells us nothing except about itself.[8] The problems of discrimination, quantification, and predictability that concern the statistical treatment of language are independent of the semantic value of the information being processed. It is words and not phonemes that carry meaning. Furthermore, words have meaning on their own account, especially such words as *liberty* or *love,* but also as elements in a whole that is not just the phrase or sentence but the entire "mother" language. To know the meaning of a word is not just a question of acquiring an appropriate phonetic motivation. It involves a familarity with an entire universe of meaning where language and society interpenetrate the lived value of words.

Language, like culture, is often regarded as a tool or an instrument of thought. But then language is a tool that accomplishes far more and yet is far less logical than we may like it to be. It is full of ambiguity and in general far too luxuriant for the taste of positivist philosophers. As a tool, language seems to use us as much as we use it. In this, it is more like the rest of our culture, which we cannot use without inhabiting it. Ultimately, language and culture defeat any attempt to conceive them as a system capable of revealing the genesis of its own meaning. This is because we *are* the language we are talking about. That is, we are the ground of language through our body. It is through our body that we can speak of the world, because the world in turn speaks to us through the body.

> "In my book the body lives in and moves through space and is the home of a full human personality. The words I write are adapted to express first one of its functions then another. In *Lestrygonians* the stomach dominates and the rhythm of the episode is that of the peristaltic movement." "But the minds, the thoughts of the characters," I began. "If they had no body they would have no mind," said Joyce. "It's all one. Walking towards his lunch my hero, Leopold Bloom, thinks of his wife, and says to himself, 'Molly's legs are out of plumb.' At another time of day he might have expressed the same thought without any underthought of food. But I want the reader to understand always through suggestion rather than direct statement."[9]

Merleau-Ponty's relation to Saussure's structural linguistics is typical of the way he treated all his "sources." He was concerned with the semantic and even more, as his own thought progressed, with the ontological implications of language. We must remember this if we are to avoid fruitless arguments over the documentation, in the conventional sense, of texts used by Merleau-Ponty. We otherwise miss the philosopher at work, improvising that new style of philosophical work for which Husserl called in *The Crisis*.[10] The concern with philosophical sources henceforth, that is, in view of the surrender of philosophy to *technique,* must be a concern with the very possibility of philosophy and its world.

I believe that we must try to understand Merleau-Ponty's patient analyses of the idealist and realist or subjectivist and naturalist accounts of perception, language, and history as efforts to understand the history of philosophy itself as the history of world domination whose substructures are science and capital accumulation. Perhaps this approach will enable us to understand the *ambiguity* of Merleau-Ponty's thought. This does not mean what it might ordinarily suggest for the reader's experience with Merleau-Ponty's writings. After all, at least since Sartre the question of how we read a text has no simple answer. The ambiguity of Merleau-Ponty's thought is properly the ambiguity in the tradition of Western philosophy that has elaborated solipsistic and intersubjectivist, nominalist and essentialist, subjectivist and objectivist accounts of the *same* phenomenal world.

If we regard the experience of ambiguity at all seriously, it means that the truth of philosophy is the work of generations of philosophers linked as much by what they reject as by what they affirm. In other words, we shall understand the *institution of philosophy*.[11] But this is a conception that appears dangerously close to the end of philosophy. The names of Kierkegaard, Marx, and Nietzsche remind us of the denial of philosophy since Hegel and that with them "we enter an age of nonphilosophy."[12] Nowadays, philosophical reflection no longer spreads its wings but must tread the earth wearily, amazed at its own variety, its own potential for barbarism. Reason must confront its own violence in the new extremes of naturalism and artificialism that seem capable of producing once and for all man's world alienation in a way that far exceeds the anticipations of nineteenth-century historicism and relativism.

But the concern with the "crisis" of Western rationalism as it is approached by Husserl does not produce an existentialist despair or an irrational reversal. These are symptomatic phenomena that threaten to divert the philosopher from the really necessary undertaking of a "teleological-historical reflection upon the origins of our critical scientific and philosophical situation." The philosopher, says Husserl, "takes something from history." But history is not a warehouse or a rummage heap from which we can take "things," because facts, documents, philosophical and literary works, are not palpably before us, apart from our own indwelling and interpretations. Furthermore, we do not, strictly speaking, transmit or hand down a scientific, literary, or historical tradition. We may be Renaissance historians without having read or researched every aspect of the Renaissance, just as we may be Platonists without a concern for every word of Plato, so that we may as well speak of a "poetic transmission" that owes as much to us as to fact. And yet none of this need imperil the teleology of knowledge, of science, history, or philosophy.

> Let us be more precise. I know, of course, what I am striving for under the title of philosophy, as the goal and field of my work. And yet I do not know. What autonomous thinker has ever been satisfied

with this, his "knowledge"? For what autonomous thinker, in his philosophizing life, has "philosophy" ever ceased to be an enigma? Everyone has the sense of philosophy's end, to whose realization his life is devoted; everyone has certain formulae, expressed in definitions; but only secondary thinkers, who in truth should not be called philosophers, are consoled by their definitions, beating to death with their word-concepts the problematic *telos* of philosophizing. In that obscure "knowledge," and in the word-concepts of the formulae, the historical is concealed; it is, according to its own proper sense, the spiritual inheritance of him who philosophizes; and in the same way, obviously, he understands the others in whose company, in critical friendship and enmity, he philosophizes. And in philosophizing he is also in company with himself as he earlier understood and did philosophy; and he knows that, in the process, historical tradition, as he understood it and used it, entered into him in a motivating way and as a spiritual sediment. His historical picture, in part made by himself and in part taken over, his "poetic invention of the history of philosophy," has not and does not remain fixed—that he knows; and yet every "invention" serves him and can serve him in understanding himself and his aim, and his own aim in relation to that of others and their "inventions," their aims, and finally what it is that is common to all, which makes up philosophy "as such" as a unitary *telos* and makes the systems attempts at its fulfillment for us all, for us [who are] at the same time in company with the philosophers of the past (in the various ways we have been able to invent them for ourselves).[13]

Understood in this way, rational argument, discovery, and criticism lie within the tradition and community of philosophers, artists, and natural and social scientists. This is a conception of the contingency of philosophical reason that avoids the postures of the alienated critic and the nihilistic dangers of cultural relativism while nevertheless providing for each thinker's style and for the local thrust of culture.

From the crisis of reason Husserl produces a conception of the limits of philosophical reflexivity that is consistent with the movement of "poetic invention" (*Dichtung*) as well as with the community in which we philosophize. This in turn underlies Merleau-Ponty's concept of reflexivity as *institution* rather than as transcendental constitution. The notion of institution is the ground of a conception of reflexivity that, instead of resting upon a transcendental subjectivity, is given in a field of presence and coexistence that situates reflexivity and truth as sedimentation and search. We must think of reflexivity as tied to the textual structures of temporality and situation through which subjectivity and objectivity are constituted as the intentional unity and style of the world.[14]

The institution of reflexivity operates through a series of exchanges between subjectivity and situation in which the polarities of means and ends or questions and answers are continuously established and renewed, thereby sedimenting ideas, truth, and culture. Reflexivity, therefore, is not an a priori but a task that we take up in order to achieve self-improvisation as well as the acquisition of a tradition or style of thought that is the recovery of an original auspices opened in the past. To this we bring a living expression, or the inauguration of a world and the outline of a future that is nothing else than ourselves, "borne only by the caryatid of our efforts, which converge by the sole fact that they are efforts to express."[15]

The institution of philosophy is the result of abandoning Husserl's attempt to construct a presuppositionless science as the correlative of an unsituated and unhistorical subjectivity, with all its problems for intersubjectivity, rationality, and philosophy itself—the realization that the corpus of knowledge, literature, art, and music is produced by individuals who take up a tradition of inquiry that is never settled and yet never wholly in doubt. Thus the philosopher, the artist, and the critic are always in debt, while giving more than they have ever received. For this reason, they proceed in their work as much by going back to the original questions in their field as by turning their backs on it, dreaming only of unheard and unseen things. This is not a simplistic argument for eternal starts any more than it is a crude rejection of the accumulation of knowledge. It is rather an attempt to interpret the solicitation and response through which tradition and rebellion are made.[16]

What phenomenology recovers for us and thus what it introduces us to is not just the freshness of perception or the novelty of language and art, though it surely reveals these as openings among the world, ourselves, and others. In Merleau-Ponty's hands, phenomenology is also the recovery of the tradition of reason in philosophy, politics, and history. In this he continues the task of *responsible rationality*[17] invoked by Husserl in *The Crisis of European Sciences*. Whether we follow Husserl in taking stock of the predicament of modern philosophy or analyzing the prejudice of the natural attitude or whether we follow Merleau-Ponty in attempting to refashion the Marxist philosophy of history on the basis of his critique of scientism,[18] we are engaged in the program of revealing the historical discourse of rationality and the philosopher's own itinerary as collective efforts to which we must be responsible without ever reducing this commitment to a methodical certitude.

For this reason, we do not find in *The Prose of the World,* any more than in other works of Merleau-Ponty, an exposition of method. By the same token, what we find of this in working notes and programmatic statements does not lie there through any failure of inclusion or organization but stands as it is—the trace of a philosopher's working life to be understood the way he himself spoke of the artist's sketches. These are not elements of some master painting the artist had in mind: that is precisely the fiction of the reviewer, whether art reviewer or philosophical reviewer. The latter presupposes some ground from which the author's intention can be viewed either in back of him or ahead of him but never given to him as it is to the critic. But this is to dispose of the author in favor of philosophy or art, to abort the artist's life and the philosopher's labor as failures of total perception, trapped in perspective and situation. In this we are bewitched, by language and its power of reification, to make prose of the world at the expense of its poetry.

The philosopher, like the painter or writer, must know how to assimilate the accumulation of tradition, style, and form in order to make an expressive use of them the way he moves his body without a precise concern for its anatomical and neurological structure without which every gesture is impossible. The true philosopher has philosophy in his bones, but these are not a dead man's bones. Philosophy is his life, the flesh of his thought through which he is open to the thoughts of other thinkers, exposed to their mood and times while still belonging to his own. The tradition in which he lives advances by a "poetic transmission" between the universal and the particular, between him and everyman.

> The Museum kills the vehemence of painting just as the library, as Sartre says, transforms writings which were once a man's gestures into *messages.* It is the historicity of death. But there is a living historicity of which the Museum offers only a broken image. It is the historicity that dwells in the painter at work when, in a single gesture, he binds the tradition he continues into the tradition he founds. It is the historicity which in a single stroke joins him with everything that has ever been painted in the world, without his having to leave either his place or time, or his blessed and accursed labor. The true history of painting is not one which puts painting in the past and then invokes superartists and fatalities—it is the history that puts everything in the present, that dwells in artists and reintegrates the painter with the fraternity of painters.[19]

It is in terms of the struggle between the two historicities of life and death that we must approach Merleau-Ponty's reflections on the algorithmic structure of language and the production of meaning in talk and literature. Although Merleau-Ponty recognized the existence of grammatical structures that subsist in our speech, he considered the Husserlian notion of an "eidetics" of language a forlorn attempt to escape the intrinsic historicity of all languages. Yet Merleau-Ponty is far from rejecting the idea of a universal discourse between men. Indeed, the very reason that he rejects a scientist linguistic base for a universal discourse is that it subverts the subjective, historical, and political responsibility that is the ground of such discourse.

Thus, as James Edie remarks, the question in Merleau-Ponty is not whether there are some linguistic universals, but what *kind* of universality we can find in language.[20] Merleau-Ponty was quite aware of the empirical facts of the translatability of languages and of their individual completeness in expressing their own worlds. But he understood the relation between the surface and deep structure of language (though these are not his expressions) in terms of a teleology of reason that is realized only through the experience of history and language in the production of a logic within contingency: an incarnate logic.

> Advent does not leave time behind: it is a promise of events. The domination of the many by the one in the history of painting, such as we have met in the exercise of the perceiving body, does not consummate succession in an eternity. On the contrary, domination demands succession; domination needs succession at the same time that it grounds its signification. Between the two problems there is more than a simple *analogy*. It is the expressive operation of the body, begun in the least perception, which amplifies into painting and art. The field of pictorial significations was opened the moment a man appeared in the world. The first sketch on the walls of a cave founded a tradition only because it gleaned from another—the tradition of perception. The quasi eternity of art compounds the quasi eternity of our corporeal existence. It is through our body that we have the first experience "of the impalpable body of history prior to all initiation into art."[21]

The transcendence of language, thought, and art is not husbanded by making it a factual transcendent. It is a *work* of ours, a task we continuously initiate and collectively elaborate, producing new sense, new perceptions upon wave after wave of meaning, which ebbs and flows nowhere else than from ourselves.

The lines between one life and another are not traced in advance. It is through the action of culture that I come to abide in lives that are not mine. I confront them, I reveal them to one another, I make them share equally in an order of truth. Responsible for all of them, I awaken a universal life—just as in one fell swoop I assume my place in space through the live and dense presence of my body.[22]

The universality and truth toward which theoretical conscious-ness aims are not an intrinsic property of the Idea. They are an acquisition continuously established and reestablished in a community and tradition of knowledge for which individuals in specific historical situations call and to which they respond. Understood in this way, history is the call of one thought to another, because each individual's work or action is created across the path of self and others toward a *public* that it elicits rather than serves. That is, history is the field that individual effort requires in order to become one with the community it seeks to build, so that where it is successful its invention appears always to have been necessary. Individual action, then, is the invention of history, because it is shaped in a present that previously was not just a void waiting to be determined by the word or deed but a tissue of calling and response that is the life of no one and everyone. Every one of life's actions, insofar as it invokes its truth, lives in the expec-tation of a historical inscription, a judgment not only of its intention or consequences but also of its fecundity: the relevance of its "story" to the present.

History is the judge—not History as the Power of a moment or of a century, but history as the space of inscription and accumulation beyond the limits of countries and epochs of what we have said and done that is most true and valuable, taking into account the circumstances in which we had to speak. Others will judge what I have done, because I painted the painting to be seen, because my action committed the future of others; but neither art nor politics consists in pleasing or flattering others. What they expect of the artist or politician is that he draw them toward values in which they will only later recognize their own values. The painter or politician shapes others more often than he follows them. The *public* at whom he aims is not given; it is a public to be elicited by his work. The others of whom he thinks are not empirical "others" or even *humanity* conceived as a species; it is others once they have become such that he can live with them. The history in which the artist participates (and it is better the less he thinks about "making history" and honestly produces *his* work as he

sees it) is not a power before which he must genuflect. It is the
perpetual conversation woven together by all speech, all valid works
and actions, each, according to its place and circumstance,
contesting and confirming the other, each one re-creating all the
others.[23]

Merleau-Ponty returns philosophy to the flux of the natural
and historical world, rejecting its compromise with the ideals of objectivism that have made the tradition of rationality an enigma to
itself. Henceforth, philosophy must abide in the life-world where
Husserl had found its roots and from there it must recover its own
ontological history. The *Crisis* is, of course, the prime example of this
effort to reflect upon the history of Western rationality *without breaking
with the natural attitude* and yet not resulting in a conventional empirical
history of philosophy. It is the model, I believe, for Merleau-Ponty's
own efforts in uncovering the ontological history of perception and
expression in art, literature, language, and philosophy.

Paul Ricoeur has seriously questioned whether Husserlian phenomenology can be turned toward the task of its own historical understanding.[24] David Carr, introducing his translation of the *Crisis*, also
draws attention to the Hegelian mode of this question but remarks
that the "crisis" theme is unthinkable in terms of the Hegelian "the-
odicy." But it is just here that we need to keep in mind Husserl's
insistence that we must rethink the past of philosophy, and in this
case with whom should we be more concerned than Hegel? It is surely
not an easy task to read Hegel. For the same reason, it is not obvious
whether Husserl is at fault in raising the Hegelian question. Merleau-
Ponty appears not to have thought so. However, he saw in *The Phenomenology of Spirit* not simply a history of ideas forced into a pro-
crustean bed of categories but the history of reason in the life-worlds
of moral, economic, political, and philosophical experience.
Throughout this history the forms of sense-certitude, understanding,
and reason are embedded in the most basic structure of the life-world,
namely, the dialectic of recognition and the struggle to death that
shapes the tragic course of human rationality as a social, historical,
and political enterprise that is not simply a goal of philosophy.

So the Hegelian dialectic is what we call the phenomenon of
expression, which gathers itself step by step and launches itself
again through the mystery of rationality. We would undoubtedly
recover the true sense of the concept of history if we acquired the
habit of modeling it on the example of the arts and language. The

close connection between each expression and every other within a single order instituted by the first act of expression effects the junction of the individual and the universal. Expression—language, for example—is what most belongs to us as individuals, for while addressing itself to others, it simultaneously acquires a universal value. The central fact to which the Hegelian dialectic returns in a hundred ways is that we do not have to choose between the *pour soi* and the *pour autrui,* between our own version of thought and the version of others, which is alienation itself, because at the moment of expression the other to whom I address myself and I who express myself are linked without concession on either side. The others, such as they are or will be, are not the sole judges of what I do. If I wanted to deny myself for their benefit, I would deny them too as "self." They are worth exactly what I am worth, and all the powers I accord to them I give simultaneously to myself. I submit myself to the judgment of another who is *himself worthy of what I have attempted,* that is, in the last analysis, to the judgment of a peer whom I myself have chosen.[25]

The recovery of the ontological history of rationality is therefore not simply gained through the critique of objectivism and naturalism exercised through the phenomenological reduction. It involves a return to the prephilosophical logos of the world that is the mystery and the wonder upon which our communally naïve and theoretical lives build equally.[26] But this need not be a further exercise in the ahistorical mystification of reason.[27] It is precisely the violent assumption of the responsibility of reason that lies nowhere else than with ourselves.

11

The Textual Cogito

I am thinking of the Cartesian *cogito;* I want to finish this
work; I can feel the coolness of the paper under my hand
and I can see the trees of the boulevard through the
window. My life is constantly thrown headlong into
transcendent things; it passes wholly outside of me. The
cogito is either this thought which took shape three centuries
ago in the mind of Descartes, or the meaning of the texts he
has left for us, or else it is an eternal truth which breathes
through them; in any case, it is a cultural being to which my
own thought reaches out but does not quite embrace, just as
my body, in a familiar surrounding, finds its orientation and
makes its way among objects without needing to have them
expressly in mind.[1]

Merleau-Ponty is said to have died at his desk while reading
Descartes's *Meditations.* We are reminded of Husserl's labors
on the *Cartesian Meditations.* Another of Merleau-Ponty's philosophers, Montaigne, hoped that when death came she would
find him at work, planting his cabbages.[2] Philosophers, like cowboys,
seem to want to die with their boots on. For much of my own life I
was schooled by Hollywood in this heroic version of death, quite un-
aware that philosophers were in love with it too, though I should have
remembered that Socrates, at least, talked himself to death. Nowadays, I am like these figures mostly at work; and work is mostly reading, writing, and talking in the midst of a myriad other jobs that do
not count. Thus the present essay has to be given shape before the
fall term opens and the summer's promises are forsaken for another
year. And this time of my life is late in other ways so that I must find
some way to bring my topic to bear, to get under way. Thus I do not

begin at any beginning. Rather, I adopt my situation as both a topic and a resource of embodied reflection linking me to a tradition of phenomenological reflection invoked in the names of Montaigne, Descartes, Husserl, and Merleau-Ponty, all of whom sat at their desk, as I do, half in thought:

> I shall now close my eyes, stop up my ears, turn away all my senses, even efface from my thought all images of corporal things, or at least, because this can hardly be done, I shall consider them as being vain and false; and thus communing only with myself, and examining my inner self, I shall try to make myself, little by little, better known and more familiar to myself.[3]

Thus begins one of the world's great explorations of philosophical and spiritual solitude to which we can hardly fail to be attracted for the sake of its promised transcendence of the limits of sensible things and their society. Such a withdrawal would, of course, be crowned on its return, bearing a certain science that would heal public opinion and restore philosophy's place in the community. To stage this movement of withdrawal and return, Descartes has to construct a double scene of separation:

1. In the isolation of the philosopher's study
2. In reflective isolation from his senses, perception, judgment, that is, in the text of the *Meditations*

Thus Descartes imagines that it might be possible to reconstruct his experience and to rearticulate it without relying upon commonsense discourse, thereby laying the foundations of certain knowledge that others might similarly enjoy, supposing they were to submit themselves to the rigors of philosophical meditation rather than to easy imitation. It is essential to the *Meditations* that the rhetorical effects of social isolation determine the philosophical effect of sensory and perceptual withdrawal by a freely inquiring mind. At the same time, the rhetoric of social withdrawal is transgressed through the philosophers' language that continues to articulate the public discourse upon the difference between waking and dream states, between certainty and uncertainty, between sight and blindness. In this way, the philosopher abrogates to his imagined private experience the authority of public knowledge, as well as its pragmatics of proof and refutation, which he conscripts through the reader's collusion.

"I am quite alone." Descartes persuades himself that in with-drawing from the world, he has nevertheless a secure place in the world from which to undertake "this general overview of my opin-ions." Descartes, then, means to conduct an assault upon himself, to attack the common man in himself with the agile arguments of the philosopher he has become through espousing doubt. Even so, he senses that he has neither the time nor the strength for doubting every one of his beliefs. In other words, it would be unreasonable for an embodied thinker to embark upon a philosophical life that would exceed the limits of ordinary living that in fact prescribes the uses of certainty and doubt within the framework of "corporeal nature in general." So far from being an object in the world of which his senses might be mistaken, or merely an image of itself as in a painting, Descartes acknowledges that his body is rather a mode of perceptual knowledge, reflexively aware of its waking and sleeping states, and as such, the constitutive ground of our being in the world:

> But, although the senses sometimes deceive us, concerning things
> which are barely perceptible or at a great distance, there are
> perhaps many other things one cannot reasonably doubt, although
> we know them through the medium of the senses, for example, that
> I am here, sitting by the fire, wearing a dressing gown, with this
> paper in my hands, and other things of this nature. And how could
> I deny that these hands and this body belong to me, unless perhaps
> I were to assimilate myself to those insane persons, persons whose
> minds are so troubled and clouded by the black vapours of the bile
> that they constantly assert that they are kings, when they are very
> poor; that they are wearing gold and purple, when they are quite
> naked; or who imagine that they are pitchers or that they have a
> body of glass. But these are madmen, and I would not be less
> extravagant if I were to follow their example.[4]

Indeed, to say that we exist, or that there is a world, or that we have a body is to say very much the same thing. Moreover, to say any of these things is ordinarily strange because they articulate the same perceptual faith in much the same way as each of our senses articu-lates the same body and its world. Questions about the infallibility of our senses, like questions about the purity of our morals, ought never to be abstracted from the ordinary contexts of our living under pain of separating us from our fellow men—and, worst of all, from our-selves. Whoever seeks absolute certainty, or absolute trust, risks hav-ing to withdraw from the world and his fellow men or to see them avoid and abandon him as they would a madman. The grammar of reasonableness in matters of perception and trust is fractured by the madman. Wholesale infringements of any local grammar and its institutional practices—rather than minor offenses readily confessed and repaired—will put any of us beyond the pale. Such exclusion is a sanctioned practice of everyday life and is incurred by children, loved ones, students, workers, and officials as ordinary members of society.[5] To invoke and to respond to such sanctions, and not to be ignorant or indifferent to them, is the ordinary mark of one's moral worth, if not of one's rational status. Thus to claim that no one knows anything or sees or hears anything for certain, or that we are asleep when we think we are awake, or hate when we think we love, or that everything might be other than what we ordinarily take it to be is to exceed even madness, for the madman makes no such distinctions.[6]

The cogito, as Merleau-Ponty observes, is in effect a *textual cogito*, that is, a verbal effect that absorbs to itself the universality of an anonymous discourse in which language holds us while effacing itself, just as our body veils the *tacit cogito* through which we are already worldly creatures before any thematization of subject and object relations:

> the true formula of this *cogito* should be: "One thinks, therefore one is." The wonderful thing about language is that it promotes its own oblivion: my eyes follow the lines on the paper, and from the moment I am caught up in their meaning, I lose sight of them. The paper, the letters on it, my eyes and body are there only as the minimum setting of some invisible operator. Expression fades out before what is expressed, and this is why its mediating role may pass unnoticed, and why Descartes *nowhere* mentions it. *Descartes, and a fortiori his reader, begin their meditation in what is already a universe of discourse.*[7]

The *Meditations* are surrendered to the ineluctable nature of language, to a play within the play written at the philosopher's table by a thinking body whose fantasy of its nonexistence merely reveals the limits of its "inexistence" distributed as a rhetorical effect of written meditation. However much Descartes resolves to objectify things in a cognitive space projected from his desk, the philosopher never leaves the greater world within which his meditations make use of his body, the page, the room, the fireside and desk whose existence presupposes the work of others greater in number and talents than the reader or writer of the *Meditations*. Thus what we witness in the *Meditations* is a *theatre of doubt*[8] in which Descartes's struggle with the evil genius (*un certain mauvais génie*) is resolved by calling in a deus ex machina, that is, a God who could not possibly allow the "philosophical seduction" of Descartes in his fantasy of universal doubt. However much Descartes pretends to remove all the props from the stage, he cannot remove the personal/public I, eye, (*je vois*) *je*, or *jeu* (play) in the *Cogito* that always addresses the reader "on stage" with the *Meditations*. Even when Descartes appears to have withdrawn body and soul, he remains with his reader all the while as the masked *narrator—larvatus prodeo*—thereby leading on the reader toward the divine goal of the *Meditations: larvatus pro deo?*[9]

What this means is that it is only the cogito as a *performance*, and not as an exteriorized *perception*, that unites thought and being. It is only by means of my exploration of things, persons, and, we should say, language, that I acquire an inner perception of self, and certainty is built upon these first uncertain relations to our world:

> certainty derives from the doubt itself as an act, and not from these thoughts, just as the certainty of the thing and of the world precedes any thetic knowledge of their properties. . . . The *cogito* is the recognition of this fundamental fact. In the proposition: "I think, I am", the two assertions are to be equated with each other, otherwise there would be no *cogito*. Nevertheless we must be clear about the meaning of this equivalence: it is not the "I am" which is pre-eminently contained in the "I think", not my existence which is brought down to the consciousness which I have of it, but conversely the "I think", which is re-integrated into the transcending process of the "I am", and consciousness into existence.[10]

Merleau-Ponty's reading of the cogito in Descartes or in Husserl persists in denying its pretention of grounding the *sum* (I am). Similarly, his reading of Husserl turns upon a distinction between the programmatic or Cartesian claims of transcendental phenomenology and the more patient text of Husserl's unfinished manuscripts in which a Cartesian nature is a possibility but inseparable from the ideal community of embodied subjects:

> Beneath Cartesian nature, which theoretical activity sooner or later constructs, there emerges an anterior stratum, which is never suppressed, and which demands justification once the development of knowledge reveals the gaps in Cartesian science. Husserl risks the description of the earth as the seat of pre-objective spatiality and temporality, as the homeland and historicity of bodily subjects

> who are not yet disengaged observers, as the ground of truth or the
> ark which carries into the future the seeds of knowledge and
> culture. Before being manifest and "objective", truth dwells in the
> secret order of embodied subjects. At the root and in the depths of
> Cartesian nature there is another nature, the domain of an
> "originary presence" (Urpräsenz) which, from the fact that it calls for
> the total response of a single embodied subject, is in principle
> present also to every other embodied subject.[11]

Things, then, are not objects enclosed in themselves any more than
we are self-possessed subjects. This is true of objects because we ad-
here to them, so to speak, and cannot withdraw from them any more
than our mind can extricate itself from our body. Rather, the mind
is the other side of the body and the body is the other side of the
mind and each is not to be found apart, any more than any single-
sided thing is to be found in our world. We might say that the object
is an opening in the subject and that the subject is entrance to the
object and that neither is at an absolute distance from the other, any
more than a child from its mother. Thus there is an interiority and
reflexivity in the visibility of things so that in seeing them we are seen
by them as a lover sees himself in seeing his beloved and is thought
by her in thinking of her.

> What there is then are not things first identical with themselves,
> which would offer themselves to the seer, nor is there a seer who is
> first empty and who, afterward, would open himself to them—but
> something to which we could not be closer than by palpating it with
> our look, things we could not dream of seeing "all naked" because
> the gaze itself envelops them, clothes them with its own flesh.[12]

It is this reversibility that Merleau-Ponty calls the *chiasm* or *interlace*
to indicate how it is that the subject of being is under erasure and
rather a modulation of being whose destiny brings the subject to
language. But this in turn needs restatement. We are not the kind of
entity that receives all of its meaning inside language. We are in meaning before language, and this prelinguistic consciousness, sensibility,
or body is what language articulates so that there can be self and
object domains, and above all the domain of languaged thought, art,
literature, and science. This is as far as we can go in turning language
and consciousness against each other, as though we might thereby
reach the origins of our being. Rather than erect a transcendental
consciousness beyond the fall into being, or language and history,
which remain intractible problems in the Husserlian formulation,

Merleau-Ponty weakens the phenomenological reduction into a mode of wonder at the world's intelligibility, its sensibility, its versatility in and for us. In the end, he brings the phenomenological reduction and the human body together as *works of art*. That is to say, each is productive of meaning and neither turns upon an external ground of sense that would be the direction of a positive phenomenology. Of course, there is a tension in these two conceptions of the reduction and it is only gradually that Merleau-Ponty adopts the vision of art as the proper mode of the reduction.[13] Thus we are the world's body and it is in us that the world thinks, sees, hears, and enunciates itself, and not at all without us who are its artists:

> there is a fundamental narcissism of all vision. And thus, for the same reason, the vision he exercises, he also undergoes from the things, such that, as many painters have said, I feel myself looked at by the things, my activity is equally passivity—which is the second and more profound sense of narcissism. . . . It is this visibility . . . that we have previously called flesh, and one knows there is no name in traditional philosophy to designate it . . . we should need the old term "element" in the sense we used to speak of water, air, earth and fire . . . a sort of incarnate principle that brings a style of being wherever there is a fragment of being.[14]

It is such subtle readings of the tradition that exemplify Merleau-Ponty's concept of the textual cogito and his larger notion of philosophy as interrogation—as deconstruction, if you will—rather than as finished truth.[15] Of course, in this way Merleau-Ponty reads Husserl against Husserl, and thus himself against his own earlier work, as the notes to the *Visible and Invisible* testify. It could well be argued that Husserl's efforts to suspend embodied thinking, as well as to separate thought from language within which sense making is even more tied to the topics of occasioned reasoning, were all the more persistent inasmuch as he was seduced by a conception of un-contaminated truth as the ideal object that constrains the philosopher in a singular vision of its wholeness and perfect adequacy. But the completeness of the philosopher's conception of and in truth cannot allow for a perspectival, temporal, and socially constructed truth that emerges within a community of thought and language whose artifacts of text, tradition, and revision give to philosophical, scientific, literary, and artistic truth its transcendental valence with respect to any of its situated, subjective, and local practices.[16] Thus we never grasp a word, thought, emotion, text, or gesture outside its historical, cultural, and institutional context that constitutes clusters of intelligibility within which these things achieve an immediate sense. The impossibility of thought outside language can only be neglected to the extent that we entertain the possibility of language before society. This, however, only tempts the philosopher who can persuade himself that such reasoning is not parasitical upon the practice of reasoning in the light of the other's presence and of the point of view of another whose demands render reason unavoidably rhetorical or public. Despite Merleau-Ponty's claims, it can be argued that Husserl remained enamored of the solitary mental life (*einsamen Seelenleben*), communicating with itself outside speech and understanding itself without the intervention of any interlocutor or thought partner, whether real or imaginary.[17] Such a philosopher knows his own mind without any horizon of ambiguity or revisability to infect the certainty of its truth and vision. And yet we can find in Husserl another sense of the tradition in which the philosopher's life is one of dispossession and his labors more akin to those of the poet:

> His historical picture, in part made by himself and in part taken over, his "poetic invention of the history of philosophy" has not and does not remain fixed—that he knows; and yet every "invention" serves him and can serve him in understanding himself and his aim, and his own aim in relation to others and their "inventions", their aims, and finally what is that is common to all, which makes up philosophy "as such" as a unitary *telos* and makes the system's attempts at its fulfillment for us all, for us who are at the same time in company with the philosophers of the past (in the various ways we have been able to invent them for ourselves).[18]

Philosophical intertextuality, as Husserl intimates, involves a certain *poetics* in which "subjectivity" and "objectivity" are relativized so that whereas the text has dimensions that only a reader can trace in it, the reader nevertheless does not discover his path except through the text. Thus Merleau-Ponty can speak of his relation to his own work in a manner similar to his relations with other texts in the phenomenological tradition. In each case, there is an opening, an occasion for philosophical reflection whose beginnings cannot determine its path independently of the tradition, while nevertheless avoiding sheer imitation or total rejection. Philosophical inquiry must move in the same plane as sensory perception and is weighted like our body:

> One sees it if one succeeds in making of philosophy a perception, and of the history of philosophy a perception of history—

everything comes down to this: form a theory of perception and of comprehension that shows that to comprehend is not to constitute in intellectual immanence, that to comprehend is to apprehend by coexistence, laterally, *by the style,* and thereby to attain at once the far-off reaches of this style and of this cultural apparatus.[19]

Here Merleau-Ponty opens up the question of *philosophical style* because it must arise once we reject the practice of interpretation exercised on the double presupposition of the self-coincidence of the text and of a self-possessed consciousness as the ground of thought and being. Thus the interpretative act must now be seen as itself inscribed in the same way as the text upon which it writes without priority, just as the act of vision yields objects only for beings that are themselves visible, that is, not entirely an object any more than a subject alone. But this means that our minds and our bodies are dimensions of one another, and irreparably so, because they belong to the same worldliness, to the same inscription of being whose destiny is in language, style, and culture.[20] The textual cogito is, of course, the result of Merleau-Ponty's inquiries into the problem of the perception of others, of the double encroachment of thought and sensibility that arises between embodied subjects. Here Merleau-Ponty shifts the pathos of influence from the anxious dependence of the *Meditations* to an expressed trust in the overlap of carnal perception:

I borrow myself from others; I create others from my own thoughts. This is no failure to perceive others; it is the perception of others. . . . Between an "objective" history of philosophy (which would rob the great philosophers of what they have given others to think about) and a meditation disguised as a dialogue (in which we would ask the questions and give the answers) there must be a middle-ground on which the philosopher we are speaking about and the philosopher who is speaking are present together although it is not possible even in principle to decide at any given moment just what belongs to each.[21]

This "undecidable" factor in any philosophical work arises on both sides of interpretation. It exceeds equally the author and the reader, privileging neither and thereby making their relationship all the more necessary. Because of this reverberation, we never can decide once and for all the question of the cogito whether in Descartes, or in Husserl, or in any of their commentators who like ourselves are drawn into philosophical inquiry. The *Meditations,* therefore, cannot reconstruct egological experience elsewhere than within the pragmatics of

intersubjective discourse and textuality. Language has no outside nature, no origins, but only a structure and history of intertextuality in
which you and I amplify each other's discourse and intelligence, en-
larging our general culture:

> I should be unable even to read Descartes' book, were I not, before
> any speech can begin, in contact with my own life and thought, and
> if the spoken *cogito* did not encounter within me a tacit *cogito*. This
> silent *cogito* was the one Descartes sought when writing his
> *Meditations.* He gave life and direction to all those expressive
> operations which, by definition, always miss their target since,
> between Descartes' existence and the knowledge of it which he
> acquires, they interpose the full thickness of cultural acquisitions.[22]

Despite the rhetorical persuasion of the *Meditations,* the very
problematic of the cogito is never wholly Cartesian. There is, of course,
a "Cartesian" cogito. But it is available only as a particular inflection
of the philosopher's question that has its peculiar style because it starts
from an obsessive *anxiety of grounds* that marks Cartesian discourse.[23]
Yet, the cogito presupposes a long history of previous philosophical
discourse that is sustained by others and that will be taken up in
future from time to time, as it has in that past that bequeathed to us
its question. Viewed in this way, the cogito does not found philosophical discourse, and could not possibly do so, except through a retrospective fiction of the historians of philosophy whose practices of
periodization are themselves only a further convention within the
philosophical community.

The inseparability of thought, language, and philosophical style
is most evident in Merleau-Ponty's own texts. They resist summary
and abstraction and invariably seduce commentators into imitation,
even to a certain intonation to convey their sensibility. Merleau-Ponty's
corpus steadfastly resists the flights of reason, idealism, and scientism—resists even phenomenology—rather bringing to bear a certain
faith in the body and in community—redefining Marxism[24]—and
always embracing the body of language, art, and music. This effect
can be seen immediately from his writings that draw at will upon
philosophy, literature, art, politics, history, and anthropology. It is
apparent, too, in Merleau-Ponty's "misreadings" of the great philosophers to whom he never pays the homage of imitation except to
work in the same field of inquiry opened by them. Here, of course,
he is most seductive since we cannot separate the tradition from his
powerful evocation of its claims upon our attention and our conse-

quent desire to understand it as he did. Merleau-Ponty stood before his philosophical forebears with the same sense of impregnation as he felt before a painting of Cezanne or in the novels of Proust. In each case, the artist's idiom, so far from being singular, embodies a perception desired in ourselves but recognized only in their expression so that in understanding them we understand ourselves. Here the eye and the mind are reconciled and an end envisaged to the long history of their separation and subordination, from Plato to Descartes. This vision of a single topography of embodied mind, of language, of visibility, of philosophy, of art, of reflected being, although unfinished in his working notes, in fact constitutes the origin of Merleau-Ponty's philosophical work and its inimitable style.[26] Here the body of thought and the body of dreams open and are opened in the same field of visibility, of the world's flesh, of the mother-body's undivided difference. Here, then, in my study at work on the *Meditations,* I am not more alone than Descartes, or Montaigne,[27] or Merleau-Ponty. The same shining world surrounds me as it did them once before, while the silence of my study murmurs with their voice in the turning pages of my reading, and their time runs into mine through this hand, writing.

Between Montaigne and Machiavelli: The Life of Politics

Merleau-Ponty's political experience is inseparable from the philosophical reflections in which he sought to express the irreducible ambiguity of thought becoming action and the blindness of action unclarified by critical thought. His meditations are identical with political action because they responded to the political situation of his time. Our politics has failed to acquire a voice of its own in which the call to freedom and intersubjectivity eschews the sterile alternatives of anticommunism and anticapitalism. History, it seems, has played upon politics the same trick that politics hoped to play upon history. The Right and the Left have failed either to stabilize or to put an end to history. Rather, each has acquired a history that includes the other. Capitalism has its future in socialism, but not by any inevitable path. Socialism, however, has its past in capitalism and is more likely to resemble capitalism than to differ from it, if all that lies between them is a vocabulary of freedom lacking an infrastructure of intersubjectivity. Thus neither the Left nor the Right possesses the truth though neither is false, except as each attempts to stand outside the other, thereby separating itself from its own history and its anchorage in a common political tradition.

Merleau-Ponty would certainly have merited all the anger, if not the awe, of his political friends and opponents had he simply found a position of political skepticism from which to expose the contradictions of the Right and the Left.[1] He knew well enough that in contemporary politics criticism of the Left is tantamount to support of the Right. Yet he could not accept that criticism of the Right meant unqualified support of the Left. This was not because Merleau-Ponty lacked political willpower or wished to indulge the rationalism of the professional intellectual. He might have chosen silence, but he thought of silence as an originary mode of expression in which meaning is fermented and solicited by the world to which it belongs. It might be mentioned that he had fought beside his fellow men, that he never ceased to argue with them, to write for them, to assume their situation as his own. But this would only add to the enigma of the distance that men felt between Merleau-Ponty and themselves. Moreover, it would be wrong to explain away that distance by an appeal to instances of comradeship. This would be to fail to see that the world and others are present to us through an *aesthetic distance* that permits us to inhabit the world and to encroach upon others without shifting our own ground. It is this very distance that is the presupposition of all secondary structures of physical and social existence. Thus Merleau-Ponty established in himself the wonder that men have for each other but that they mistake for skepticism in those individuals who excel in that wonder.

It is understandable then that Merleau-Ponty's political meditations drew inspiration from Montaigne and Machiavelli and that in reflecting upon them he sought to unravel the ambiguities of skepticism, humanism, and terror in order to clarify that "astonishing junction between fact and meaning, between my body and myself, myself and others, my thought and my speech, violence and truth" that is the originary ground of social and political life.

I shall attempt to interpret Merleau-Ponty's conception of the ambiguity of politics developed in the essay *Humanism and Terror*[2] by situating that essay between his meditations on Montaigne[3] and Machiavelli.[4] It is hoped that these reflections illuminate the larger essay inasmuch as they reveal Merleau-Ponty's conception of political reflection and save it from criticisms of skepticism and noncommitment that I think quite alien to Merleau-Ponty's philosophical thought.

On reading Montaigne it is not enough simply to say of him that he was a skeptic. For skepticism has two aspects. It means that nothing is true, but also that nothing is false. Thus we cannot conclude that skepticism abandons us to an utter relativism of truth. Rather, it opens us to the idea of a totality of truth in which contradiction is a necessary element in our experience of truth. Montaigne's skepticism is rooted in the paradox of *conscious being*, to be constantly involved in the world through perception, politics, or love and yet always at a distance from it without which we would know nothing of it. *"What is taken to be rare about Perseus King of Macedonia—that his mind attached itself to no rank but went wandering through all kinds of life and representing customs to itself which were so vagabond and flighty that it was not known to himself or others what man this was—seems to me more or less to apply to everyone. We are always thinking somewhere else."*[5] And, as Merleau-Ponty adds, "it could not possibly be otherwise. To be conscious is, among other things, to be somewhere else." Thus the skeptic only withdraws from the world, its passions and follies, in order to find himself at grips with the world, having as it were merely slackened the intentional ties between himself and the world in order to comprehend the paradox of his being-in-the-world. Whenever Montaigne speaks of man he refers to him as "strange," "monstrous," or "absurd." What he has in mind is the paradoxical mixture of mind and body that we are, so that a prince can kill his beloved brother because of a dream he has had.

The variety of human practices produces in Montaigne something more than anthropological curiosity or philosophical skepticism. *"I study myself more than other subjects. It is my metaphysics and my physics."* Because of the mixture of being that he is, the explanation of man can only be given by himself to himself, through an experience of the problematic nature that he is. Man does not borrow himself from philosophy or from science. He is the treasure upon which the sciences draw. Nevertheless, man has to make his own fortune and in this the folly of a treasure laid up in a religious heaven is no better, nor for that matter any worse, than the treasures of Eldorado. For the enthusiasm of religion is a mode of our folly and our folly is essential to us. "When we put not self-satisfied understanding but a consciousness astonished at itself at the core of human existence, we can neither obliterate the dream of an other side of things nor repress the wordless invocation of this beyond."[6]

Montaigne can, however, speak as though we should remain indifferent to the world and in love or politics never allow ourselves to play more than a role. *"We must lend ourselves to others and give ourselves only to ourselves."* And yet we must adopt the principles of family and state institutions for they are the essential follies of life with others. To attempt to live outside the state and the family reveals the abstraction of the stoic distinction between what is internal and what is external, between necessity and freedom. "We cannot always obey if we despise, or despise always if we obey. There are occasions when to obey is to accept and to despise is to refuse, when a life which is in part a double life ceases to be possible, and there is no longer any distinction between exterior and interior. Then we must enter the world's folly, and we need a rule for such a moment."[7] But this is not a desperate attempt to achieve certainty. It would only be this if we assumed the standpoint of a finished truth toward which we could move from doubt only by a leap. But that would be to exchange our nature for some other existence, whether animal or angel; *"the extinction of a life is the way to a thousand lives."* If we abandon such a notion then we come back to the ground of opinion, to the fact that there is truth and men have to learn doubt. *"I know what it is to be human better than I know what it is to be animal, mortal or rational."* Skepticism with respect to the passions deprives them of value only if we assume a total self-possession, whereas we are never wholly ourselves but always interested in the world through the passions that we are. Then we understand the passions as the vehicle by which truth and value are given to us and we see that the critique of the passions is the rejection of false passions that do not carry us toward the world and men, but close us in a subjectivity we have not freely chosen.

Although it is the evil of public life to associate us with opinions and projects we have not chosen for ourselves, the flight into the self only reveals the self as openness toward the world and men so that among other things, what we are for others and their opinion touches the very core of our being.

> The fact of the matter is that true skepticism is movement toward the truth, that the critique of passions is hatred of false passions, and finally, that in *some* circumstances Montaigne recognized outside himself men and things he never dreamed of refusing himself to, because they were like the emblem of his outward freedom, and because in loving them he was himself and regained himself in them as he regained them in himself.[8]

Skepticism and misanthropy, whatever the appearances, are misbegotten political virtues for the reason that the essential ambiguity of politics is that its vices derive from what is most valuable to men: the idea of a truth that each intends for all because men do not live side by side like pebbles, but each lives in all. It is the evidence of the vital truths that men hold intersubjectively that provides the infrastructure of social and political life. This is not to say that this prepolitical suffrage ever exists in abstraction from political and social institutions, nor to deny that it is weighted by ideology. Our task is to make it function as the *norm* of political society; to communicate it through criticism, information, and publicity. This is a difficult task and one that demands a philosophy that is free of political responsibilities because it has its own. Such a philosophy can be free and faithful because it does not play at reconstructing politics, passions, and life, but devotes itself to the disclosure of the basic meaning-structures through which we inhabit the world.

Merleau-Ponty's essay *Humanism and Terror* is an exercise in political philosophy that is true to itself as philosophy because it dwells within the problematic of communism and anticommunism in order to reveal the latent structures of political action, truth, and violence, which are the foundations of all social existence. The starting point of Merleau-Ponty's reflections on the Communist problem, as it is raised by the Moscow Trials, seems to defeat all progress in the argument and almost ensures that it will win converts from neither side. The argument runs the risk of being dismissed for its hesitation, its noncommitment, or even flatly rejected as an ill-timed invitation to skepticism at a moment when the Third World seems bent upon learning the ideologies of the Right or the Left. And yet it is precisely to the problem of the genesis of political community and the clarification of the historical option that it involves that the essay on humanism and terror addresses itself. It cannot therefore be dismissed as a local tract nor be ignored by those whose hope is for an end of ideology.[9]

"Communism does not invent violence, it finds it established." Communism has no monopoly on violence. All political regimes are criminal, however liberal the principles to which they subscribe. Liberal societies are compatible with domestic and international exploitations in which their principles of freedom and equality participate as mystifications. The liberal cannot salve his conscience with the myth that violence has been completely legalized in his own society, and for that reason he cannot identify terror with communism. But the communist sympathizer is in no better position. Violence cannot be understood historically or statistically. The death of a single individual is sufficient to condemn an entire regime. "The anticommunist refuses to see that violence is universal, the exalted sympathizer refuses to see that no one can look violence in the face."[10] The nature of political action is not contained by the alternatives of the yogi and the commissar, for men are neither entirely interior beings nor wholly the objects of external manipulation. This is not to deny that Rubashov might provide himself with the objectivist arguments of Marxian scientism and historicism. From this point of view the self remains an

empty category until the Party has fulfilled its historical task of providing the economic infrastructure of authentic subjectivity. But this
is a position motivated by a conception of consciousness as either
everything or nothing. Even if we understand this alternation simply
as a political strategy, the question arises, What does Rubashov make
of his personal consciousness in the days after the trial when, after
publicly saving his past, he is faced with the existential difference
between the judgment of universal history and his own self-esteem?
To answer this question we must understand something of the relation between political reason and political passions.

"One does not become a revolutionary through science, but
out of indignation. Science comes afterwards in order to fill in and
determine that empty protestation."[11] Rubashov and his comrades
had started from the evident truth of the value of men and only later
learned that in the course of building its economic infrastructure they
would have to subject individuals to the violence generated in the
distance between the specific circumstances of the revolution and its
future. The paradox of the revolutionary is that the recognition of
the value of intersubjectivity engages a struggle to the death that
reproduces the alienation of the individual between the options of a
subjectivism and an objectivism neither of which can reach its proper
conclusion. Marxism does not create this dilemma; it merely expresses it. Koestler, on the other hand, poses the problem in such a
way that he neglects what is *moral* in the Marxist decision to treat the
self solely from outside, from the standpoint of the objective requirements of history. He thereby misses the essential ambiguity of the
distinction between the subjective and the objective standpoints. The
values of the yogi are not simply the reverse of those of the commissar
because each experiences an internal reversal of the values of subjectivism and objectivism whenever either standpoint is assumed as an
absolute. We can understand then that, once in prison, Rubashov
experiences the value of the self in the depths of its interiority where
it opens toward the White Guard in the neighboring cell *as someone
to whom one can talk.*[12] The tapping on the prison walls is the first
institution of that communication between men for the sake of which
Rubashov had embarked upon his revolutionary career. Between the
beginning and the end of his life there is, however, a continuity that
is possible only through the contradiction that it embraces.

It is this openness toward its own past and future that prevents
political action from ever being unequivocal. Hence the historical
responsibility that the revolutionary assumes can never be established
as a matter of brute fact. The trials therefore never go beyond the

level of a "ceremony of language" in which meaning is sensed entirely within the verbal exchanges and not through reference to an external ground of verification.

> The Trials do not go beyond the subjective and never approach what one calls "true" justice, objective and timeless, *because they bear upon facts which are still open toward the future, which consequently are not yet univocal and only acquire a definitively criminal character when they are viewed from the perspective on the future held by the men in power.*[13]

What the trials reveal to us are the form and style of the revolutionary. The revolutionary judges what exists in terms of what is to come: he regards the future as more vital than the present to which it owes its birth. From this perspective there can be no subjective honor; we are entirely and solely what we are for others and our relation to them. The revolutionary masters the present in terms of the future, whereas the counterrevolutionary binds the present to the past. The revolutionary shares in an intersubjective conviction of making history, which is, of course, an arbitrary conviction, but with respect to the *future* of which we cannot in principle be certain. However, the evidence of the value of a future society of comrades suffices for a revolutionary decision, and its lack of certainty has nothing to do with the individual hesitation that belongs to prerevolutionary sensibilities. For the revolutionary there exists no margin of indifference; political differences are acts of objective treason. In such circumstances government is terror and humanism[14] is suspended. It is this state of affairs that arouses the greatest offense.

The liberal conscience rejects the barbarism of communism. But this amounts to nothing more than a refusal to give violence its name. Civilization is threatened as much by the nameless violence institutionalized in liberal society as it is by terror exercised openly in the hope of putting an end to the history of violence. In the liberal ideology, justice and politics assume a division of labor between concern for ends and calculation of means. But this is an abstraction from political reality where conflict is generated in the definition of ends because this activity determines what shall be identified as means. In other words questions of justice are identified in terms of so-called abstract values. In reality, truth and justice are inseparable from the violence of possession and dispossession. This is evident in every revolutionary situation where society cannot be assumed but has yet to emerge from its origins in "the passional and illegal origins of all legality and reason,"[15] where for a time humanism is suspended precisely because it is in genesis.

It is the problem of the genesis of collective life that is the fundamental theme of Merleau-Ponty's reflections upon the ambiguity of humanism and terror in revolutionary societies. But, of course, he is not dealing here with the fiction of a presocial state of nature introduced in order to rationalize revolt or order according to whether the presocial condition of man is pictured as benign or brutish. Indeed, it is just these alternatives that are not open in the state of nature because it is a genetic state in which violence and justice, truth and contradiction, are the very matrix from which the option of a specific historical form of society emerges. Marxists themselves lose sight of the essential contingency in that genesis of a revolutionary praxis to the extent that they treat history as an object of knowledge, ignoring their own attempt to *make* history. The Marxist intervention of history inserts into history a norm of intersubjectivity generated through the very conflict and contingency that a scientific law of history seeks to eliminate.

At the same time Merleau-Ponty does not intend to conclude that history is simply a field of radically contingent action: "this irrationalism is indefensible for the decisive reason that *no one lives it, not even he who professes it.*"[16] That the whole of reality for man is only probable whether in the appearance of things or of the future does not mean that the world lacks a style of physiognomy in its appearance to us. We live in subjective certainties that we intend universally and practically and that are in no way illusory unless we posit some apodictic certainty outside the grounds of human experience. "The future is only probable, but it is not an empty zone in which we can construct gratuitous projects; it is sketched before us like the beginning of the day's end, and its outline is ourselves."[17] We do not experience uncertainty at the very core of our existence. The center of our experience is a common world in which we make appraisals, enlist support, and seek to convince our opponents, never doubting the potential permutation of subjective and objective evidence.

Although it is true that our perspectives depend upon our motives and values, it is just as true that our values are derived from concrete experience and not drawn from some preestablished sphere. Thus contradiction and conflict do not stem from abstractly opposed principles or perspectives but presuppose a fundamental community of experience that gives meaning to such conflict. "The dialectic of the subjective and objective is not a simple contradiction which leaves the terms it plays on disjointed; it is rather a testimony to our rootedness in the truth."[18] This fundamental ambiguity of truth and contradiction, far from being destructive of intersubjectivity, in fact presupposes a community of men as its originary ground. This presupposition differs from the liberal assumption of a finished human nature. In terms of the latter it is impossible to understand conflict and error as anything but historical accidents, rather than as elements in a matrix from which truth and community emerge. Marxism differs from liberalism and anarchism[19] in that it can account for violence in history, not in the sense of providing it with excuses but in the sense that it situates violence within the ambiguous origins of truth and justice, in the birth of reason from unreason that is the mark of a new society. The notions of truth and freedom arise only in certain cultures and are not historical laws as is pretended in the liberal version of history. Truth and freedom are options of history whose matrix is violence. The option that history opens up for us is ourselves, and this option remains irreducibly what it is whether we contemplate it as a spectacle or implement it through action.

The foundations of history and politics are inseparable from the dialectic between man and nature and between man and his fellow men. It is the nature of human consciousness to realize itself in the world and among men, and its embodiment is the essential mode of its opening toward the world and to others. The problem of community and coexistence only arises for an embodied consciousness driven by its basic needs into a social division of labor and engaged by its deepest need in a life and death struggle for intersubjective recognition. Embodied consciousness never experiences an original innocence to which any violence would be an irreparable harm; it knows only different kinds of violence. For consciousness finds itself already engaged in the world, in definite situations in which its resources are never merely its own but derive from the exploitation of its position as the husband of this woman, the child of these parents, the master of these slaves. As such the intentions of embodied consciousness already presuppose a common matrix of justice and injustice, truth and deception, out of which they emerge as acts of love, hate, honesty, and deceit. This is the ground presupposed by political discussion and political choice. We never act upon isolated individuals, as the liberal imagines, but always within a community that possesses a common measure of the good and evil it knows. As soon as we have lived we already know what it means for subjects to treat one another as objects, placing into jeopardy the community of subjectivity that is the originary goal of embodied consciousness. None of us reaches manhood outside this history of the violence we hold for one another. None of us can bear it apart from the attempt within this violence to establish love and communion.

The prospects of humanism are wholly bound up with the *meaning* that Marxism introduces into violence as a polarity within a structure of truth and intersubjectivity against which all other forms of violence are retrograde. But the norm of intersubjectivity is not itself a law of history, and its own genesis has no guarantee precisely because it lies in the revelation of man to himself and finds, as it were, its natural limit in man. The attempt to establish harmony within ourselves and with others as an existential truth is not routed by conflict and error, but assumes them as something we can overcome as fellow men.

This last reflection raises once again the question of the relation between truth and community. The problem is that the emergence of truth seems to presuppose a community, and in turn the emergence of a community assumes a concept of truth. The Marxist criticism of the liberal truth lies in the exposition of its lack of correspondence with the objective relations between men in liberal society. The problem of communism is similar, since it has failed so far to make the historical road repairs that were written into its political charter. Marxism claims to be a truth in the making; it overturns liberal society in order to clear the way for the genesis of a society grounded in authentic intersubjectivity. The birth of communist society, however, is no less painful than the birth of man himself, and already from the earliest years it is familiar with violence and contradiction.

Merleau-Ponty's thought dwells within the circle of this problem, and it seems natural that he should have turned toward Machiavelli, whose own meditations embraced the same problematic. "For he describes that knot of collective life in which pure morality can be cruel and pure politics requires something like a morality."[20] Had either Montaigne or Machiavelli stood outside politics in order to contemplate political action, then they might easily have succumbed to the conclusions of skepticism and cynicism. But then they would have broken the circle of being that we inhabit, whereas they chose to dwell and to meditate within it. They would not otherwise have provided a model for Merleau-Ponty's reflections upon their experience, which, we suggest, is indirectly his own political experience.

If the cynic is right and humanity essentially an accident, then it is difficult to see what else besides sheer force could uphold collective life. In this mood Machiavelli is obsessed with violence and oppression. But there is a deeper reflection in Machiavelli that discovers something other than sheer force in the phenomenon of conflict and aggression. "While men are trying not to be afraid, they begin to make themselves feared by others; and they transfer to others the aggression that they push back from themselves, as if it were absolutely necessary to offend or be offended."[21] Human aggression is not simply a conflict of animal or physical forces, but a polarity within a dialectic of intersubjective recognition or alienation. Political power never rests upon naked force but always presumes a ground of opinion and consensus within a margin of potential conflict and violence that is crossed only when this common sense is outraged. "Relationships between the subject and those in power, like those between the self and others, are cemented at a level deeper than judgment. As long as it is not a matter of the radical challenge of contempt, they survive challenge."[22] The exercise of power succeeds best as an appeal to freedom rather than as an act of violence that only reinforces itself through the aggression that it arouses. The art of the Prince is to maintain the free consent of his subjects, and in this we discover a touchstone for a humanist politics inasmuch as the people at least seek to avoid oppression if not to aim at anything greater. The *virtue* of the Prince is a mode of living with others such that their opinion is consulted without being followed slavishly nor merely heard without effect. At such times there is always the possibility that the originary conflict of will and opinion will arise, and yet it is only under these conditions that there can be genuine consultation and real leadership. Within such a community the exercise of power is tied to the realm of appearances, for only the Prince can know how the people are and only they know him.

> What sometimes transforms softness into cruelty and harshness into value, and overturns the precepts of private life, is that acts of authority intervene in a certain state of opinion which changes their meaning. They awake an echo which is at times immeasurable. They open or close hidden fissures in the block of general consent, and trigger a molecular process which may modify the whole course of events. Or as mirrors set around in a circle transform a slender flame into a fairyland, acts of authority reflected in the constellation of consciousness are transfigured, and the reflections of these reflections create an appearance which is the proper place—the truth, in short—of historical action.[23]

Machiavelli is a difficult thinker because he forces upon us the ambiguity of virtue from which self-styled humanists so often shrink, preferring the history of principles to the history of men. Among Montaigne, Machiavelli, and Marx, on the other hand, there is common effort to consider the nature of history and politics within the boundaries that men set for themselves. That is to say, human action always achieves something more and something less than it envisages and yet political man must assume the consequences. Far from being a fatal flaw in the nature of action, this essential ambiguity is what makes human actions neither blindly impulsive nor divinely efficacious. At the same time, the ambiguity of political action is not a justification for the lack of political conviction or fidelity. For what introduces ambiguity into political action is precisely the metamorphoses of truth and justice experienced in putting them into practice without any absolute guarantee that this project will not be attacked, sabotaged, and even undermined from within. It is, in short, the denial of political innocence even at the birth of freedom.

Finally, Merleau-Ponty teaches us the lesson that truth and justice are alien to history and politics in the sense that they can never be completely realized and yet never exist entirely apart from the life and vicissitudes of community and power. The expression of truth and justice is never a solitary confrontation of the philosopher and a truth that he expresses, unless we lose sight of the community to which the philosopher belongs and before whom he expresses the truth. This is not to say that the philosopher expresses the truth solely in accordance with others, any more than for himself alone, or as the voice of a truth in itself an abstraction from himself and others. The enigma of philosophy is that sometimes life has the *same* face for us and for others and before the truth, so that the philosopher is called to share a life whose truth and goodness are evident and he would never think of opposing himself to his fellow men or setting truth against life. And yet the philosopher knows the limits of other men and must refuse them, but with all the more peace that comes from sharing the same world. "Hence the rebellious gentleness, the thoughtful adherence, the intangible presence that upset those around him."[24]

To pose the problem of truth and opinion in this way opens memory to what is close to us from the past and lends immediacy to the life and death of Socrates, who bore men the same love that he bore philosophy. If Socrates had simply denied the gods of the polis he would have shown his fellow men nothing more than their daily practice. But Socrates sacrificed to the gods and obeyed the law of the polis to his death. Or if Socrates had claimed to believe more than his fellow men he might well have scandalized them; but in either case, whether through excess or revolt he would not have conveyed his esssential irony, which is to have thought religion true but not in the way it understood itself to be true, just as he believed the polis to be just but not for reasons of state. Socrates could speak as though he obeyed the laws out of the conservatism of age and the gradualism it calls hope. But his inertia is more truly that of his daimon or the absolute standpoint of an internal truth that admonishes through joining man to his own ignorance. Only by engaging his judges in the example of an obedience that is simultaneously a resistance, in an encounter with a truth that is proved whether they sentence him or acquit him, can Socrates introduce into the polis the principle of philosophy that transforms the certainty of religion by bringing both religion and philosophy to the same ground. Thus the Socratic irony does not lie in the exploitation of the differences of level between philosophy and religion but in the experience of their reversal. The significance of Socrates' obedience to the laws is that henceforth the polis is the guardian of the individual soul; it has become a citadel without walls and hence no longer needs the laws of religion and the state—it needs men.

There is no complacency or self-sufficiency behind the Socratic irony. "The irony of Socrates is a distant but true relation with others. It expresses the fundamental fact that each of us is himself only when there is no escape and yet can recognize himself in the other. It is an attempt to release us together for freedom."[25] There would be no tragedy in Socrates' stand before the Athenian Assembly if he had not believed that his fellow men could understand him or that no one after him would take a similar stand. Not everyone voted to condemn Socrates; for truth and error, justice and injustice, are never whole and have always to be taken up again in every age and by every man. It is the same faith that inspired Merleau-Ponty's meditations on the true distance that is the source of meaning and poetry within the fold and flesh of the world.

Situation, Action, and Politics in Sartre and Merleau-Ponty

Much of Merleau-Ponty's thought can only be grasped if we understand something of his continuous reflections upon and differences with Sartre's phenomenology of the body and political action. Here I shall restrict myself for the most part to Sartre's essays collected in the volumes *Situations*,[1] since what follows is intended largely as an introduction to *Situations IV*,[2] and in particular to the long essay therein on Sartre's relation to Merleau-Ponty. The ultimate purpose of the discussion is to suggest that there is perhaps a greater similarity in the views of Sartre and Merleau-Ponty on the phenomenology of action, expression, history than is likely to appear if one relies upon a number of conventional interpretations of Sartre and then turns away in order to study Merleau-Ponty. I am aware, of course, that the two friends became enemies over their differences. But I am suggesting that Merleau-Ponty's preoccupation with Sartre as late as *The Visible and the Invisible* requires us to find some common ground out of which their differences grew.

It has been argued that Sartre's identification of consciousness and imagination condemns individual consciousness to a comedy of errors, degeneration, and self-enchantment. Similarly, Sartre's conception of individual freedom as any awareness of the conflict between *L'être-en-soi-pour-soi* and the being that lacks being opens up an abyss that individual freedom can never overleap.[3] Together these views involve the difficulty that the flux of individual consciousness and the futility of its passions resist identification with any historical process that aims at the realization of political values willed as such for all men. The Sartrean individual is crippled by the burden of a radical freedom that is essentially indifferent to the structures of language, history, economy, and society.

In my own view much of the critical literature has concentrated upon the antithetical nature of Sartre's philosophy of action because it has dealt only with its epistemological and/or ontological ekstasis, but has not attempted to understand these as secondary structures within the temporal ekstasis that is the diasporatic unity of all the intramundane multiplicities of being. Time is the opening in being, through which there can be meaning (*sens*) that is neither transcendental nor opaque, but rather a schema of the practical truth or physiognomy of things. Thus time is the hollow in being in which is conceived the value of being-in-itself for the being who lacks being or self-coincidence. Time is the arrow of being, the dialectical surge that continuously sweeps up its starting points into fresh, but equally distant, totalizations of the human act.

> Thus Temporality is not a universal time containing all beings and in particular human realities. Neither is it a law of development which is imposed on being from without. Nor is it being. But it is the intra-structure of the being which is its own nihilation—that is, the *mode of being* peculiar to being for itself. The For-itself is the being which has to be its being in the form of Temporality.[4]

We shall not properly understand Sartre's concept of situation as a matrix in which the act is born in a revelation and recovery of being unless we preserve its temporal ekstasis. Situation is a secondary structure that can be made and unmade in the temporalization of an original project that is never present in a global view, but reveals being at the place where being opens to gesture, expression, and conduct. It is thus the appropriation of a world that is present to a being that undertakes to make itself through acts that polarize the world as value and instruments: that is, the human world.

The structure of the human world is essentially linguistic. It is through language that we assume responsibility for events either

in the past or in the future that are the necessary but otherwise in-
sufficient conditions of the *act;* hence the unities of time, place, and
action.[5] It is the task of the play and the novel, as employed by Sartre,
to recuperate the mysterious depth that the decision to act opens up
in the commonplace world that otherwise bears us away from our acts
and covers them over as soon as they are done. Literature is action
because of the intentional structure of the word, and its situations are
correlative with the historical structure of the world. There are, however, at the extreme limits two literary techniques that are alien to the
intention of the authentic novel. Though they seem to be opposites,
naturalism and *l'art pour l'art* are in practice two species of objectivism,
that is, an unsituated perspectivism that produces a decomposition of
time and duration. Writers who employ either technique construct
novels according to what Sartre calls the eidetic imagery of bad faith:
handing over the freedom of their characters to the past, or moving
them like creatures who have pawned their future in order to maintain their author's omniscience. The true novelist draws the reader
into the situation of his characters as an accomplice to actions that
unfold with the characters and polarize the flow of events as acts
polarize the scenes in a play.

The technique of the naturalist or neorealist does not, according to Sartre, produce genuine novels. The naturalist fails because he
attempts to construct the novel out of events that have only a Humean
history and never any intrinsic meaning. But then it might be argued
that Hume is the first philosopher of the absurd, as Camus, Hem-
mingway, and Dos Passos are the great novelists of the absurd. What
each reveals to us is that man's customs are merely veils that hide the
abyss between man and nature. None of our routines ever succeeds
in establishing a "qualitative ethic." Outside the idea, we experience
only a sequence of radically contingent events that turn up without
qualitative adhesions, yet with a density of their own in the feelings.
Although the philosophy of the absurd scrupulously avoids the ori-
entations of bad faith, Sartre nevertheless denies the status of the
novel to Camus's *The Stranger,* as he does for similar reasons to Hem-
ingway's *Death in the Afternoon.* In each case, Sartre's objection is that
the technique of these writers is not to use words to integrate the
absurd into a human order, but to juxtapose a transparent sequence
of events and an order of meaning correspondingly opaque. Similarly,
in Dos Passos, the technique of accumulation by conjunction is employed to represent events that borrow prefabricated meanings
through the public declarations of the characters. But in Dos Passos
("the greatest writer of our time") the characters maintain a hybrid

existence between their own lived time and the collapsed time of reported events into which they are driven in the conflict between character and the destiny that is their lot in capitalist society.

The lack of transcendence in the writings of the naturalists, which has its source in their metaphysical decomposition of time, is likewise the defect of an author such as Mauriac, who views his characters sub specie aeternitatis, a technique that also fails to grasp the nature of lived time essential to the novel as the unfolding of action.

> A novel is a series of readings, of little parasitic lives, none of them longer than a dance. It swells and feeds upon the reader's time. But in order for the duration of my impatience and ignorance to be caught and then moulded and finally presented to me as the flesh of these creatures of invention, the novelist must know how to draw it into the trap, how to hollow out in his book, by means of the signs at his disposal, a time resembling my own, one in which the future does not exist. If I suggest that the hero's future actions are determined in advance by heredity, social influence or some other mechanism, my own time ebbs back into me; there remains only myself, reading and persisting, confronted by a static book. Do you want your characters to live? See to it that they are free.[6]

Characters whose future is congealed in the gaze of the author are reduced to *things* that have a *destiny* but no life that the reader can share from the inside.

The fate of Mauriac's characters is revealed in his use of third-person statements. The latter function ambiguously to designate the other, viewed solely from the outside, and simultaneously, while preserving a certain *aesthetic distance,* to draw us into the intimacy of the subject on the basis of shared experience. But in Mauriac's use the ambiguity of the third person loses the dimension of aesthetic distance and is employed to set us up in judgment over the characters. Suddenly, out of his own omniscience, Mauriac gives us the key to his characters. Thereafter, "Therese's 'pattern of destiny', the graph of her ups and downs, resembles a fever curve; it is dead time, since the future is spread out like the past and simply repeats it".[7] In Mauriac there are no time-traps, objects have no resistance or impenetrability, and conversations never stumble, meander, or grope toward meaning: everything is lucid. But lucidity is the novelist's sin of pride. It is the denial of the principle of relativity that applies both to physical and to fictional systems (the novel as a whole, as well as the partial systems of which it is composed, the minds of the characters, their psychological and moral judgments). In short, "novels are written *by* men and *for* men. In the eyes of God, Who cuts through appearances and goes beyond them, there is no novel, no art, for art thrives on appearances. God is not an artist."[8]

Sartre's conception of action and the novel may be further illustrated by turning to his comments upon the novels of Nathalie Sarraute and André Gorz that, like those of Nabakov, Waugh, and Gide, represent an attempt to use the novel against itself in order to reflect upon the genuine nature of the novel. The result is what Sartre calls the *antinovel*,[9] understood as a creative experiment that explores the novel as a metaphysical trap for the storyteller and the reader. Sarraute, much like Dos Passos, takes as her theme the realm of the *commonplace*. The trick of the novelist is to shuffle off the problem of the relation of the individual to the universal by resorting to the commonplaces of character, moral opinion, and art, especially the novel itself. Through such devices the threat of subjectivity is contained within the realm of the objective. Feeling is centrifugal and consensual, feeding upon the exchange of generalities, in flight from itself.

Sarraute subjects the novel to a confrontation with its possibility of inauthenticity. Gorz, however, pushes the novel into an extreme situation in which the words have yet to inhabit its principal character. We witness the birth of an order in which every moment involves the risk of a regression. The pages of the book murmur to us, but they do not speak in the first person for the very reason that they are in search of a self.

> What reassures us, however, is that we perceive, behind the hesitations of life and language, an arid, trenchant and frozen passion, a steel wire stretched between the lacerations of the past and the uncertainty of the future. An inhuman passion ignorant of itself, an uneasy seeker, a lunatic silence within the heart of language. It bores a hole through the reader's time, dragging this stream of words behind. We shall have faith in it.[10]

The experiment undertaken in Gorz's novel is the search for the *act* that justifies the shift from the third person to the first person. Otherwise we all remain kidnapped by the other. "They spoke of us as 'He' years before we were able to say 'I'. We had our first existence as absolute objects."[11] It is this circumstance that causes us to be careless of our human nature, whereas Gorz's Traitor, by the effort he has to appropriate every human emotion, reminds us that the human species does not exist.

The error common to those writers whom Sartre refuses to recognize as novelists is that they adopt a position external to their characters. This in effect involves a double error, namely, that the writer fails to understand his own immersion in time as well as that of his characters. These writers treat time as a datum, as either a sociological or a theological assumption. The result is that their art is reduced to the revelation of the spectacle of being and falls into the category of consumption rather than production, or *praxis*. The genuine novelist is obliged to analyze his own historical situation and its effects upon his metaphysical assumptions and literary techniques. This is the task that Sartre undertook in a lengthy essay, *What Is Literature?*, where he makes it clear that the novelist's creation of character is an integral factor in the historical process in which man makes himself at the risk of losing himself.

The intention of Sartre's survey of the history of literature is not to separate its future from its past or near-present. Indeed, Sartre is not *surveying* the history of literature in any ordinary sense at all. It is only in the light of a literature that is for-itself that its separation from its modality as action identifies it as *having been* a literature of *hexis* and consummatory destruction. The task of literature is to reveal the human situation in order to surpass it toward a community of freedoms. Its own history is internal to the ideal relationship of generosity and freedom that it forges between the writer and the public. In the past literature fell into the category of consumption because it had adopted a metaphysics in which being and having were identical. Thus literature professed to offer through indulgence the fulfillment of being, the appropriation of being through the spectacle of being. By contrast, the literature of praxis starts from the metaphysical assumption that being is appropriated only through the act of making itself. The literature of praxis is always a literature *en situation*. It inserts itself into the world of gestures and instruments that reveal the world in the act of transforming it.

The late nineteenth-century bourgeoisie had employed artists and writers to convince itself that it was capable of useless, gratuitous passions, such as adultery and stamp collecting. For a class that practiced honesty out of interest, virtue through unimaginativeness, and fidelity from habit, it was satisfying to be told that its daring exceeded that of the seducer or highwayman. Under these conditions the writer, himself formerly a useless passion, became a functionary in producing a *literature of alibis,* titillating the bourgeoisie with a fictional identity of the categories of production and consumption.

Surrealist literature that followed attempted to recreate the identification of literature with consumption radicalized as the pure act of destruction. It embarked upon the destruction of bourgeois subjectivity by pushing its rationality to the limit, in an automated irrationalism that consumes the contours of every object in a radical self-contradiction. In reality, the surrealists merely bracketed the world in order to celebrate its symbolic destruction. Their conception of violence was instantaneous, gratuitous, and scandalous, but not such as could undertake a protracted struggle in which the categories of means and ends are essential to the definition of the political situation.

It was the forties that altered the pace of history and the ratios of good and evil so as to confront every individual with a situation in which to act was to play one's hand irredeemably in the certainty that destruction and evil were absolute realities. For previous generations evil had been only an appearance, a detour for freedom. Henceforth good and evil were equally absolute because their consequences for collective destruction could no longer be foreseen contemplatively, but required deliberation through action for resistance. Under these conditions the individual lived on the frontier between his own humanity and man's inhumanity to man. In these circumstances, the relativity of things could be conveyed only through a *literature of extreme situations* that involved the reader in the predicament of characters without guarantees. It was no longer possible to create a literature of ordinary situations when each day a man somewhere chose between humiliation and heroism, between the polarities of the human condition.

Finally, in the period of postwar capitalist reconstruction, literature had once again to situate itself relative to the processes of production and consumption. In a context characterized equally by the highest levels of production in history and the most profound sense of alienation it becomes the task of literature to reveal the power of the productive process over the producer, as did Hesiod in an earlier day, and to relate this alienation within the total project whereby man makes history his own history. The writer engaged in such a task must create what Sartre calls *a total literature* that is simultaneously a literary and a political activity in which the writer and the reading public communicate man to man, on the model of a socialist society.

The power of nihilation or freedom whereby consciousness becomes aware of what is lacking in its condition is not an act of pure reflection or simple withdrawal. The fundamental project that I am is progressively revealed through an ensemble of real existents that simultaneously separate me from my ends and are structured secondarily as means or obstacles to my purposes. Values come into the world only through the being that carves into the plenitude of being its own lack of being.

> We shall use the term *situation* for the contingency of freedom in the *plenum* of being of the world inasmuch as this *datum,* which is there only *in order not to constrain* freedom, is revealed to this freedom only as already *illuminated* by the end which freedom chooses. Thus the *datum* never appears to the for-itself as a brute existent in itself; it is discovered always *as a cause* since it is revealed only in the light of an end which illuminates it. Situation and motivation are really one. The for-itself discovers itself as engaged in being, hemmed in by being, threatened by being; it discovers the state of things which surrounds it as the cause for a reaction of defence or attack. But it can make this discovery only because it freely posits the end in relation to which the state of things is threatening or favourable.[12]

My situation is never reducible to the deadweight upon me of my body, my place, my past, my environment, my death, my relation to the other. The significance of each of these structures unfolds only within my situation as a practical field in which my decision to act qualifies the facticities of place or environment. It is only in the light of my undertaking that things acquire a coefficient of adversity, that is to say, are designated simultaneously as *data* that have to be assumed by my action and as *possibilities* that are illuminated by my needs. It is through the exigency that I exist in order to become what I am that nothingness is added to the plenitude of being.

> It is because freedom is condemned to be free—i.e., can not choose itself as freedom—that there are things; that is, a plenitude of contingency at the heart of which it is itself contingency and by its surpassing that there can be at once a *choice* and an organization of things in *situation;* and it is the contingency of freedom and the contingency of the in-itself which are expressed *in situation* by the unpredictability and the adversity of the environment. Thus I am absolutely free and absolutely responsible for my situation. But I can never be free except *in situation.*[13]

Thus we are in language as we are in the body, that is, as a vehicle of expression, an excarnation of particular purposes or de-totalizations of the total human project. In speech we unveil the world, name its objects, and describe situations in order to transcend them. It is the poet who does not pass beyond words to the practical utilities that they furnish. To the poet these connections are purely magical. He uses words to produce word-objects or images of the world, but not to *express* a certain situation like the writer of a political pamphlet who intends to transform the situation in the light of his description. Every creation of the genuine artist, far from being a finished object, opens on to the entire world, calling forth the freedom of his public.

> Each painting, each book, is a recovery of the totality of being. Each of them presents this totality to the freedom of the spectator. For this is quite the final goal of art: to recover this world by giving it to be seen as it is, but as if it had its source in human freedom. But since what the author creates takes on objective reality only in the eyes of the spectator, this recovery is consecrated by the ceremony of the spectacle—and particularly of reading. We are already in a better position to answer the question we raised a while ago: the writer chooses to appeal to the freedom of other men so that, by the reciprocal implications of their demands, they may readapt the totality of being to man and may again enclose the universe within man.[14]

The artist's creation, therefore, appeals to a kingdom of ends for which terror and beauty are never simply natural events but simultaneously an *exigency* and a *gift* to be integrated into the human condition. Whenever the artist is separated from his public, his work loses its quality as an imperative and is reduced to a purely aesthetic object. In turn the artist is forced to substitute the formal relationship between himself and his art for the relationship of commitment and transcendence between the artist and the public. Under these conditions, works of art function not as outlines of the total man, but as treasures whose scarcity is the measure of the absolute poverty of man, whose eternity is the denial of human history.[15]

Together Sartre and Merleau-Ponty were the enemies of "high-altitude thinking." But, as Sartre tells the story, the two became estranged by everything they had in common. The thought of Merleau-Ponty is labyrinthine; its anchorage in the body, its passion unity. By contrast, Sartre allows his own thought to appear overlucid, dialectical, and, even worse, optimistic in the face of Merleau-Ponty's brooding silence. The events of history forced the two to quarrel over the spontaneity of the proletarian revolution and its organization, the nature of individual and group life, in the course of which they embroiled everything each had ever stood for.

> Beneath our intellectual divergences of 1941, so calmly accepted when Husserl alone was the cause, we discovered, astounded, that

our conflicts had, at times, stemmed from our childhood, or went
back to the elementary differences of our two organisms; and that
at other times, they were between the flesh and the skin; in one of
us hypocrisies, complicities, a passion for activism hiding his
defeats, and, in the other, retractile emotions and desperate
quietism.[16]

Sartre generously conceded that it was from Merleau-Ponty
that he "learned History," and the testimony to this is his *Critique de
la raison dialectique.* To some this may suggest the relative inferiority
of *Being and Nothingness* to the *Phenomenology of Perception* and the con-
sequent failure of Sartre's identification of the categories of literature
and politics. This is the old criticism of Sartrean lucidity that I suggest
is unjust to Sartre's phenomenology of action and situation that is the
foundation of his novels and plays and his most recent studies of
history and social structure. I think my argument for a certain continuity in the approaches of Sartre and Merleau-Ponty, despite their
political quarrels, can be seen if we turn now to Merleau-Ponty's phenomenology of freedom.

Merleau-Ponty's views on action, choice, and determinism underwrite, so to speak, Sartre's position by grounding them in a conception of the body as generality rather than particularity. Sartre
speaks as though embodiment were fundamentally a mode of alienation, that is, a purely external object for the gaze of another body
similarly isolated by its other. If this were the body of history and
politics, then the latter would indeed be subject to an extreme form
of voluntarism whose figure is the Party intellectual as played by
Sartre himself. Curiously enough, it is this voluntarist and idealist
account of political action that confines the proletariat to the passivity
of materialism and determinism. Against this conception of the "lum-
pen-body," Merleau-Ponty develops this phenomenology of the body
that is a mode of being-in-the-world, at once self and other, and a
general schema upon which we articulate the domain of our psychosocial and political history. Thus the world of things and persons is
not the primary model of what is external any more than we, or our
minds, are the model of what is internal. Each of these domains is
relativized through the kind of body that is the human body, that is,
neither a separable thing nor a transcendental thought or percipient,
each with a problem of their relationship:

The solution of all problems of transcendence is to be sought in the
thickness of the pre-objective present, in which we find our bodily

being, our social being, and the pre-existence of the world. That is,
the starting point of "explanations", in so far as they are
legitimate—and at the same time the basis of our freedom.[17]

In short, there are action and history because there is in the world an
autoaffective being whose mode of being-in-the-world requires no
existential leap but a continuous hermeneutic of its experience and
relationships. This human being is never given wholly to itself, nor
to others, any more than it is possessed of thought and language prior
to the general conversation of mankind that is its element. By the
same token, human action requires a field of being in which there
can be possibilities and obstacles to its operation. In this case, we
should rather speak of our freedom as the opportunity to modify a
tradition, a habit, or a situation in which we have hitherto lived; and
it is quite impossible to gauge the relative weights of freedom and
situation:

> The idea of situation rules out absolute freedom at the source of
> our commitments, and equally, indeed, at their terminus. No
> commitment, not even commitment in the Hegelian state, can make
> me leave behind all differences and free me for anything.[18]

We shall develop this phenomenology of tradition and criticism
in Chapter 15. In the next chapter we shall be concerned more fully
with Merleau-Ponty's conception of phenomenology and Marxism and
with the sharper differences that arose between him and Sartre. Here
we should conclude with some remarks on the broad philosophical
anthropology shared by Sartre and Merleau-Ponty through their ap-
prenticeship to Kojève's lectures on Hegel's *Phenomenology*.[19] The crux
of the matter lies in the interpretations of the dialectic of Desire, that
is, whether or not history releases a humanizing desire of one's own
humanity and coproduced and reflected in the desire of the other
person's humanity. Sartre appears to have reduced the Master's inability
to recognize the Slave's self-hood, and thereby his own potential for
self-development, to the narrow lack of recognition in selves that are
locked into their bodies as mere objects of an alienating gaze. Sartrean
bodies are unrecognizable, vertiginous objects of a repulsive subjective
gaze that drains the world of familiarity and intersubjectivity.
Although we have tried to modify this exaggerated existentialist posture, it nevertheless seems to color Sartre's voluntarist re-
bound into social and political relationships that he never quite releases
from the uncanniness of the practical-inert. By contrast, as Kojève

reads Hegel, it is precisely in the world of the practico-inert, that is, where the Slave submits to the laws of the materials to which he is bound, that an emancipatory possibility arises. Yet it would require the sort of analysis made by Habermas, as we shall see in Chapter 15, to articulate the levels of cognitive and emancipatory interest within a higher level of communicative practice and to bring forth the full sense of this "labor of recognition," if we may put it this way. For it may well be that Marx's emphasis upon the "recognition of labor" would only reverse the dialectic of Lordship and Bondage without releasing any communicative community. The resultant *political nausea* is precisely what Merleau-Ponty suspected to be the effect of Sartre's ultrabolshevism. One might say that Sartre's voluntarism collapses the historical narrative in Hegelian Marxism, reducing it to the strategical diversions and opportunism of a Party whose organization and propaganda repeat on the political level the nonrecognition experienced by the proletariat in its economic relations with capital and the market.

The medium of alienation and of the failed dialectic of recognition on the political level is language. Hence Merleau-Ponty is a careful critic of Sartrean political vocabulary. We can be brief about this in view of our broad exposition of Merleau-Ponty's ideas.[20] The main thing to say is that in Merleau-Ponty the body-politic is grounded in the anonymously knowledgeable body through which each of us shares the world and an intersubjectivity of perception, commonsense knowledge, and values. Conflict and justice arise because we are already social beings in virtue of that specific vicissitude of human embodiment that entails all our senses and is a function of our collective history. This collectivity is not a political invention required by correction of individual justice. It is prefigured in the operation of the human senses as historical universals without which consciousness is an empty gesture and lacks any measure of good and evil:

> When one says there is a history one means precisely that each
> person committing an act does so not only in his own name,
> engages not only himself, but also others whom he makes use of, so
> that as soon as we begin to live, we lose the alibi of good intentions;
> we are what we do to others, we yield to the right to be respected as
> noble souls.[21]

Thus, although Merleau-Ponty is concerned to show that Marxist humanism cannot escape the violence encountered in its own determination to end exploitation, he simultaneously develops a critique of the Party's management of one-way controls in the creation of social revolution. In short, the Party acquires its own history of violence. Because of this misadventure of the dialectic, Merleau-Ponty increasingly resigned himself to a politics of the possible, a politics more like a craft than a science, one more responsive to the limits of the community in which it works, more inclined to compromise than to the Sartrean heights of consciousness. Such a voice will be lost where the circumstances appear to require hard ideological lines; it will be treasured whenever our ideologies collide without common ground.

14

The Phenomenological Critique of Marxist Scientism

n the immediate postwar period of hardening East-West relations, Merleau-Ponty began to rethink Marxism from a phenomenological perspective. In *Humanism and Terror,* he studied the Moscow Trials in order to understand from the standpoint of the revolutionaries their notions of individual and collective responsibility. He also opened up the larger study followed in *Adventures of the Dialectic* in which Marxist scientism is criticized in terms of a Leninist and Weberian conception of the philosophy of history. In the present chapter, these arguments are set out descriptively, or as nearly as possible in Merleau-Ponty's own terms. I have, of course, organized the arguments and made explanatory comments where necessary. Merleau-Ponty did not write in the discursive style favored by the social sciences. This reflects the difference between hermeneutical and causal analysis. Rather than reduce Merleau-Ponty's thought to a mode of discourse of which he was extremely critical, not only on epistemological grounds, but also because of its attempt to reduce the autonomy of language and style, I have chosen to preface the argument with some analytic reading rules that I believe underlie its construction. I believe that a discussion over the responsibility of reading and writing would not be alien to Merleau-Ponty's thought and would also contribute to the critique of literary scientism.

Analytic Reconstruction of the Following Argument

Merleau-Ponty's argument relies upon the history of Marxism, while claiming that Marxism confers upon history a meaning without which history would be sheer violence. *Humanism and Terror* announces in its very title the twin birth of man and violence. In *The Rebel* Camus has argued that the birth of man is the beginning of endless violence. When Merleau-Ponty makes the *Adventures of the Dialectic* his topic, he has again to find a thread to history, avoiding the extremes of premature closure or of senseless ups and downs. It may be said that, after all, both *Humanism and Terror* and *Adventures of the Dialectic* are topical works outside the interests of political philosophy. But then we have surrendered the world to violence in order to preserve the harmony of history. Alternatively, we may risk the face of philosophy in search of truths that will be found to be partial, and possibly even destructive, when held in competition with other values and beliefs. Merleau-Ponty is a valuable thinker because he refused to separate politics and philosophy. He could do this because as a philosopher he was not wedded to the ideal of absolute knowledge, and because in politics he was just as opposed to historical fatalism as to senseless violence. Merleau-Ponty struggled to comprehend his times. He was not withdrawn. Nor did he surrender himself to aesthetic revulsion. He claimed no privileged theory of action, and so he avoided sloganizing the issues of rethinking Marxism at a time when positions were hardening in the East and West.

I want now to formulate the narrative that follows in the form of a number of rules of procedure that I believe furnish an analytic reconstruction of the arguments of Marxist humanism. These are the rules that I believe can be abstracted from the history of rethinking Marx in terms of Hegel, in order to provide a critique of Marxist scientism. By the same token, these rules may be interpreted as rules for anyone participating in the community of argument since Lenin read Marx in the light of Hegel. We may then think of the Marxist tradition as a set of rival reading practices that have to be understood as the very issues of Marxist politics, and not simply as glosses upon events intelligible apart from such practices. I consider this the basic postulate of Marxist humanism. It is challenged by Marxist scientism, such as that of Althusser, inasmuch as the latter espouses a conception of historical events whose life would be independent of the hermeneutical continuity of rival interpretations.

I Thus, in the first place, we must subject our own discussion of Marxism to the *humanist rule* that the nature of Marxism is not given to Marxists as the simple negation of bourgeois liberalism and capitalism. This is the Marxism of commissars. It lacks its own voice. In other words, Marxism has no monopoly over criticism. Humanist Marxism must keep itself in question, and it can only do this by means of a lively recognition of the limitations facing both socialist and liberal discourse.

II We may then treat the first rule as a procedure for reconstructing the history of Marxist thought since Marx himself read Hegel, through Lenin, into the Hegelian Marxism of Lukács and Kojève (we should also include Korsch, who is closer to Kant) as the work of eliciting the Hegelian dialectic of recognition as:

a. An ideal telos of history
b. A method of hermeneutical analysis

III The test of these rules is offered in Merleau-Ponty's treatment of violence. We cannot consider violence as limited to either communism or capitalism, nor can we be sure that proletarian violence is only a temporary revolutionary expedient. For where the Party intervenes to bring the proletariat into history, there is always the risk that the Party will subject the proletariat to its own rule.

a1. History and politics are made by men.
a2. Men themselves must be made human in the objective course of history and politics.
a3. Let us call the Party the action of bringing together (a1) and (a2) and the tension between (a1) and (a2) the field of justice and violence.

Thus, a phenomenological approach to the Soviet trials will proceed hermeneutically, so as to prevent false antitheses in the construction of the member's praxis in trying to resolve the double commitment to historical inevitability and political responsibility.

b1. The trials are not to be treated a priori as illegal or corrupt justice.
b2. Nor can we justify collectivization ex post facto.
b3. We must let stand members' rival readings of the primacy of economic and political decisions.

IV In light of the preceding rules we are necessarily engaged in a double task:

a. The critique of Marxist scientism
b. A hermeneutic of history and politics

V We may treat both tasks as the elicitation of a historical and political norm of *intersubjectivity;* specifically, the question is, How are free men to be led to freedom? Marxist humanism is thus (broadly conceived) a *pedagogical problem.* Consequently, all future Marxist discussion should contribute to the development of socialist education and to an understanding of the relationship between truth and justice.

Waiting for Marx

It is impossible to think of modern political history apart from the Russian Revolution. At the same time, it is hard not to be ambivalent toward the history and politics of Marxism itself. In the days before communism ruled a major part of the world, one could believe that communism would shunt all forms of political and economic exploitation into the siding of prehistory. In those days Marxism was emancipatory knowledge wonderfully scornful of the "iron laws" of history and economics. This is not to say that Marxist critique failed to recognize the weight of historical structures. Indeed, we owe Marx much of the credit for a structuralist analysis of historical development. By the same token, there has always been an uncertain relation between Marxist analysis of the determinism of historical structures and its prophecy of a proletarian fulfillment of historical law. Prior to the actual experience of the revolution, it was easy enough to think of it as a temporary, albeit violent, intervention on the side of justice against a moribund but destructive ruling class. But the revolution is itself an institution, and it soon acquires a history of its own, leaders and enemies, priorities and policies that could not be foreseen. In view of these complexities, Communist practice inevitably hardened and Marxism soon became the intellectual property of the Party, which abandoned the education of the proletariat in favor of slogans and dogma. This is the context of what we call Marxist *scientism.*[1] That is to say, once Marxism became Party knowledge and a tool for the industrialization of Soviet society, Marxism identified with economic determinism and the values of scientific naturalism at the expense of its own radical humanism. This is variously described as the difference between communism and Marxism, the difference between theory and practice, or the difference between the early, Hegelianized Marx and the later, scientific Marx.[2]

Today socialism and capitalism are equally in question insofar as the same ideology of technological domination underlies their apparently opposed political and ideological systems. We can no longer assume that Marxism challenges capitalism and justifies the sufferings of revolution unless we can be sure that Marxism possesses the philosophical resources for rethinking the logic of technical rationality and the Party practices that have forced this logic upon the proletariat in the name of the revolution. The task we are faced with is a reflection upon the very Logos of Western rationality. It is only against this broad background that we can understand the historically specific goals and ambitions of Western Marxism. In particular, it is in this way that we can best understand the phenomenon of recent attempts to rethink Marxism in terms of Hegelian phenomenology in order to liberate Marxist praxis from the limitations of positivist knowledge.[3] To rethink Marxism, however, means that we put it in abeyance as the only "other" answer that we have to the uncertainties of our times. In other words, it means that we need to examine the categories of Marxist thought such as man, nature, history, party, and revolution, in order to recover a proper sense of their dialectical relations so that they are not organized around a simple logic of domination. What this will involve is a recovery of the relation between the already meaningful world of everyday life and the specific practices of science, economics, and politics through which we attempt to construct a socialist society, mindful of the historical risks and responsibilities of such a project. In short, by placing Marxism in abeyance while we rethink the meaning of socialism we educate ourselves into a permanently critical attitude toward the Party of history as guarantors of socialist rationality and freedom.

Merleau-Ponty's critique of Marxist scientism cannot be well understood unless we situate it in the intellectual history of France and the post–World War II rejection of communism by leftist intellectuals who at the same time turned to the revival of Marxism.[4] This renaissance of Marxist thinking in part reflected the task of catching up with Central European thought—Korsch and Lukács—as well as with German phenomenology—Hegel, Husserl, Heidegger, not to mention Weber and Freud. The task was to separate the radical humanist philosophy of Marx from the Engels-Lenin orthodoxy of positivism and scientism.[5] In practice this meant reading Hegel anew and on this basis interpreting Marx's early writings. Merleau-Ponty was among many like Sartre and Hyppolite[6] who listened to Alexandre Kojève's lectures[7] on Hegel's *Phenomenology of Mind*. It was not until the mid-1950s that the rift between communism and Marxism, a difficult distinction for outsiders, let alone insiders, became wide open. Apart from other broken friendships, the friendships of Merleau-Ponty and Sartre and of Sartre and Camus were destroyed in the wake of *Humanism and Terror, Adventures of the Dialectic,* and Camus's *The Rebel.*[8] Later, in his *Critique de la raison dialectique,* Sartre attempted to learn from this the "lesson of history," as he himself puts it, in a massive effort to construct an adequate Marxist history and sociology.

It is much easier for us four decades after World War II to consider capitalism and socialism as subcultures of industrialism rather than as mortal antagonists. But in 1945 it was possible to hope that communism was the solution to the capitalist syndrome of war and depression. For leftist intellectuals in Europe the Soviet war effort and the Communist resistance promised a renewal of life once peace came. But peace never came, except as what we call the cold war. In such an atmosphere, intellectual attitudes were forced to harden. Capitalists and socialists increasingly blamed each other for all the violence and oppression in the world. The price of loyalty either to socialism or to capitalism became a blind and uncritical faith.

The argument of *Humanism and Terror* is especially difficult to understand if the radical alternative forced upon French politics by the cold war split between America and the Soviet Union is accepted without question. In 1947 there was still a chance, at least in mind of a non-Communist leftist intellectual like Merleau-Ponty, that France and Europe would not have to become a satellite either to America or to the Soviet Union. The hopes of the Resistance for immediate revolutionary change after the war had withered away in the tripartist tangles of the Communists, Socialists, and Christian Democrats. In March 1947 the Truman doctrine was initiated, and in April the Big Four discussions on Germany failed. The introduction of the Marshall Plan in June of the same year, condemned by Molotov's walkout on the Paris Conference in July, hastened the breakdown of tripartism. Suspicion of the anti-Soviet implications of the Marshall Plan caused many of the Left to look toward a neutralist position for Europe, but made them uncertain whether to build this position around the Socialist party, which had failed so far to take any independent line, or the Communist party, which could be expected to follow a Soviet line. But the drift was toward a pro-Western, anti-Soviet European integration led by the center and Right elements of the French

Third Force, including the Gaullists. Within two years, the formation of the Brussels Treaty Organization, the North Atlantic Treaty Organization, and the Soviet Cominform brought down the iron curtain of which Winston Churchill had spoken in his Fulton speech in March 1946.

The intellectual French Left was in an impossible situation that no combination of Marxism or existentialism seemed capable of remedying. French capitalism was bad, but American capitalism was even more anathema to the Left, if only because it was in the rudest of health internationally, though perhaps not at home. At the same time, French socialism was anything but independent and its chances looked no better with Communist help. In such a situation it was impossible to be an anti-Communist if this meant being pro-American, witnessing the Americanization of Europe, and foreswearing the Communists who had fought bravely in the Resistance. On the other hand, it was not possible to be a Communist if this meant being blind to the hardening of the Soviet regime and becoming a witness to the Communist brand of imperialism that broke so many Marxist minds. It is not surprising that many on the Left as well as the Right were unable to bear such ambiguity and therefore welcomed any sign to show clearly which side to support, even if it meant a "conversion" to the most extreme Left and Right positions.

I want to argue that in *Humanism and Terror*[9] Merleau-Ponty does more than illustrate the fateful connection between revolution and responsibility as it appears in the drama of the Moscow Trials. I think it can be shown that Merleau-Ponty develops a theory of the relations among political action, truth, and responsibility that is the proper basis for understanding his approach to the problem of the relation between socialist humanism and revolutionary terror. *Humanism and Terror* was prompted by Koestler's dramatization of the Moscow Trials in *Darkness at Noon*. Merleau-Ponty's reply to Koestler's novel takes the form of an essay in which he develops a phenomenology of revolutionary action and responsibility in order to transcend Koestler's confrontation of the Yogi and the Commissar. The argument depends upon a philosophy of history and truth that draws upon Merleau-Ponty's phenomenology of perception, embodiment, and intersubjectivity. Here I shall restrict myself to the political arguments without entering into the structure of Merleau-Ponty's philosophical thought, which in any case is better revealed in a certain style of argument rather than through any system.[10]

> Politics, whether of understanding or of reason, oscillates between
> the world of reality and that of values, between individual judgment

and common action, between the present and the future. Even if one thinks, as Marx did, that these poles are united in a historical factor—the proletariat—which is at one and the same time power and value, yet, as there may well be disagreement on the manner of making the proletariat enter history and take possession of it, *Marxist politics is, just like all the others, undemonstrable.* The difference is that Marxist politics understands this and that it has, more than any other politics, explored the labyrinth.[11]

It is typical of Merleau-Ponty to speak factually whereas he is addressing an ideal that his own work brings to reality. It was necessary for Merleau-Ponty among others to take Marxist thinkers through the labyrinth of politics for them to understand the true nature of political trial and error. The philosopher of ambiguity,[12] as Merleau-Ponty has been called, prefers to raise questions rather than offer answers. This is not because he is nerveless but precisely because he wishes to bring to life the historical presumptions of Marxist thought. It is not literally the case that Marxists consider their knowledge undemonstrable. From the *Communist Manifesto* to the Russian revolution there is a fairly straight line, at least doctrinally. But in fact such a line represents a colossal abstraction from the doctrinal debates and historical contingencies that shaped these debates and in turn were interpreted through them. Merleau-Ponty believed it was possible to discern in the terrible reality of the Moscow trials the places where the life of Marxist thought was larger than the simplistic moral antithesis of the Yogi and the Commissar. Of course, Merleau-Ponty's purpose is easily misunderstood. Koestler's *Darkness at Noon* is certainly true to Soviet practice from the time of the Trials to the later revelations in the Cominform campaign against Tito, the Rajk-Kosov trials, the Soviet labor camps and mental hospitals. Like many on the Left, Merleau-Ponty himself had to open his eyes to Communist practice. Yet at the same time he begins to rethink Marxist philosophy of history and politics along the lines that have led to a renaissance of Marxist-Hegelian thought while only the most blind could have held on to the romance with Soviet institutions.

In *Humanism and Terror* Merleau-Ponty is concerned with revolution as the genesis of political community and with the dilemma of violence that in the name of fraternity becomes self-consumptive. This is the moral dilemma to which the Yogi responds by spiritualizing political action and that the Commissar handles by objectivizing his conduct in the name of historical forces. These alternatives, as posed by Koestler, are rejected by Merleau-Ponty on the grounds that they lose the essential ambivalence of political action and revolutionary responsibility. The science and practice of history never coincide.

Because of this contingency, political action is always the decision of a future that is not determined uniquely by the facts of the situation. Thus there enters into political conduct the need to acknowledge responsibility and the fundamental terror we experience for the consequences of our own decisions as well as for the effects of other men's actions upon ourselves.

> We do not have a choice between purity and violence but between different kinds of violence. Inasmuch as we are incarnate beings, violence is our lot. There is no persuasion even without seduction, or in the final analysis, contempt. Violence is the common origin of all regimes. Life, discussion and political choice occur only against a background of violence. *What matters and what we have to discuss is not violence but its sense or its future.* It is a law of human action that the present encroaches upon the future, the self upon other people. This intrusion is not only a fact of political life, it also happens in private life. In love, in affection, or in friendship we do not encounter face to face "consciousness" whose absolute individuality we could respect at every moment, but beings qualified as "my son", "my wife", "my friend" whom we carry along with us into common projects where they receive (like ourselves) a definite role with specific rights and duties. So, in collective history the spiritual atoms trail their historical role and are tied to one another by the threads of their actions. What is more, they are blended with the totality of actions, whether or not deliberate, which they exert upon others, and the world so that there does not exist a plurality of subjects but an intersubjectivity and that is why there exists a *common measure* of the evil inflicted upon certain people and of the good gotten out of it by others.[13]

Yet Merleau-Ponty refuses to draw the skeptical conclusion that violence and conflict derive from the essentially antisocial nature of the human passions. In his essay on Montaigne,[14] which allows us to anticipate here his differences with Sartre, he interprets Montaigne's skepticism in terms of the paradox of embodied consciousness, namely, to be constantly involved in the world through perception, politics, or love and yet always at a distance from it, without which we could know nothing of it. The skeptic only withdraws from the world, its passions and follies, in order to find himself at grips with the world, having, as it were, merely slackened the intentional ties between himself and the world in order to comprehend the paradox of his being-in-the-world. Skepticism with regard to the passions only deprives them of value if we assume a total, Sartrean self-possession, whereas we are never wholly ourselves, Merleau-Ponty would say, but always interested in the world through the passions that we are. Skepticism and misanthropy, whatever the appearances, have no place in Marxist politics for the reason that the essential ambivalence of politics is that its violence derives from what is most valuable in men: the ideas of truth and justice that each intends for all because men do not live side by side like pebbles but each in all.

Marxism does not invent the problem of violence, as Koestler would suggest, except in the sense that it assumes and attempts to control the violence that bourgeois society tolerates in the fatalities of race, war, domestic and colonial poverty. The Marxist revolutionary is faced only with a choice between different kinds of violence and not with the choice to forgo violence. The question that the revolutionary poses is not whether any one will be hurt but whether the act of violence leads to a future state of society in which humanist values have been translated into a common style of life expressed as much in low levels of infant mortality as in solipistic, philosophical, and literary speculation. If consciousness were a lonely and isolated phenomenon, as it is pictured in the individualist tradition of philosophy and the social sciences, and above all in Sartre, then the Yogi's horror at a single death is enough to condemn a whole regime regardless of its humanist or socialist aims. But this is an assumption that Marxist-Hegelianism challenges. We never exist even in splendid philosophical isolation let alone social isolation. We exist through one another, in specific situations mediated by specific social relations in which we encroach upon others and are committed by others so that our intentions are rarely entirely our own any more than their results. In these exchanges we necessarily prevail upon one another and one generation necessarily commits the future.[15]

The Marxist revolutionary starts from the evident truth of the embodied values of men and of the evil of human suffering. Only later does he learn that in the course of building the economic foundations of a socialist society he has to make decisions that subject individuals to forms of violence upon which the future of the revolution may depend. Marxism does not create this dilemma; it merely expresses it. Koestler, on the other hand, poses the problem in such a way as to miss the essential ambivalence of the subjective and objective options of the Yogi and the Commissar. The values of the Yogi are not simply the reverse of those of the Commissar because each experiences an internal reversal of the subjective and objective values whenever either is assumed as an absolute end. It is for this reason that Commissar Rubashov, once imprisoned, experiences the value of the self in the depths of its inner life, where it opens up to the White Guard in the next cell as someone to whom one can speak. The tapping on the prison walls is the primordial institution of human communication for whose sake Rubashov had set out on his revolutionary career.

In the debate over the alternatives of industrialization and collectivization there were facts to support the various arguments of Stalin, Bukharin, and Trotsky. But their divergences arose within the very Marxian conception of history that they all shared. Each regarded history as a reality made through action in line with yet altering the shape of social forces, just as a landscape is progressively revealed with each step we take through it.

> History is terror because we have to move into it not by any straight line that is always easy to trace but by taking our bearings at every moment in a general situation which is changing, like a traveller who pushes into a changing countryside continuously altered by his own advance, where what looked like an obstacle becomes an opening and where the shortest path turns out the longest.[16]

But the leaders of a revolution are not on a casual stroll. They walk on the wild side and must accept responsibility for the path they choose and be judged by it as soon as they open it up. For this reason Merleau-Ponty argued that the Moscow Trials have to be understood in terms of the Marxist philosophy of history, in which history is a drama open toward the future in such a way that the significance of the action at any point of time is never unequivocal and can only be established from the futurist orientation of those in power. The trials therefore never go beyond the level of a "ceremony of language" in which the meaning of "terrorism," "wrecking," "espionage," "defeatism," "responsibility," and "confession" has to be sensed entirely in the verbal exchanges and not through reference to an external ground of verification.

The trials reveal the form and style of the Marxist revolutionary. The revolutionary judges what exists in terms of what is to come; he regards the future as more vital than the present to which it owes its birth. From this perspective there can be no purely subjective honor; we are what we are for others and our relation to them. So often in the Court Proceedings the "capitulators," while presenting themselves in the light of enemies of the Party and the masses, hint at the discrepancies between the subjective and objective aspects of their careers. Their statements are to be understood not as formulations of the facts alleged in them except reflectively and by means of certain rules of translation. Consider the following exchange between Vyshinsky and Bukharin:

> Vyshinsky: Tell me, did Tomsky link up the perpetration of a hostile act against Gorky with the question of the overthrow of the Soviet government?
> Bukharin: In essence he did.
> Vyshinsky: In essence he did?
> Bukharin: Yes, I have answered.
> Vyshinsky: I am interested in the essence.
> Bukharin: But you are asking concretely. . . .
> Vyshinsky: Did your talk with Tomsky provide reason to believe that the question of a hostile act against Alexei Maximovich Gorky was being linked up with the task of overthrowing the Stalin leadership?
> Bukharin: Yes, in essence this could be said.
> Vyshinsky: Consequently, you knew that some hostile act against Gorky was under consideration?
> Bukharin: Yes.
> Vyshinsky: And what hostile act in your opinion was referred to?
> Bukharin: I gave no thought to the matter at all at that time and I had no idea. . . .
> Vyshinsky: Tell us what you did think.
> Bukharin: I hardly thought at all.
> Vyshinsky: But was it not a serious matter? The conversation was about what?
> Bukharin: Permit me to explain in a few words. Now, *post factum,* now, during the investigation, I can say. . . .
> Vyshinsky: Not during the investigation but during your conversation with Tomsky.
> Bukharin: But this was only a fleeting conversation, a conversation which took place during a meeting of the Political Bureau and lasted only a few seconds.
> Vyshinsky: I am not interested in how long this conversation lasted; you could have spoken to Tomsky for a whole hour somewhere in a corner, therefore your arguments are of no importance to me. What is important to me are the facts, and these I want to establish.[17]

It is not possible to understand these verbal plays apart from the Hegelian-Marxist expressions of the hypostases through which the logic of social forces reveals the essence of a situation or fact and its relevance for revolutionary action.[18] They will otherwise only seem to be the result of a corrupt legal process and as such the pure expression of Soviet terror. If *Humanism and Terror* were merely engaged in an ex post facto justification of Stalinism then Merleau-Ponty would simply have been doing bad historiography. But he understood himself to be involved in trying to comprehend Stalinism *ex ante* or from the political agent's standpoint, in other words, in the subjective terms of a Marxist philosophy of history and not just a Stalinist rewrite.

Responsible History

It is, then, Merleau-Ponty's interpretation of the Marxist philosophy of history that must concern us. His method of presentation in this case, as elsewhere, involves the familiar alternatives of determinism and voluntarism. As a complete alternative, determinism is incompatible with the need for political action, though it may be extremely effective in the rhetoric of politics to be able to reassure one's comrades that history is on their side; and similarly, a voluntarism that does not take into account the social preconditions of revolution is likely to waste itself in abortive action. Political reflection and political action occur in a milieu or interworld that is essentially ambiguous because the facts of the situation can never be totalized and yet we are obliged to act upon our estimation of them. Because of the double contingency of the openness of the future and the partiality of human decision, political divergences, deception, and violence are irreducible historical phenomena, accepted as such by all revolutionaries.

> There is no history where the course of events is a series of episodes without unity, or where it is a struggle already decided in the heaven of ideas. History is where there is a logic *within* contingence, a reason *within* unreason, where there is a historical perception which, like perception in general, leaves in the background what cannot enter the foreground but seizes the lines of force as they are generated and actively leads their traces to a conclusion. This analogy should not be interpreted as a shameful organicism or finalism, but as a reference to the fact that all symbolic systems—perception, language, history—only become what they were although in order to do so they need to be taken up into human initiative.[19]

Marxism is not a spectacle secure from its own intervention in our common history. Marxists need a philosophy of history because human history is neither open in an arbitrary way nor so closed that we are relieved of the responsibility of reading its signs and implementing our own chances. The future is not stillborn in the present, nor does the past lie unalterably upon the present. Between the past and the future there is our presence, which is the chance we have of testing our limits. In the human world men cannot be the object of their own practice except where oppression rules: that is to say, where some men subject others to the rule of things. Yet men need leaders as much as leaders need men. Thus there arises for Marxism the dreadful problem, once men are determined to be free, of how it is free men are to be led along the path of freedom. For freedom is not the absence of limits that would make knowledge and leadership unnecessary. Freedom is only possible in the real world of limits and situated possibilities that require the institution of thoughtful and responsible leadership.[20]

In confronting the problematic of freedom and truth, Merleau-Ponty reflected upon man's options in terms of Max Weber's response to the historical task of understanding. He saw in Weber one who tried to live responsibly in the face of conflicting demands of knowledge and action. This was possible, in the first place, because Weber understood that history is not the passive material of historiography any more than the practice of historiography is itself free of historical interests and values. There is no neutral material of history. History is not a spectacle for us because it is our own living, our own violence, and our own beliefs. Why then are revolutionary politics not an utterly cynical resort to violence and nothing but a skeptical appeal to justice and truth? For the very reason, says Merleau-Ponty, that no ones lives history from a purely pragmatic standpoint, not even he who claims to do so. Skepticism is a conclusion that could only be reached if one were to draw, as does Sartre, a radical distinction between political knowledge and political action. But allowing that we only experience things and the future according to a probable connection does not mean that the world lacks a certain style or physiognomy for us. We live in terms of subjective certainties that we intend as practical and universal typifications that are in no way illusory unless we posit some apodictic certainty outside the grounds of human experience. We do not experience uncertainty at the core of our being. The center of our experience is a common world in which we make appraisals, enlist support, and seek to convince skeptics and opponents, never doubting the fundamental permutation of subjective and objective evidence.[21]

If we accept the Marxist view that there is meaning in history as in the rest of our lives, then it follows that Marxist politics are based upon an objective analysis of the main trends in history and not simply on the will of the Communist party. In other words there is a materialist foundation to Marxist politics. At the same time, the trends in history do not lead necessarily to a socialist society. History is made through human action and political choices that are never perfectly informed, and thus there is always a contingent factor in history. It is necessary to avoid construing these materialist and ideological factors too crudely. Marxian materialism is not the simple notion that human history consists in the production of wealth; it is the project of creating a human environment that reflects the historical development of human sensibility. Similarly, the Marxist claim that ideological systems are related to economic factors is not a simple reductionist argument; it is the claim that ideological factors and the mode of production are mutually determining expressions of a given social order. At any given moment the mode of production may be the expression of the ideological superstructure just as the physical movements of the body may express a person's life-style. But in the long run it is the economic infrastructure that is the medium of the ideological message, just as our body is the structure underlying all our moods. Because we do not inhabit the present as a region totally within our survey, nor yet as a zone of pure possibility, history has familiar contours for us, a feel that we recognize in our daily lives, where others share the same conditions and the same hopes. This daily life is something that we shape through our desires and that in turn acquires an institutional reality that conditions the future limits and possibilities that are our life chances. In short, we bring a life-style to political action, a lifetime of suffering, with others and for others, and together, for better or worse, we decide to act. But it is neither an open nor a closed calculation. It is more like the decision to live from which we cannot withdraw, a decision that we never make once and for all and yet for which we are uniquely responsible. And like the decision to live, the choice of a politics entails the responsibility for the contingency of violence that is the "infantile disorder" in our private and public lives.

> One can no more get rid of historical materialism than of psychoanalysis by impugning "reductionist" conceptions and causal thought in the name of a descriptive and phenomenological method, for historical materialism is no more linked to such "causal" formulations as may have been given than is

psychoanalysis, and like the latter it could be expressed in another language. . . .

There is no one meaning of history; what we do always has several meanings, and this is where an existential conception of history is distinguishable from materialism and from spiritualism. But every cultural phenomenon has, among others, an economic significance, and history by its nature never transcends, any more than it is reducible to, economics. . . . It is impossible to reduce the life which involves human relationships either to economic relations, or to juridical and moral ones thought up by men, just as it is impossible to reduce individual life either to bodily functions or to our knowledge of life as it involves them. But in each case one of the orders of significance can be regarded as dominant: one gesture as "sexual", another as "amorous", another as "warlike", and even in the sphere of coexistence, one period of history can be seen as characterized by intellectual culture, another as primarily political or economic. The question whether the history of our time is preeminently significant in an economic sense, and whether our ideologies give us only a derivative or secondary meaning of it is one which no longer belongs to philosophy, but to politics, and one which will be solved only by seeking to know whether the economic or ideological scenario fits the facts more perfectly. Philosophy can only show that it is *possible* from the starting point of the human condition.[22]

The foundations of Marxian history and politics are grounded in the dialectic between man and nature (domination) and between man and his fellow men (recognition). It is the nature of human consciousness to realize itself in the world and among men; its embodiment is the esential mode of its openness toward the world and toward others. The problems of conflict and coexistence only arise for an embodied consciousness driven by its basic needs into the social division of labor and engaged by its deepest need in a life and death struggle for identity through mutual recognition and solidarity. Embodied consciousness never experiences an original innocence to which any violence would do irreparable harm; we experience only different kinds of violence. For consciousness only becomes aware of itself as already engaged in the world, in definite and specific situations in which its resources are never entirely its own but derive from the exploitation of its position as the child of these parents, the incumbent of such and such a role, or the beneficiary of certain class and national privileges. We rarely act as isolated individuals, and even when we seem to do so our deeds presuppose a community that possesses a common measure of the good and evil it experiences.

The problem that besets the Marxist theory of the proletariat is that the emergence of truth and justice presupposes a community while the realization of a genuine community presupposes a concept of truth and justice. The Marxist critique of the liberal truth as a mystification that splits the liberal community starts from the exposure of its lack of correspondence with the objective relations between man in liberal society. By contrast, Marxism claims to be a truth in the making; it aims at overthrowing liberal society in the name of an authentic community. However, the birth of Communist society is no less painful than the birth of man himself, and from its beginnings communism is familiar with violence and deception. It might be argued that the violence of Marxist revolutionary politics arises because the Party forces upon the proletariat a mission for which history has not prepared it. The proletariat is thus the victim of the double contingency of bourgeois and Communist deception and exploitation. The constant shifts in Party directives, the loss of socialist innocence, the reappearance of profit and status in Communist society may be appealed to as indications of the failure of Marxism to renew human history. Merleau-Ponty was aware of these arguments and indeed explicitly documents them with findings on conditions in the Soviet Union, including the shattering discovery of the labor camps.[23]

Nevertheless, Merleau-Ponty argued that the proper role of Marxist violence is to be the midwife of a socialist society already in the womb of capitalist society. The image is essential to his argument. For it was intended to distinguish Marxist violence from historically arbitrary and authoritarian forms of violence.[24] The image of birth suggests a natural process in which there arises a point of intervention that is likely to be painful but is aimed at preserving a life that is *already there* and not entirely at the mercy of the midwife. In the language of the *Communist Manifesto,* the argument is that the birth of socialist society depends upon the full maturation of capitalism that engenders a force whose transition from dependency to independence is achieved through a painful transition in which dramatic roles are assigned to the bourgeoisie, the proletariat, and the Party. There are, of course, features of the imagery of birth that lead to outcomes rather different from those that Merleau-Ponty wishes to draw. The human infant achieves maturity only after a long period of tutelage in which if anything social dependency becomes far more burdensome than umbilical dependency, as we have learned from Freud. Understood in this way the image involves a greater political dependency of the proletariat upon the Party and its commissars than is compatible with the aims of socialist humanism. Merleau-Ponty's ideal for the childhood of the revolution is the period of Lenin's frank and open discussions with the proletariat concerning the reasons for the New Economic Policy. This was a time when words still had their face meaning, when explanations for changes of tactics that left the proletariat with an improved understanding of events and with heightened revolutionary consciousness were given.

> Marxist Machiavellianism differs from Machiavellianism insofar as it transforms compromise through awareness of compromise, and alters the ambivalence of history through awareness of ambivalence; it makes detours knowingly and by announcing them as such; it calls retreats retreats; it sets the details of local politics and the paradoxes of strategy in the perspective of the whole.[25]

Marxist violence is thus an integral feature of the theory of the proletariat and its philosophy of history. To be a Marxist is to see meaning taking shape within history. Anything else is to live history and society as sheer force. To be a Marxist is to believe that history is intelligible and that it has a direction that encompasses the proletarian control of the economic and state apparatus, along with the emergence of an international brotherhood. Whatever the lags on any of these fronts, it is the Marxist persuasion that these elements delineate the essential structure or style of communist society. It is this structure of beliefs that determines the Marxist style of historical analysis and political action.

Even before he turned to Max Weber for his conception of responsible history, Merleau-Ponty had anticipated those adventures of the dialectic that had made it necessary to rethink Marxism as a philosophy of history and institutions. Unless this task is undertaken, Marxism must either continue to hide from its own history or else see its universal hopes thrown into the wasteland of historical relativism. Only an absolutely relativist conception of history as the milieu of our own living can keep alive what Merleau-Ponty called *Western Marxism*.

> History is not only an object in front of us, far from us, beyond our reach: it is also our awakening as subjects. Itself a historical fact the true or false consciousness that we have of our history cannot be simple illusion. There is a mineral there to be refined, a truth to be extracted, if only we go to the limits of relativism and put it, in turn, back into history. We give a form to history according to our categories; but our categories, in contact with history, are themselves freed from their partiality. The old problem of the relations between subject and object is transformed, and relativism

is surpassed as soon as one puts it in historical terms, since here the object is the vestige left by other subjects, and the subject—historical understanding—held in the fabric of history, is by this very fact capable of self-criticism.[26]

We have to understand how it is that Marxism that arises as a movement within history can be the fulfillment of history rather than a phase subject to its own laws of historical transition. How is it possible that men who are driven by material circumstances in general, the proletariat in particular, are capable of the vision of humanity freed from exploitation and alienation? However these questions are answered, we have to face the fact that the proletariat is given direction by the Communist party and that with respect to this relationship we face new questions about Marxist knowledge and the freedom of the masses. In his analysis of these questions Merleau-Ponty extended his reading of Weber through Lukács's studies in Marxist dialectics.[27] In terms of this reading Merleau-Ponty came to a reformulation of Marx's historical materialism. If materialism were a literal truth it is difficult to see how the category of history could arise. For matter does not have a history except by metaphorical extension. Men live in history. But their history is not external to themselves in the same sense that the history of a geological stratum might be susceptible to observation. Men inhabit history as they do language.[28] Just as they have to learn the specific vocabulary of Marxism, so they have to bring their everyday experiences of poverty, power, and violence under the notion of the "proletariat" and to interpret their experiences through the projection of "class consciousness" and "revolution." Thus "class consciousness" does not inhere in history either as a pre-existing idea or as an inherent environmental force. What we can say is that despite all its contingencies the history of society gathers into itself the consciousness that is dispersed in all its members so that it fosters their consciousness as civic knowledge:

As a living body, given its behavior, is, so to speak, closer to consciousness than a stone, so certain social structures are the cradle of the knowledge of society. Pure consciousness finds its "origin" in them. Even if the notion of interiority, when applied to a society, should be understood in the figurative sense, we find, all the same, that this metaphor is possible with regard to capitalist society but not so with regard to precapitalist ones. This is enough for us to say that the history which produced capitalism symbolizes the emergence of a subjectivity. There are subjects, objects, there are men and things, but there is also a third order, that of relationships between men inscribed in tools or social symbols. These relationships have their development, their advances and their regressions. Just as in the life of the individual, so in this generalized life there are tentative aims, failure or success, reaction of the result upon the aim, repetition or variation, and this is what one calls history.[29]

Despite its detours and regressions, Merleau-Ponty retains his conviction of the overall meaning of human history as an emancipatory process but allows for the successes and failures in this project to lie in one and the same historical plane. History is the growing relationship of man to man. This does not mean that all previous societies are to be judged by today's standards because at every stage history is threatened with loss and diversion. What we can properly regard as today's developments really only take up problems that were immanent in the previous period. Hence the past is not merely the waste of the future. If we can speak of an advance in history it is perhaps only in the negative sense that we can speak of the elimination of non-sense rather than of the positive accumulation of reason. The price we must pay for history's deliverance of reason and freedom is that freedom and reason never operate outside the constraints of history and politics. Therefore Marxism cannot simply claim to see through all other ideologies as though it alone were transparent to itself. Indeed, Marxism is itself open to the danger of becoming the most false ideology of all inasmuch as its own political life will require changes of position that can hardly be read from the state of its economic infrastructure.

If Marxism is not to degenerate into a willful ideology and yet not claim absolute knowledge, it must be geared to the praxis of the proletariat. But this is not an easy matter since the proletariat does not spontaneously realize its own goals and by the same token the Party cannot easily avoid a specious appeal to the allegedly objective interests of the proletariat. If like Sartre we force the distinction between theory and praxis, then the Party is reduced to either a democratic consultation of the momentary thoughts and feelings of the proletariat or else to a bureaucratic cynicism with regard to the gap between the present state of the proletariat and the Party's idea of its future. So long as we think of consciousness as a state of individual minds then we cannot get around the problem of locating the synthesis of knowledge in an absolute consciousness called the Party. This means that the proletariat is really not the subject of its own deeds but the object of what the Party knows on its behalf. To understand

Merleau-Ponty's critique of Sartre's "ultrabolshevism" we need to have some notion of how they were divided even over a common philosophical background. The opposition between Sartre and Merleau-Ponty derives in the first place from their fundamentally opposite phenomenologies of embodiment. For Sartre the body is a vehicle of shame, nausea, and ultimate alienation caught in the trap of the other's look.[30] In Merleau-Ponty the body is the vehicle of the very world and others with whom together we labor in love and understanding and the very same ground to which we must appeal to correct error or overcome violence. In Sartre the body is the medium of the world's decomposition; in Merleau-Ponty the body symbolizes the very composition of the world and society. In each case there follow radically different conceptions of political life. In Merleau-Ponty, the extremes of collectivism and individualism, labor and violence, are always historical dimensions of our basic social life. To Sartre, nothing unites us with nature and society except the external necessity of scarcity that obliges us to join our labor and individual sovereignty into collective projects that are always historically unstable.

> The "master", the "feudal lord", the "bourgeois", the "capitalist" all appear not only as powerful people who command but in addition and above all as *Thirds;* that is, as those who are outside the oppressed community and *for whom* this community exists. It is therefore *for* them and *in their freedom* that the reality of the oppressed class is going to exist. They cause it to be born by their look. It is to them and through them that there is revealed the identity of my condition and that of others who are oppressed; it is for them that I exist in a situation organized with others and that my possibles as dead-possibles are strictly equivalent with the possibles of others; it is for them that I am a worker and it is through and in their revelation as the Other-as-a-look that I experience myself as one among others. This means that I discover the "Us" in which I am integrated or "the class" *outside,* in the look of the Third, and it is this collective alienation which I assume when saying "Us". From this point of view the privileges of the Third and "our" burdens, "our" miseries have value at first only as a *signification;* they signify the independence of the Third in relation to "Us"; they present our alienation to us more plainly. Yet as they are nonetheless *endured, as in particular our work, our fatigue are nonetheless suffered,* it is across this endured suffering that I experience my being-looked-at-as-a-thing-engaged-in-a-totality-of-things. It is in terms of my suffering, of my misery that I am collectively apprehended with others by the Third; that is, in terms of the adversity of the world, in terms of the facticity of my

condition. Without the Third, no matter what might be the adversity of the world, I should apprehend myself as a triumphant transcendence; with the appearance of the Third, "I" experience "Us" as apprehended in terms of things and as things overcome by the world.[31]

In Sartrean Marxism it is therefore the role of the Party to unite an ever disintegrating proletariat to which it plays the role of the other or Third analogous to the role of the capitalist as the Other who unites the atomized labor of the workshop or assembly line. In effect, Sartre constructs the Party as the sole source of historical intelligibility because he denies any basis for intersubjectivity to arise at other levels of conduct. The result is that Sartre is obliged to idealize the notions of fact, action, and history as nothing but what is determined by the Party. Hence the Party is subject to permanent anxiety since it is deprived of any middle ground between itself and a proletarian praxis from which it might learn to formulate, revise, and initiate plans that do not risk its whole life. Because he can understand expression only as pure creation or as simple imitation, Sartre loses the real ground of political communication.

> If one wants to engender revolutionary politics dialectically from the proletarian condition, the revolution from the rigidified swarm of thoughts without subject, Sartre answers with a dilemma: either the conscious renewal alone gives its meaning to the process, or one returns to organicism. What he rejects under the name of organicism at the level of history is in reality much more than the notion of life: it is symbolism understood as a functioning of signs having its own efficacy beyond the meanings that analysis can assign to these signs. It is, more generally, expression. For him expression either goes beyond what is expressed and is then a pure creation, or it copies it and is then a simple unveiling. But an action which is an unveiling, an unveiling which is an action—in short, a dialectic—this Sartre does not want to consider.[32]

Properly speaking, praxis is not divided between theory and practice but lies in the wider realm of communication and expression. Here Merleau-Ponty's argument already anticipates Habermas's later correction of Marx's confusion of the emancipatory orders of labor and symbolic interaction.[33] The everyday life of the proletariat makes the notion of a class a possibility long before it is formulated as such. When the occasion for the explicit appeal to class consciousness arises, its formal possibility does not lie in the power of the Party's theoreticians but in the ordinary capacity of men to appraise their situation, and to speak their minds together because their thoughts are not locked behind their skulls but are near enough the same in anyone's experience of exploitation and injustice. Of course, the Party has to give these thoughts a political life, to realize their truth as a common achievement in which the proletariat and the Party are mutually enlightened. "This exchange, in which no one commands and no one obeys, is symbolized by the old custom which dictates that, in a meeting, speakers join in when the audience applauds. What they applaud is the fact that they do not intervene as persons, that in their relationship with those who listen to them a truth appears which does not come from them and which the speakers can and must applaud. In the communist sense, the Party is this communication; and such a conception of the Party is not a corollary of Marxism—it is its very center."[34] Thus we see that the heart of Marxism is not just the communalizing of property but the attainment of an ideally communicative or educative society whose icon is the Party. At the same time, this ideal society of labor and speech is obliged to resort to violence since its truths reflect only a reality that has to be brought into being. Marxist truth is not hidden behind empirical history waiting to be deciphered by the Party theoreticians. Ultimately, the issue here is the question of the education of the Party itself in its role of educating the masses. It was first raised by Marx himself in the Third Thesis on Feuerbach. If the Party is not above history then it is inside history like the proletariat itself. The problem is how to relativize the opposition between Party and proletarian consciousness so that their mutual participation in history is not organized in terms of a (Party) subject and (proletariat) object split. The argument between Sartre and Merleau-Ponty parallels the difference between the political practices of Lenin and Stalin, at least insofar as Merleau-Ponty like Lukács can argue for a period in Lenin's own use of the Party as an instrument of proletarian education and party self-critique. In his book *Lenin*,[35] Lukács argues with respect to Lenin's political practice much the same thesis that Merleau-Ponty later espoused, namely, that it must not be confused with realpolitik. "Above all, when defining the concept of compromise, any suggestion that it is a question of knack, of cleverness, of an astute fraud, must be rejected. 'We must,' said Lenin, 'decisively reject those who think that politics consists of little tricks, sometimes bordering on deceit. *Classes cannot be deceived.*' For Lenin, therefore, compromise means *that the true developmental tendencies of classes* (and possibly of nations—for instance, where an oppressed people is concerned), which under specific circumstances and for a certain period run parallel in determinate areas with the interests of the proletariat, are exploited to the advantage of *both.*"[36] In the postscript to his essay on Lenin, Lukács repeats the argument for the unity of Lenin's theoretical grasp of the political nature of the imperialist epoch and his practical sense of proletarian politics. In trying to express the living nature of that unity in Lenin's own life, Lukács describes how Lenin would learn from experience or from Hegel's *Logic,* according to the situation, preserving in himself the dialectical tension between particulars and a theoretical totality. As Lenin writes in his *Philosophic Notebooks:* "Theoretical cognition ought to give the Object in its necessity, in its all-sided relations, in its contradictory movement, in- and for-itself. But the human Concept 'definitively' catches this objective truth of cognition, seizes and masters it, only when the Concept becomes 'being-for-itself' in the sense of practice."

It was by turning to Hegel that Lenin sought to find a way to prevent making theory the mere appendage of state practice, while reserving to practice a more creative political role than the retroactive determination or revision of ideology. But this meant that Marxist materialism could never be the simple enforcement of political will, any more than political will could be exercised without a theoretical understanding of the specific class relations it presupposed. Thus Lenin remarks that "The standpoint of life, of practice, should be first and fundamental in the theory of knowledge. . . . Of course, we must not forget that the criterion of practice can never, in the nature of things, either confirm or refute any idea *completely.* This criterion too is sufficiently 'indefinite' not to allow human knowledge to become 'absolute', but at the same time it is sufficiently definite to wage a ruthless fight against all varieties of idealism and agnosticism." Of course, in these later Hegelian formulations Lenin is modifying his own version of Engels's dialectical materialism as set forth in *Materialism and Empirio-Criticism,* thereby rejoining the challenge set to this work by Lukács's own *History and Class Consciousness,* as well as by Karl Korsch's *Marxism and Philosophy,* both published in 1923. Lukács's essay on Lenin was published on the occasion of Lenin's death in 1924. What died with Lenin was orthodox Marxism, although its dead hand was to be upon socialism for another thirty years or more. But although it is clear that scientific socialism was not ready for Lukács, the same must be said of the West, where only today is the critique of scientific praxis entering into a properly reflexive or critical social science. What *History and Class Consciousness* made clear was that living Marxism is inseparable from its idealist and Hegelian legacy. The

Hegelian concept of totality furnishes a matrix for the integration of ethics and politics through the restless dynamics of man's attempt to measure his existential circumstances against the ideal of his human essence, which he achieves through the struggle against self and institutional alienation. The Hegelian Marxist totality is thus the basis for the integral humanism of Marxist social science.[37]

What Merleau-Ponty adds to Hegelian Marxism from his own phenomenology of perception is an unshakable grasp of the "interworld" (*intermonde*) of everyday living and conduct that is far too dense and stratified to be a thing of pure consciousness. This is the world of our species-being, a corporeal world whose deep structures of action and reflection are the anonymous legacies of the body politic.[38] The interworld is never available to us in a single unifying moment of consciousness or as a decision whose consequences are identical with the actor's intentions. But then none of us thinks or acts outside a life whose ways have molded us so that what "we" seek is never entirely our own and therefore borrows upon the very collective life that it advances or retards. Thus we never have anything like Sartre's absolute power of decision to join or withdraw from collective life. What we have is an ability to shift institutions off center, polarizing tradition and freedom in the same plane as creativity and imitation. Our freedom, therefore, never comes to us entirely from the outside through the Party, as Sartre would have it. It begins inside us like the movements of our body in response to the values of a world that it opens up through its own explorations and accommodations. It follows that Sartre's conception of the Party expropriates the spontaneity of all life in the name of the proletariat, having first separated the proletariat from what it shares with men anywhere engaged in the struggle for life.

> The question is to know whether, as Sartre says, there are only *men* and *things* or whether there is also the interworld, which we call history, symbolism, truth-to-be-made. If one sticks to the dichotomy, men, as the place where all meaning arises, are condemned to an incredible tension. Each man, in literature as well as in politics, must assume all that happens instant by instant to all others, he must be immediately universal. If, on the contrary, one acknowledges a mediation of personal relationships through the world of human symbols, it is true that one renounces being instantly justified in the eyes of everyone and holding oneself responsible for all that is done at each moment. But since consciousness cannot in practice maintain its pretension of being God, since it is inevitably led to delegate responsibility—it is one

abdication for another, and we prefer the one which leaves consciousness the means of knowing what it is doing.[39]

The universality and truth toward which political consciousness aims are not intrinsic properties of the Party. They are acquisitions continuously established and reestablished in a community and tradition of knowledge for which individuals in specific historical situations call and to which they respond. Understood in this way, history is the call of one thought to another, because each individual's work or action is created across the path of self and others toward a public that it elicits rather than serves. That is, history is the field that individual effort requires in order to become one with the community it seeks to build so that where it is successful its invention appears always to have been necessary. Individual action, then, is the invention of history, because it is shaped in a present that previously was not just a void awaiting to be determined by the word or deed but in a tissue of calling and response that is the life of no one and everyone. Every one of life's actions, insofar as it invokes its truth, lives in the expectation of a historical inscription, a judgment not only of its intention or consequences but also of its fecundity, which is the relevance of its "story" to the present.

> History is the judge—not History as the Power of a moment or of a century—but history as the space of inscription and accumulation beyond the limits of countries and epochs of what we have said and done that is most true and valuable, taking into account the circumstances in which we had to speak. Others will judge what I have done because I painted the painting to be seen, because my action committed the future of others; but neither art nor politics consists in pleasing or flattering others. What they expect of the artist or politician is that he draw them toward values in which they will only later recognize their own values. The painter or politician shapes others more than he follows them. The *public* at whom he aims is not given; it is a public to be elicited by his work. The others of whom he thinks are not empirical "others", nor even *humanity* conceived as a species; it is others once they have become such that he can live with them. The history in which the artist participates (and it is better the less he thinks about "making history" and honestly produces *his* work as he sees it) is not a power before which he must genuflect. It is the perpetual conversation woven together by all speech, all valid works and actions, each according to its place and circumstance, contesting and confirming the other, each one recreating all the others.[40]

Merleau-Ponty returns Marxist politics to the flux of the natural and historical world, rejecting its compromise with the ideals of objectivism that have made the tradition of rationality an enigma to itself. Henceforth, politics must abide in the life-world where Husserl found its roots, and from there it must recover its own ontological history.

Today history is hardly more meaningful because of the advent of socialism in the Soviet Union or elsewhere. Indeed, the potential nuclear confrontation of world ideologies has brought human history to new heights of absurdity. Marxism has become a truth for large parts of the world but not in the sense it intended. The question is what conclusion we should draw from this. Writing in 1947 and the decade following, Merleau-Ponty was afraid that the West would try to resolve the Communist problem through war. To this he argued that the failures of communism are the failures of Western humanism as a whole and so we cannot be partisan to it, far less indifferent. The Marxist revolution can lose its way. This is because, as Merleau-Ponty puts it, it is a mode of human conduct that may be true as a movement but false as a regime. But it is the nature of political action to offer no uniquely happy solution. Political life involves a fundamental evil in which we are forced to choose between values without knowing for certain which are absolutely good or evil. In the Trojan wars the Greek gods fought on both sides. It is only in modern politics that, as Camus remarks, the human mind has become an armed camp. In this situation Merleau-Ponty wrote to overcome the split between good and evil that characterizes the politics of crisis and conflict. Above all, he raised the voice of reason that despite skepticism and error achieves a truth for us that is continuous with nothing else than our own efforts to maintain it.

> For the very moment we assert that unity and reason do not *exist* and that opinions are carried along by discordant options that remain below the level of reason the consciousness we gain of the irrationalism and contingency in us cancels them as fatalities and opens us to the other person. Doubt and disagreement are facts, but so is the strange pretension we all have of thinking of the truth, our capacity for taking the other's position to judge ourselves, our need to have our opinions recognized by him and to justify our choices before him, in short, the experience of the other person as an *alter ego* in the very course of discussion. *The human world is an open or unfinished system and the same radical contingency that threatens it with discord also rescues it from the inevitability of disorder and prevents us*

from despairing of it, providing only that one remember that its various machineries are actually men and try to maintain and expand man's relations to man.

Such a philosophy cannot tell us *that* humanity will be realized as though it possessed some knowledge apart and were not itself embarked upon experience, being only a more acute consciousness of it. But it awakens us to the importance of daily events and action. For it is a philosophy that arouses in us a love for our times, which are not the simple repetition of human eternity nor merely the conclusion to premises already postulated. It is a view that, like the most fragile object of perception—a soap bubble or a wave—or like the most simple dialogue, embraces indivisibly all the order and all the disorder of the world.[41]

15

Can Phenomenology
Be Critical?

What is the task that I mean to set in asking whether phenomenology can be critical? I am raising the question whether we can be authentically aware of the reflexive limits of the corpus of social science knowledge due to its implicit ties with the order of history and politics. The very question is evidence of a certain uneasiness, but also of a determination to dwell within its circle at least as much as to drive for a solution. How shall I proceed then? For to begin, I cannot settle the nature of phenomenology. Of course, I am aware that I might attempt to repeat some of the principal features of Husserlian phenomenology. But the question of authoritative procedures for introducing phenomenology is problematic in view of the developments in phenomenology from Husserl to Heiddeger, Scheler, and Jaspers; or through Sartre and Merleau-Ponty; not to mention Schutz. Faced with a similar problem, Merleau-Ponty has remarked that "we shall find in ourselves, and nowhere else, the unity and true meaning of phenomenology."

I want to develop a phenomenological conception of critique and argument under a rule of limit and cosmic order that is simultaneously the ground of political order and rebellion. Habermas has argued[1] that Husserl's critique of positivist science does not go far enough in simply denying the separation between knowledge and the life-world, insofar as science and philosophy, including the social sciences, separate the activity of theorizing from the world of human interests and values. The unfortunate practical consequences of separation of science and values can only be corrected through an understanding of the true relation between knowledge and interest, in other words, of praxis. Husserl's critique of the objectivism of science and the natural attitude that is its prescientific ground may be taken as an obvious sense in which phenomenology is critical. But it does not go far enough to free transcendental phenomenology itself from practical interest. Habermas invokes the etymology of θεωρία in order to trace a development in the concept of theory from the original activity of the representative sent by a polis to witness the sacred festival of another city to the philosopher's μίμησις or representation in the order of his soul of the natural κοσμος.

> Husserl rightly criticizes the objectivist illusion that deludes the sciences with the image of a reality-in-itself, consisting of facts structured in a lawlike manner; it conceals the constitution of these facts, and thereby prevents consciousness of the interlocking of knowledge with interests from the life-world. Because phenomenology brings this to consciousness, it is itself, in Husserl's view, free of such interests. It thus earns the title of pure theory unjustly claimed by the sciences. It is to this freeing of knowledge from interest that Husserl attaches the expectation of practical efficacy. But the error is clear. Theory in the sense of the classical tradition only had an impact on life because it was thought to have discovered in the cosmic order an ideal world structure, including the prototype for the order of the human world. Only as *cosmology* was *theoria* also capable of orienting human action. Thus Husserl cannot expect self-formative processes to originate in a phenomenology that, as transcendental philosophy, purifies the classical theory of its cosmological contents, conserving something like the theoretical attitude only in an abstract manner. Theory had educational and cultural implications not because it had freed knowledge from interest. To the contrary, it did so because it derived *pseudo-normative power* from *the concealment of its actual interest*. While criticizing the objectivist self-understanding of the sciences, Husserl succumbs to another objectivism, which was always attached to the traditional concept of theory.[2]

Whether or not Husserl neglected the original connection between θεωρία and its consequences for the philosophical way of life, as Habermas argues, it is important to stress the ambivalence in classical philosophical knowledge with respect to the idea of Beauty and Goodness. Habermas tends to overlook this tension. Hannah Arendt, however, has argued that the subordination of life in the pursuit of human affairs (βιος πολιτικός) to the "theoretical way of life" (βίος θεωρητικός) is a result of the Platonic subordination of the contemplative love of the true essence of Being, under the idea of the Beautiful, to the idea of Good, or an art of measurement that provides a rule to the philosopher's potential disorientation in everyday political life.[3] In other words, there is an essential ambivalence in Western knowledge between the values of the recognition and domination of Being that has been consequential for its political tradition, particularly when the pattern of domination is based upon modern scientific knowledge that breaks once and for all the connection between κοσμός and θεωρία.

Modern social science knowledge has reduced its independence as a form of theoretical life to a rule of methodology founded upon the auspices of technical rationality. This results in a disenchanted objectivism or rationalization of the interests and values that guide technological domination as a form or "conduct of life," to use Max Weber's phrase. However, Weber's formal rationality, so far from resting upon "value-free" auspices, is in fact a historical constellation whose precondition is the separation of the orders of knowledge, work, and politics. In the period of the bourgeois ascendency, the value-free conception of rationality furnishes a critical concept of the development of human potential locked in the feudal world of "traditional" values. Weber makes a fatality of technical rationality, thereby identifying its historical role with political domination as such,[4] whereas Marx's critique of class political economy showed the critical limits of economic rationality. Social science knowledge must be grounded in a limited but authentic reflexivity through which it recognizes its ties to individual values and community interests, notwithstanding its attempts to avoid bias and ideology. Habermas himself furnishes five theses that I shall interpret as the auspices of a limited reflexivity responsible to the project of *homo faber*:

1. The achievements of the transcendental subject have their basis in the natural history of the human species.
2. Knowledge equally serves as an instrument and transcends mere self-preservation.
3. Knowledge-constitutive interests take form in the medium of work, language, and power.
4. In the power of self-reflection, knowledge and interest are one.
5. The unity of knowledge and interest proves itself in a dialectic that takes the historical traces of suppressed dialogue and reconstructs what has been suppressed.

Together these five theses reveal the axiological basis of human knowledge as a pattern of communication, control, and decision, predicated upon man's self-made and thus largely symbolic project of creation and freedom. The human project is a structure of biological, social, and, I would add, libidinal values, which are institutionalized through the media of language, work, and politics.[5] The vehicle of the human project is a common tradition and identity tied to speech, creation, and citizenship that relate individual expressions to everyday social life and culture. In each of these realms there is practical metaphysics of the relation of particulars to universals, within the limits of common speech, the exchange of labor, and the pursuit of the common good. Moreover, there is, as Habermas argues, an essential relation among the orders of language, work, and politics. The man who is not free in his labor is not free to speak, and thus freedom of speech presupposes an end of economic exploitation as well as of political repression. Dialogue and poetry are therefore the primary expressions of the bond between speech and politics; it is through them that knowledge achieves reflexive awareness of the values of the human community to which it belongs and is thus able to play its role in the constitution of the body politic. I have mentioned the work of the poet in the politics of freedom because he, as well as the novelist and musician, is the guardian of tradition and creativity. I think it is necessary to relate the knowledge-constitutive interests to the expressive, libidinal interests of the body politic in order to extend political dialogue into the street, the songs, and the everyday confrontations within the body politic. For these are the life-world understandings of the traditions of need and rebellion.

Modern consciousness is tied to the standpoints of anthropology and historicism that reveal that all knowledge about man, including scientific knowledge, presupposes some metaphysical position on the relation among human facticity, knowledge, and values.[6] Thus we can only speak of the reflexive ties between subjectivity and the regional ontologies of the worlds of science, economics, politics, and everyday life, and not of a naïve realist, subject-object dichotomy.

It may help to clarify the conception of limited reflexivity that I am proposing as the auspices for a mode of political theorizing that has its community in the body politic, if I contrast it with the consequences of a total reflexivity of absolute knowledge. There is, for example, a conception of reflexivity that is very close to the limited notion I am fostering, but that is quite alien to it in its consequences for the orders of language, thought, and politics. I have in mind the sociological conception of reflexivity as the awareness of the infrastructures of knowledge in culture, class, and biography. At first sight, the consequences of the sociology of knowledge and ideology may appear to make for a moderation of political argument through an understanding of the intervening circumstances of class and history. But in practice it has brutalized political awareness and obscured the science of politics for which Mannheim had hoped. It was to these issues that both Husserl and Weber addressed themselves in their reflections on the vocations of science and politics. Both were concerned with the nihilism that was a potential conclusion from historicism and the sociology of knowledge. Husserl and Weber approached these problems in terms of an inquiry into the very foundations of Western knowledge or science. Let us recall briefly Weber's reflections, which are perhaps better known to sociologists and political scientists, and then turn to Husserl's struggles with these problems in *The Crisis of European Sciences.*[7]

At first sight, the connections among Weber's reflections on the vocations of science, politics, and capitalism are not evident. Superficially, modern economics, politics, and science present us with an exotic competition of goods and values without a rational standard of choice. We accumulate knowledge much as we do money, and the result is a vast obsolescence of commonsense knowledge and values. Any attempt to introduce order into this process is as disturbing to it as the occasions for these very attempts, so that our politics is snared in a polytheism of value. "And with this," says Weber, "we come to inquire into the meaning of science. For, after all, it is not self-evident that something subordinate to such a law is sensible and meaningful in itself. Why does one engage in doing something that in reality never comes, and never can come to an end."[8] Weber's question about the auspices of modern science is simultaneously a question about the grounds of modern community and personality in a world from which God is absent and order thereby an enigma to a disenchanted world of value accumulation. Weber compares his own questioning of the meaning of science with Tolstoy's question about the meaning of death in the modern world, where man is pitted against himself in a self-infinitude of want and desire. "And because death is meaningless, civilized life as such is meaningless; by its very 'progressiveness' it gives death the imprint of meaninglessness."[9] In this way Weber made sociology aware of its own reflexive need to embed in a community of purpose whose institution is as much a charismatic hope as a goal of rationality.

Weber's conclusions, though they do not satisfy Marcuse's conception of critical theory, are in striking contrast with the Parsonian interpretation of Weber that serves to make sociological knowledge an irony of functionalist practice. That is to say, the Parsonian version of sociological knowledge invents a utopia of social system and pattern-variable action congruence in order to embed its own instrumentalist rationality as a precipitate of utilitarian culture. Whether it starts from Hobbes's nasty vision or from Luther's excremental vision, Parsonian sociology reduces the problem of its own reflexivity to the anodyne of instrumental knowledge, hoping thereby to substitute affluence for the glory of love's risen body. Although we cannot dwell upon Parsonian sociology in any detail, it may not be amiss, in view of its adoption into political science, to comment that Parsons's latest generalization of the instrumentalist vision, based upon the master metaphor of money as the most generalized means of exchange and efficacy, serves only to further mystify the grounds of political order by neglecting the ways in which the behavior of money is nothing else than the algebra of the system of stratification and exploitation for which Parsons pretends to account. In short, and in contrast with the critics of Parsonian ideology, I would argue that it is Parsons's conception of theorizing as an activity grounded in the means-end schema that generates his intrinsic notions of social structure and personality as a functionalist utopia of congruent orders of individual and collective reality. Yet the unconscious merit of Parsons's classical study of the corpus of utilitarian social science knowledge[10] is to have focused on the ambivalence of the instrumental and ritual values of human knowledge, subordinated to the a priori of individual interest.

I have turned my argument toward the topic of sociological reflexivity not for the purpose of engaging in criticism as it is conventionally understood, but for the purpose of coming to terms with the very phenomenon of sociological reflexivity, namely, *how it is that we can show the limits of sociology and still be engaged in authentic sociological theorizing.* This is the question that I began with when I set myself the task of asking whether phenomenology could be critically aware of its own limits and its implicit ties with history and politics. I shall not pursue this topic in Husserl's later writings, acknowledging that my reading of them is a continuation of an earlier reading by Merleau-Ponty. More concretely, my reading of Husserl and Merleau-Ponty is essentially a borrowing from them both, continuous with everything else we borrow in life. For, indeed, as Merleau-Ponty remarks, "I borrow myself from others; I create others from my own thoughts. This is no failure to perceive others; it is the perception of others."

We need a conception of the reflexive grounds of social science knowledge that will be grounded in the facts of institutional life and yet remain equally true to the claims of science and poetry, or to what is general as well as what is unique in our experience. It is this task that I shall address in my concluding essay on communicative sociology. Reflecting upon the crisis of the European sciences, Husserl remarked that *"the dream is over"* of there ever being an apodictic or rigorous science of philosophy. Some have thought that it is only those who set such goals for philosophy who are likely to turn to philosophical disbelief and despair. In such circumstances, it is the task of phenomenological philosophy to take its historical bearings, to acknowledge its debts to the life-world that it presupposes so long as there is no total threat to civilization, but that must then concern it.

The philosopher, says Husserl, "takes something from history." But history is not a warehouse, or a rummage heap from which we can take "things," because facts, documents, philosophical and literary works, are not palpably before us, apart from our own indwelling and interpretations. Furthermore, we do not, strictly speaking, transmit or hand down a scientific, literary, or historical tradition. We may be Renaissance historians without having read or researched every aspect of the Renaissance, just as we may be Platonists without a concern for every word of Plato, so that we might as well speak of a "poetic transmission" that owes as much to us as to fact. And yet none of this need imperil the teleology of knowledge, of science, history, or philosophy.

> Let us be more precise. I know, of course, what I am striving for under the title of philosophy, as the goal and field of my work. And yet I do not know. What autonomous thinker has ever been satisfied with this, his "knowledge"? For what autonomous thinker, in his philosophizing life, has "philosophy" ever ceased to be an enigma? Everyone has the sense of philosophy's end, to whose realization his life is devoted; everyone has certain formulae, expressed in definitions; but only secondary thinkers who in truth should not be called philosophers, are consoled by their definitions, beating to death with their word-concepts the problematic *telos* of philosophizing. In that obscure "knowledge", and in the word-concepts of the formulae, the historical is concealed; it is, according to its own proper sense, the spiritual inheritance of him who philosophizes; and in the same way, obviously, he understands the others in whose company, in critical friendship and enmity, he philosophizes. And in philosophizing he is also in company with himself as he earlier understood and did philosophy; and he knows that, in the process, historical tradition, as he understood it and used it, entered into him in a motivating way and as a spiritual

sediment. His historical picture, in part made by himself and in part taken over, his "poetic invention of the history of philosophy", has not and does not remain fixed—that he knows; and yet every "invention" serves him, and can serve him in understanding himself and his aim, and his own aim in relation to that of others and their "inventions", their aims, and finally what it is that is common to all, which makes philosophy "as such" as a unitary *telos* and makes the system's attempts at its fulfilment for us all, for us (who are) at the same time in company with the philosophers of the past (in the various ways we have been able to invent them for ourselves).[11]

Merleau-Ponty remarks how well Husserl's term *Stiftung,* foundation or establishment, captures the fecundity of cultural creations by which they endure into our present and open a field of inquiry to which they are continuously relevant.

It is thus that the world as soon as he has seen it, his first attempts at painting, and the whole past of painting all deliver up a *tradition* to the painter—*that is,* Husserl remarks *the power to forget origins* and to give to the past not a survival, which is the hypocritical form of forgetfulness, but a new life, which is the noble form of memory.[12]

Through language, art, and writing, what was only an ideal meaning in the mind of an individual achieves an objective and public status and enters a community of thinkers, which is the presupposition of truth. Thus we witness the event of that circuit of reflection in which what was first recognized as neither local nor temporal "according to the meaning of its being," comes to rest upon the locality and temporality of speech, which belongs neither to the objective world nor to the world of ideas.

Ideal existence is based upon the document, not, of course, as a physical object, or even as the vehicle of one-to-one significations assigned to it by the language in which it is written, but upon the document in so far as, again by an "intentional transgression", it solicits and brings together all lives in pursuit of knowledge—and as such establishes and re-establishes a "Logos" of the cultural world.[13]

We need, then, a conception of the auspices of philosophical reflexivity that is consistent with "poetic invention" (*Dichtung*), as well as with the community in which we philosophize. Such a notion may be present to us in the concept of *reflexivity as institution* rather than as transcendental constitution. By means of the notion of institution we may furnish a conception of reflexivity that, instead of resting upon a transcendental subjectivity, is given in a field of presence and co-existence that situates reflexivity and truth as sedimentation and search. We must think of reflexivity as tied to the textual structures of temporality and situation through which subjectivity and objectivity are constituted as the intentional unity and style of the world. "Thus what we understand by the concept of institution are those events in an experience which endow it with durable dimensions, in relation to which a whole series of other experiences will acquire meaning, will form an intelligible series or a history—or again those events which sediment in me a meaning, not just as survivals or residues, but as the invitation to a sequel, the necessity of a future."[14] The institution of reflexivity is founded upon a series of exchanges between subjectivity and situation in which the polarities of means and ends or question and answer are continuously established and renewed, no less than the institution of ideas, truth, and culture. Reflexivity, therefore, is not an a priori, but a task that we take up in order to achieve self-improvization, as well as the acquisition of a tradition or style of thought that is the recovery of an original auspices opened in the past. To this we bring a living expression, or the inauguration of a world and the outline of a future, that is nothing else than ourselves, "borne only by the caryatid of our efforts, which converge by the sole fact that they are efforts to express."[15]

The notion of *critique* that we may derive from the concept of reflexivity as institution is one that is grounded in a contextual environment that lies open horizontally to the corpus of social science knowledge rather than through any transcendental reflection. This notion of critique is the result of abandoning Husserl's attempt to construct an eidetic of any possible corpus of knowledge as the correlative of a universal and timeless constituting reflexivity and the problems it raises for intersubjectivity, rationality, and philosophy itself. The corpus of the historical and social sciences is not, properly speaking, constituted through any object or any act of reflection. It arises from a continual production or verification (*reprise*) that each individual undertakes according to his situation and times. Thus each one's work must be continually reviewed to unearth its own auspices sedimented in the archaeology of human science. This is not a simplistic argument for eternal starts, any more than a crude rejection of the accumulation of human knowledge. It is rather an attempt to interpret the *rhetorical* nature of the appeal of knowledge and criticism through which tradition and rebellion are made.

"Reading" a text is inevitably an essay in rhetoric; that is to say, if we follow Aristotle, leaving aside Plato's insistence on the mastery of truth, it requires a profound knowledge or care for the souls one seeks to persuade. This concern to suit one's speech or argument to the other person's soul is the anthropological ground of all talk, argument, and criticism. It is at the heart of what is serious in our concern to discuss with one another, to correct, and to persuade. It is for this reason that we elaborate upon one another's speech and thought. And we never argue so fiercely as between ourselves, because what is at stake is the utopian connection of truth, justice, and beauty. We sense implicitly the style of the world from a manner of speaking and thinking, so that we are drawn by its resonance, or else confused and repulsed. The error in modern communication and information theory is that it overlooks the rhetorical vehicle of speech, reading, and writing. It does this because in turn it lacks any conception of the intention to institute solidarity and a just social order in the relations between the partners to human speech.

What emerges from these examples is that the universality and truth aimed at by theoretical consciousness are not intrinsic properties of the idea. They are acquisitions continuously established and reestablished in a community and tradition of knowledge called for and responded to by individuals in specific historical situations. Understood in this way, history is the call of one thought to another, because each individual's work or action is created across the path of self and others toward a *public* that it elicits rather than serves.[16] That is to say, history is the field that individual effort requires in order to become one with the community it seeks to build so that, where it is successful, its invention appears always to have been necessary. Individual action, then, is the invention of history, because it is shaped in a present that previously was not just a void waiting to be determined by the word or deed, but a tissue of calling and response that is the life of no one and everyone. Every one of life's actions, insofar as it invokes its truth, lives in the expectation of a historical inscription, a judgment not of its intention or consequences but of its fecundity, which is the relevance of its "story" to the present.

> True history thus gets its life entirely from us. It is in our present that it gets the force to refer everything else to the present. The other whom I respect gets his life from me as I get mine from him. A philosophy of history does not take away any of my rights or initiatives. It simply adds to my obligations as a solitary person the obligation to understand situations other than my own and to create a path between my life and that of others, that is, express myself.[17]

The object of human knowledge is not, strictly speaking, an object; it is the institution within human space and historical time of artifacts, tools, services, institutions that are depositaries of what men before us have thought, needed, and valued. Cultural objects, in this sense, are the vestiges of embodied beings who live in society and communicate with one another as embodied minds. It is such human beings who have opened up for us the hearth of culture and institutions, which it is our first duty to tender. And this we do, not as mere drudgery, but as the cultivation of our own growth, the basis for our departures and the source to which we return for fresh inspiration. Human institutions are the ground of our common and individual achievements, enriching us and impoverishing us with a legacy that was never quite intended for us and is yet never totally rejected by us, even when we refuse it. This human legacy is never fully ours until we learn to alter it through our own inventions, our personal style.

Human experience and vision accumulate only in the circle of social relations and institutions, which enlarge and deepen the sense of our sentiments, deeds, and works through the symbiosis of solidarity and personaltiy. Human action is essentially the unfolding of a cultural space and its historical dimensions, so that in a strict sense we never accomplish anything except as a collective and historical project. For the individual action involves, therefore, a constant dialogue with others, a recovery of the past, and the projection of breaks that are never entirely successful. But this is not a source of irremediable alienation; it is the feature of our experience that calls for its completion through a collectivity, with a history that knows a tradition as well as a future. Such a collectivity or institution is never wholly reified; it is made and unmade, with a particular grain in each of us who lives and alters what he draws upon for his life. And this is a feature not only of human institutions, but of our thoughts, of our sentiments, and, above all, of human talk. Understood in this way, human institutions are the sole means that we have of keeping faith with one another, while being true to ourselves.

The ultimate feature of the communicative institution of reflexivity is that it grounds critique in membership and tradition. Thus the critic's auspices are the same as those of anyone working in a community of language, work, and politics. In the critical act there is a simultaneity of authorship and authenticity that is the declaration of membership in a continuing philosophical, literary, or scientific community. The critic does not alienate himself from his community; that would be the consequence of an absolute knowledge and ultimate nihilism. This is not to say that the critic is not rebellious; it is to remark upon the consequences of solitude and solidarity as the starting points of criticism.

Criticism in our sense is very close to Camus's conception of rebellion and order under the sun. Criticism reflects an aspiration to order under the auspices of the things that are present and of our fellow men, under a limit that is reflexively the recognition of solidarity and a rule of memory as an antidote to revolutionary absurdity.

> At this meridian of thought, the rebel thus rejects divinity in order to share in the struggles and destiny of all men. We shall choose Ithaca, the faithful land, frugal and audacious thought, lucid action, and the generosity of the man who understands. In the light, the earth remains our first and our last love. Our brothers are breathing under the same sky as we; justice is a living thing. Now is born that strange joy which helps one live and die, and which we shall never again postpone to a later time. On the sorrowing earth it is the unresting thorn, the bitter brew, the harsh wind off the sea, the old and the new dawn. With this joy, through long struggle, we small remake the soul of our time, and a Europe which will exclude nothing. Not even that phantom Nietzsche, who for twelve years after his downfall was continually invoked by the West as the blasted image of its loftiest knowledge and its nihilism; nor the prophet of justice without mercy who lies, by mistake, in the unbelievers' pit at Highgate Cemetery; nor the deified mummy of the man of action in his glass coffin; nor any part of what the intelligence and energy of Europe have ceaselessly furnished to the pride of a contemptible period. All may indeed live again, side by side with the martyrs of 1905, but on condition that it is understood that they correct one another, and that a limit, under the sun, shall curb them all. Each tells the other that he is not God; this is the end of romanticism. At this moment, when each of us must fit an arrow to his bow and enter the lists anew, to reconquer, within history and in spite of it, that which he owns already, the thin yield of his fields, the brief love of this earth, at this moment when at last a man is born, it is time to forsake our age and its adolescent furies. The bow bends; the wood complains. At the moment of supreme tension, there will leap into flight an unswerving arrow, a shaft that is inflexible and free.[18]

I have tried, then, to outline a notion of criticism as a mode of theoretical life that is reflexively tied to the communicative institutions of philosophy, art, and the sciences. The heart of this conception is its adherence to the presence of the things around us and of our fellow men in recognition of the institutional life that they share through the work of language, labor, and politics. It is a notion of critical theorizing whose auspices lie nowhere else than in the community of knowledge and value that are its claim to any contribution. The voice of such criticism is neither fanatical nor cynical, although it is in no way a simple affirmation of the claims of the community and tradition in which it belongs. What I have in mind is a conception of criticism that does not exploit the differences between the way things are and the way they might be but rather leaves itself open to the experience of their reversal and to the care for what is sublime as well as of what is desperate in the human condition and the times through which it passes. It is this conception of the human sciences that I shall address in the following pages.

PART   2

AN INTRODUCTION TO COMMUNICATIVE SOCIOLOGY

Preface

An Introduction to
Communicative Sociology

I want to present a conception of sociology that follows, though without explicit deduction, from Merleau-Ponty's conception of social phenomenology. Elsewhere I have addressed the analytic issues in what is now known as phenomenological sociology.[1] Here my purpose is to develop a persistent reflection upon the issue of fidelity in the practice of sociology as a science and the integrity of the lived society that exceeds the social sciences whose uses it trusts. In short, I am concerned with a phenomenological approach to the calling of sociology in a way that will preserve both its professional vocation and its religious motives. The latter may be filled in by the reader in the terms of his or her own religion's teachings on the preservation of society, its reform and renewal. It may also be read in terms of any broadly humanistic perspective upon society in which the hard lines of socialism and conservatism are softened in favor of a refusal of omnipotence and omniscience. As Merleau-Ponty might have said, it is the reversibility of science and society that is the mark of a phenomenological sociology:

Thus philosophy is not defined by a peculiar domain of its own. Like sociology, it only speaks about the world, men, and mind. . . . Philosophy is nature in us, the others in us, and we

are in them. Accordingly, we must not simply say that
philosophy is compatible with sociology, but that it is necessary
to it as a constant reminder of its tasks. . . . Philosophy is not a
particular body of knowledge; it is the vigilance which does
not let us forget the source of all knowledge.[2]

This essay, then, is especially devoted to the task of sustaining that vigilance that Merleau-Ponty urges. To do so,
I have construed the notion of *wild sociology*. At first sight,
such a term seems quite improper. It is potentially offen-
sive both to the adherents of scientific sociology and to
those whose humanism is attached to an order of cultivation that wild sociology appears to threaten. My purpose is rather to remind these two sides of sociology of
their common source. Yet it is not simply to insist upon
what they have in common but rather to make their differences more vital, or more charismatic, in the sense that
each labors toward a society that is not wholly its own.
Such a principle of humility is the conclusion to be drawn
from the phenomenological revision of the place of philosophy and science within the life-world that gives rise
to them, suffers them, and asks to be served rather than
to be subordinated by them. This *charismatic principle* is
what is radical about the conception of wild sociology.
Here, we think of others differently than they do themselves. But we do so with a duty to give back to them an
understanding in which we are also increased but as one
of them. Merleau-Ponty spoke of the integrity of Being,
which is before philosophy and science, as "wild Being"
(*être brut*), or as the "flesh of the world." We might also
call it ourselves inasmuch as we live from one another
without priority and despite all vicissitudes of difference.
This is our communal life in whose observance we honor
one another as best we can.

Introitus: A Phenomenology of Approach

E very approach must presume upon its reception. And, so, in
beginning we never fear that we shall be wholly misunderstood;
we trust that our hesitancy, our stumbling talk, and our choice
of words are not a search in the dark. To begin confidently is
part of the work of building and sharing an understanding. It is
ideally the institution of making sense together within a common life
and a common world.

Any approach asks for an understanding. In this sense our
approach is rarely just a casual opening, any more than the opening
of a Platonic dialogue or the break of dawn is irrelevant to the experiences that are to follow. An opening is never just a beginning
except in retrospect. We begin in the midst of things, that is to say,
when it is already late and we are caught irrevocably in the web of
understandings, borrowed back and forth against the time we have
spent together: in thought, in work, in play, in love, or in hate. Our
approach is self-consciously a presentation: the presence of others
and of ourselves to them. Thus it is we who are latently the resource
and circumstance that permit us to choose our ground, to start here
rather than there, to abide and concede, to question and answer. And
we would never get under way were it not for a certain surrender to
the tide of presence, the invitation of a look or of a word that launches

us on a voyage of meaning and truth in which each will have different tasks and different dreams, yet all come safely to the shore. For such a voyage the irresistible call is that of truth to which we must fit our talk and all it involves; just as we fit out our ships, not knowing everything they will encounter but trusting everything men have learned from the sea to build into themselves and into their ships in order to sail. In this enterprise we can be confident of ourselves only in the chain of work. We have not to start from the posture of loneliness, nor amid any babel of tongues. This does not mean that in search of truth we may not keep lonely watch or fall upon exotic islands and strange sights. Yet all these things can be told in our tales, which are somehow suited to bringing back and keeping memory for the telling of things unseen and deeds unheard.

Nor can we set out until we are ready, and thus our voyage begins at home in the world of familiar objects, among friends and everyday scenes. We cannot take our leave without a word or a smile; without checking the ropes, our trusty knife, the matches, the salt, the back door, the tickets, and the passports. Whether we leave for the Orient, the cottage, or the moon, we do not expect to encounter a totally alien scheme of things. We take along toothpaste, a clean shirt, and everyone's best wishes for our new life, whether in marriage or in Canada. We remember all we have been told by friends, novelists, poets, wise men, and even science-fiction writers. We never go alone; we are always ambassadors, representatives of the people, missionaries, or anthropologists. And something of the sort must be true. Or else by what right do we leave home and friends? By what right do we exchange day and night and wander into regions where our own language and customs become self-conscious, strained, and perhaps unusable? What is it that drives us to know more, or to know anything else than what those around us know, those who have always known us and loved us and never thought we would leave or want anything else than what we had between us? For this is a difference at the heart of things, greater than all the variations of man and woman, of childhood and maturity, of race or class or history. Once we no longer believe that all knowings and misunderstandings and all loves or hates lie within the same flesh and fold of humanity, we do not simply invite the philosopher's loneliness: we suffer the agony and ridicule of solipsism. This is not just to think bravely on one's own, as it might seem to be, but to betray the bond between us and man that, for all it has cost him, God himself has never wholly broken.

We shall have to deal with the temptations of solipsism, but not as a beginning. First we must make our preparations for leaving. For then the bustle of getting ready pushes loneliness into a sentiment of things to come, an adventure within our journey rather than the ground from which we start.

To begin is to approach our work; to be alone is to be at work. Yet we must remember the variety and seasons of work to understand its common load. We must remember the terraced vineyards, the railroads, and the docks; we must not forget the insides of factories, mines, and ships; we must be able to hear the roar of trucks, the screech of sawmills. We must feel the fisherman's cold, the weight of things, the way they tear and waste those who work them. But if we wish to start right, it is not enough to remember these things in a casual glance, the way we might thumb through an atlas. We must think of the joys of labor as well as its pains, its celebration in things as well as its struggle with them. We must know what it is people do in their work; how they feel; what they see; what they hear; what they need from steel, or marble, or bread; and how all this is metamorphosed into everyday life and in the simplest exchange between us, in friendship, in families, in love, in fear, in anxiety, in cruelty, in strikes, and in reconciliations.

In approaching our own task of developing a communicative sociology, we naturally reach backward and forward, and in this we heighten our sense of commitment to the commonplaces of meaning, habit, and community to which we have been accustomed. We start from a simple conviction that the sense of things is not alien and that knowledge and truth have only messengers and no experts. Truth has a face: it is the work of man and earns his bread. Thus in the work of knowledge we intend only to open paths that others can follow. Messengers, of course, carry news that they do not know will be well received in the community. But at first they are made welcome, brought in from the cold and rain, given food and drink and a place to rest from their journey. And it is the same when we get our news from the morning paper over a cup of coffee. We think of the truth as part of the well-being of our community; we receive it as sustenance or as a friend or guest. That is why the truth is painful when it reveals that things are not well in the land, in our lives, or in our community. To begin a work is to solicit an encounter between ourselves and others present to us here and now, or through their work and its legacy. Such a beginning is of the order of intimacy and revelation in which we discover a primitive sense of closeness. Yet our approach would be unbearable if it were not like the meeting of eyes in which there can be no primacy of the self or of the other but only a kind of alternating life. Our approach is rather an invitation to friendship and love, unsure yet certain. It is a warm embrace in which we are caught up in that overlap in which we spend our lives together and that invites comparison and understanding as much as fear or uncertainty. This is the ground for starting with one another. The encounter with someone or something new to us awakens in us a sense of openness, the sharing of need, that provides the horizon to our own vocation and is prior to all motivations of love, anonymity, creativity, or destruction. In this sense the encounter with beginnings, or first times, is not a radical break with everyday life. It is like a breath we draw more deeply at first and then let go, just as the fullness of life may rush in upon us and then recede, returning us to the ordinary absorption of living. This encounter of first things involves both a nostalgia and an ideal to which we compare our everyday experience without willfully courting either terror or ennui, yet not without longing and yearning:

> We are talking now of summer evenings in Knoxville, Tennessee, in the time that I lived there so successfully disguised to myself as a child. . . . All my people are larger bodies than mine, quiet, with voices gentle and meaningless like the voices of sleeping birds. One is an artist, he is living at home. One is a musician, she is living at home. One is my mother who is good to me. One is my father who is good to me. By some chance, here they are, all on this earth; and who shall even tell the sorrow of being on this earth, lying, on quilts, on the grass, on a summer evening, among the sounds of night. May God bless my people, my uncle, my aunt, my mother, my good father, oh, remember them kindly in their time of trouble; and in the hour of their taking away.
>
> After a little I am taken in and put to bed. Sleep, soft smiling, draws me unto her: and those receive me, who quietly treat me as one familiar and well beloved in that home: but will not, oh, will not, not now, not ever; but will not ever tell me who I am.[1]

There is a kind of sufficiency to things in which they realize themselves, neither falling short nor exceeding their limits. Here we have begun the enterprise of exploring our need of one another, thereby making thematic something we always assumed. We are engaged in an exercise that will involve us in mentioning what might never need to have been said and in falling short, or rather falling back into that embrace that surpasses all reason. Our task then is one of memory, of the care of first and last things, and in this the world and those around us are our support. We wish to understand and love one another, to be understood by others and by ourselves. We look about for certainties and find the memory of a summer evening on the grass among our family invading us with the presence that comes in the weight and lift of our bodies, in the sight and sound of our brother and sister and the goodness of our mother and father. And we borrow our own presence from theirs who in all the comings and goings of their own lives are here with us this evening and dwell in our heart by a marvelous chance of warmth and love. These are arrangements that are lasting like a family that lasts against its own troubles and dyings, as summer evenings last all the while that they, too, are dying. It is certain that we are not deceived in these familiar memories and do belong to them. Yet in the slip of time we do not hold and so become a question to ourselves, even while those around us still care and treat us as one so well loved and known to them, but who will not now or ever tell us who we are. And who can ever forget the places of memory?

We need to understand what moves us, what it is in the way a table is set, a garden cared for, or a mother dresses her child, that holds us and makes us either cry or sing somehow to tell about it— to hold it against time, against profusion, against our own indifferences or the times we are not watchful. In part this is what we can mean by simplicity, that is to say, a way of allowing ourselves to be the occasion of the fullness of things, of the world, of man. For the rest, it is the transcendence or transfiguration of things through us that is love's union of the mind and heart in love's thought (*amor intellectualis*).[2] What I have in mind here is the "world-building" character of love that makes its objects absolutely necessary, sometimes in themselves but also altogether, so that we feel we shall burst with the world inside us. It is sometimes thought that the thinker is a man without passions, a homeless figure. But this is false to the passionate understanding that is the very circumstance of things; it is false to the world that the thinker beholds and moreover shares in principle, though for want of company he may appear to hoard his love.[3]

Since Descartes we have been persuaded that a solitary and sedentary thinker could achieve certain and public knowledge of the world. The price of such subjective certainty, namely, the split between mind and nature, including the thinker's own embodiment, has been considered "proper" to thinking. Indeed, insofar as embodiment enters thinking or the effort to think, it has been only as something to be put out of play. The techniques of disembodied thinking have varied from closing one's eyes in order to shut out the fleeting world of the senses, or raising one's eyes toward heaven in thought or prayer, in order at least to be in the right way of what is noble and abiding, not to mention the practice of more ascetic spiritual disciplines of the body and soul. These gestural and postural choreographies of thought, to which must be added a number of other seclusive devices, such as the study cell lined only with the silent voices of the past, or the habit of working at night when the world shuts down and the senses in particular are handicapped, run deeper than the behavioral quirks of philosophers. For all kinds of work result in a certain physiognomy, in the peasant's bent back, the waitress's varicose veins, the heavy shoulders of the truck driver. Indeed, certain kinds of work, such as surgery, piano playing, tightrope and high wire walking, are essentially body work and as such demand a regimen that can no more be reduced to a technique than can thinking in the true philosopher. The activities of the body, whether proper to such work as that of the acrobat, or apparently circumstantial, as in the work of the philosopher, cannot be reduced to a lower order, except as a metaphysical posture: as the determination to redeem nature, or to dominate it by means of an ascesis.

Once we understand the world-building nature of love, we can make sociological thinking a daily practice that does not isolate us before things or them before us—which is the favorite mode of contemplation—but is instead beholden to the scenes in which we live, in streets, in gatherings, in labors, in ways and customs. In other words, we shall understand love's thought as a mode of everyday care. In addition, we can see that it is ordinarily improper to separate knowledge and morals. For we do not look upon things indifferently but rather for the goodness that is in them, and we measure our own maturity by what it is we can appreciate in this life. In this sense, then, the simplest heart is the most learned; for it knows how to take account of the ways of things and of people in their ways.

What is the direction of such thinking? To some it will be quite beside the concern with the accumulation of sociological knowledge and the domination of the world. To others it will seem to ignore the hierarchy of being and concern that has been the essence of philosophical thought. Well, this thinking, like love itself, does not move out of the plenitude in which it finds itself; it dwells in a concern with the things and people around us. Such thought does not treat its circumstances as a background for its own act; it does not abstract from its circumstances, rising above them. Today, more than ever, we need to cultivate what is near to us, to make of thought a garden rather than a bypass or a perishable collection that can only land us on the moon. Such a retreat would not weaken the universality of sociological thought. "We must try to find for our circumstance, such as it is, and precisely in its very limitation and peculiarity, its appropriate place in the immense perspective of the world. We must not stop in perpetual ecstasy before hieratic values, but conquer the right place among them for our individual life. In short, the reabsorption of circumstance is the concrete destiny of man."[4]

We make our lives from what is around us, from our family, our house, street, playmates, school, teachers, friends, books, comics, and church. But we forget this. Our projects take us away from home; they sweep everything behind us as a past we hardly remember. We move on, looking for wider perspectives, new experiences, unseen things. Our thoughts destine us for utopia, and in this we are for a time heroic figures, resisting the inertia of things, giving them our own extraordinary accent. But things beckon us back—the weight of things, their touch, their smell; the time of things, their seasons; the way of things, their uses—all these offer us a chance of salvation, a redemption rooted in things, often comically, but in an ultimate wisdom. For the truth of the life-world is that the way of things is the way of ourselves with them, like the friendship of a man and his dog: a bond of faith, a mutual need, each unthinkable apart from the other, even in argument and anger.

To think sociologically is to dwell upon a question we have answered long ago: How it is that men belong to one another despite all differences? This is the task of a *wild sociology*, namely, to dwell upon the platitudes of convention, prejudice, place, and love; to make of them a history of the world's labor and to root sociology in the care of the circumstance and particulars that shape the divine predicaments of ordinary men.[5] The work of communicative sociology, because it hearkens to its ground in wild sociology, is to confront the passionless world of science with the epiphany of family, of habit, and of human folly, outside which there is no remedy. This is not to reject scientific sociology. It is simply to treat it as a possibility that has yet to convince the world. Wild sociology is mindful of the poverty of sociology, of its ambitions and its easy alliances. It sees no other way than to remain in the world it needs for its own vocation and for the particulars of its reasoning. It has no unprecedented claims, and its meditations draw ever deeply from the very ground they seem to make strange. Wild sociology exhibits without end its appeal to the ancestral orders of our everyday conventions. Yet this does not mean that sociological thinking lacks any election. It simply means that the vocation of sociology is never in hand as a hard and fast beginning but is to be found over its way and through its concerns. It is therefore never reducible to a matrix of procedural rules. The success of wild sociology lies in the integrity of its concerns and not in the division of its labor.

Our approach to communicative sociology cannot be hasty with the imperatives of science if we are ever to know its worth. What is the necessity of sociology; in what need do we stand of its particular concern? This is a question of fulfillment, like asking someone we love what it is he is doing so as to bring his labor closer to us than our very eyes because we want to take it in and hold it to our heart. Communicative sociology cannot be self-serving. Nor should it borrow from others mindlessly. Either way, we accumulate with nothing to call our own. We need to start conscious of others, willing to learn; to be overwhelmed, to struggle, to fight back, and to stand. But this is a time of waiting even when it hides itself as worldly success. True growth needs origins, a return to first things: to place, time, and pattern. Intellectual order is not simply an instrument of domination; it involves just as much a capacity for reliving our thoughts. It is perhaps more like housecleaning, a rearrangement that in welcoming others leaves more room for ourselves. In such welcome there is a yield of being that is achieved in the arrangement of simple things to do honor to one like us. The integrity of our beginnings is the source of our welcome. It also strengthens our speech and the commitment of our interests and thereby reminds us of our freedom. For in thinking and speaking we choose paths much as in life we choose careers and marriages, that is, as ways of resolving the history and geography of our lives.

17

The Place of Sociology in the Conversation of Mankind

T he language and history of sociology will seem far removed
from my concern. It is, indeed, if we think of our approach to
sociology as an initiation into a logic of generalization and precision to which we have no native claim. But it is just this way
into sociology of which I do not want to take advantage; I do not
want to settle before I begin the question of the relation of scientific
languages to everyday speech and talk. I have begun by trying to
show a concern for how it is we manage any departure together, how
we approach understanding by building upon the great platitudes of
our experience as embodied beings, with our speech set in local needs
and circumstances. To say that we are sociologists is only to remark
on the materials at hand, on the necessity of working on this rather
than that. We must first raise the question of what it is that is presupposed by the field we have chosen to work. The practice of sociology, like that of any other discipline, is precarious. It soon leaves us
unable to remember our first motives for doing it at all. The aim of
method, as I understand it, is to test in us that strange distance between our work and those for whom we intend it. Sociologists are

particularly attached to methods for the sake of their claim to scientific status; I am concerned with the poetic claims of method. I think these two belong together in our working lives. Method plays the music in what is of interest to us; it shapes our sensibilities, determines our passions, and defines our world. Method is our practical idealism; it is the opening in things and of ourselves toward them. This is possible because we are able to convert our private enthusiasms into objective enterprises that, in turn, are never accomplished once and for all and so require of us a constant response according to our own need.

In what follows I shall adopt the commonplace method, as I understand it. The notes and texts upon which I have relied, whether shown for themselves or through my own reflection, are intended as places of embellishment. Their work is to celebrate the world's own appeal rather than to defend the authority of science. They are copied as holy works seeking the redemptions of correct spelling in the salvation of divine and human reading.[1]

Like Vico we believe poetry is essential to our living and is not to be overlooked by wild sociologists. Or, at least, poetry cannot be overlooked by sociologists once we do not begin with the assumption that our speech is governed by language in its literal, or scientific, form.[2] It is time for sociology to consider how it means to connect language and reason once it sheds the outworn conception of science and poetry as two hostile knowings. We are aware, of course, that societies vary in the respect they accord to the works of knowledge and imagination. What we know of this makes it conventional for sociology to aspire to the status of scientific knowledge and thus to shun the fall into poetry as a failure of power and control. Because we know this we need to find out that, all along, this organization of knowledge and language has been a conventional arrangement and that other visions have gathered around it, if not inside.[3]

We should not overlook the attractive power and pride of science, its ability to keep ranks and well-ordered speech. In comparison, other knowledge is a poor thing and common sense sounds like the babble of children and elders or of the scrambled wits of the careerless. Yet we know very well that language is not all of a piece. We know this because we know that ordinary men are neither obsessed nor privileged with a single vision. Language is not outside the variety of human conditions. The generalities men care for are more like the hills and valleys they see around them, more like the fates of their children, their animals, and homes, than the high-sounding generalizations of science and mathematics: more like prayer and poetry.

But then sociology ought to exercise care in its own speech, since it cannot presume upon its scientific allegiances to hold it in faith with its proper place in men's lives.

The sociologist's speech is not separable from his manner of speaking, for sociology accumulates no determinate body of knowledge outside the need of society to be persuaded of its use. To the extent that the sociologist is forgetful of this dependence, he speaks to himself only. But this is the source of his pride. Such pride may comfort the sociologist in his distance from the daily conversation of mankind. This attitude is more likely due to the sociologist's loss of ability to handle the tension between what is urgent and what is easy in everyday life. Yet to live with this tension is the mark of ordinary maturity. Fortunately, nothing preserves sociological speech from foolishness and banality once its content is known. Nothing is more vain than a sociology whose content cannot be found except as the promise of science. Yet the sociologist cannot wholly avoid these dangers if he is to respect common sense while nevertheless urging its improvement.

The sociologist is in danger of speaking as though only scientific utterances were true to the practical bearing of life. Because of the necessity of making himself heard among the other voices of science, history, and economics, the sociologist seeks to persuade common sense that the spirit of science lies in the voice of inquiry and discussion, thereby allowing for the possibility of his own place in the conversation of mankind. This is an insidious argument. For once it is admitted, it easily serves the usurpation of genuinely different modes of discussion by the high-sounding voice of expertise. Yet sociology, more than any other voice, should be concerned with the preservation of that meeting place of mankind for which Michael Oakeshott has so marvelously furnished us with the image of conversation rather than of inquiry or argument:

> This, I believe, is the appropriate image of human intercourse— appropriate because it recognizes the qualities, the diversities, and the proper relationships of human utterances. As civilized human beings, we are the inheritors, neither of an inquiry about ourselves and the world, nor of an accumulating body of information, but of a conversation, begun in the primeval forests and extended and made more articulate in the course of centuries. It is a conversation which goes on both in public and within each of ourselves. Of course there is argument and inquiry and information, but wherever these are profitable they are to be recognized as passages in this conversation, and perhaps they are not the most captivating

of the passages. It is the ability to participate in this conversation, and not the ability to reason cogently, to make discoveries about the world, or to contrive a better world, which distinguishes the human being from the animal and the civilized man from the barbarian. Indeed, it seems not improbable that it was the engagement in this conversation (where talk is without a conclusion) that gave us our present appearance, man being descended from a race of apes who sat in talk so long and so late that they wore out their tails. Education, properly speaking, is an initiation into the skill and partnership of this conversation in which we learn to recognize the voices, to distinguish the proper occasions of utterance, and in which we acquire the intellectual and moral habits apppropriate to conversation. And it is this conversation which, in the end, gives place and character to every human activity and utterance. I say, "in the end," because, of course, the immediate field of moral activity is the world of practical enterprise, and intellectual achievement appears, in the first place, within each of the various universes of discourse; but good behaviour is what it is with us because practical enterprise is recognized not as an isolated activity but as a partner in a conversation, and the final measure of intellectual achievements is in terms of its contribution to the conversation in which all universes of discourse meet.[4]

Science, common sense, and poetry are varieties of language rather than declensions of controlled communication. Man does not always seek things poetically. He may equally seek to dominate things, to subject them to his will and control, to construct them. In this case, the presence of things recedes in favor of their analytic composition, which together with their laws of combination permits man's assembly of the world. Or else things are subject to traditional use and need and concern us only insofar as they serve our purposes. Language is anchored upon ourselves, our relations to others, to God and nature; and upon the history and stories that accumulate in our communities. Our care for language shapes our responsibility to ourselves and others; it is the mark of our faithfulness to the nature of things, to their shape and drift. Our use of language is not ruled by the scandals of philosophy and science. Yet its patient task of shaping common sense into good sense is often hurried by the claims of logic and method to inaugurate a republic of knowledge. Language suffers in all this because clarity is the enemy of ornament and epiphany and throws out poetry in favor of public knowledge, health, and security.

Method is hostile to the gratuities of poetry and myth. Thus science seeks to conscript sociology to its ideals of well-ordered speech. Sociology in turn is tempted to regard the efficiency of speech as the workings of an external order of progressive revelation moving from magic and myth to science and plain sense. Moreover, sociology is enamored with mastery and technique. But these are equally the responses of speech in addressing nature, language, and society as the others of dialogue. The acquisition of sociological speech does not begin with the postulate of social facts. In Durkheim and Weber the birth of sociology owes as much to prayer—society is God, society is spirit—as to the method of its fathers. In this, sociology is tied to singing itself as much as the world it furnishes. Where would sociology find any other path to knowledge than science, and how would this shape its speech? It is not even possible to raise this question so long as sociology clings to the skirts of science without any knowledge of the place of science itself in the conversation of mankind. Rather, sociology must learn, as King Lear learned, that it is in ourselves that we encounter the division of reason working irresistibly against the kingdom of love, mutilating the power of language in its prayers, its names, and its truth telling. Sociology must learn that in the end it is we who gather the world and are its true metamorphosis. For even in our asylums God's spies gather up the heavens against the day when they will prevent the Machiavellians and charlatans who twist the grain of our humanity:

> No, no, no, no! Come, let's away to prison;
> We two alone will sing like birds i'th'cage:
> When thou dost ask me blessing, I'll kneel down,
> And ask of thee forgiveness: so we'll live,
> And pray, and sing, and tell old tales, and laugh
> At gilded butterflies, and hear poor rogues
> Talk of court news; and we'll talk with them too,
> Who loses and who wins; who's in, who's out;
> And take upon's the mystery of things,
> As if we were God's spies: and we'll wear out,
> In a wall'd prison, packs and sects of great ones
> That ebb and flow by the moon.[5]

King Lear's lesson is the lesson of communicative sociology. For what he has to learn against the demands of Hobbesian will and utility is the regeneration of the bonds of service and family, of the generics of natural society. Lear's tragedy is the tragedy of relation to which we are born, on which we depend for love, friendship, truth, and service. In youth we challenge relation; in old age we depend upon it for our peace. In all else we define it, defend it, resist it, even to honor or destroy it. Relation is the metaphysics of our humanity; it is our alliance with the world's fools. Sociological knowledge is a knowledge of metamorphosis. For it is we who are the substance and form of social life whose structure is in turn commentary upon its methodology and matter. "One cannot come back too often to the question what is knowledge and to the answer knowledge is what one knows."[6]

The conversable attitude of daily life is grounded in the monumental achievements of the commonsense perception, knowledge, and values. These are the work of everyone and no one, furnishing the considerations and relevances of our living that lie upon us as a daily and sacred part of the mind. For the most part rationalism in science and philosophy consists in the demand that things and action be conformable to the standards of rationality. Properly speaking, however, theory is only rational when it abides by the troublesome contingency of things and human conduct. The rationality of wild sociology, unlike scientific rationalism, refrains from imposing reason upon reality: it seeks rather to make sociological theory rational in the acceptance of the contingent modes of social reality. All this keeps our talk to itself in the small gatherings of our lives, between families and among friends, in kitchens as in high places, protected only by the warmth of our own people and remembered kindly despite its pain and injuries:

> And thus, too, these families, not otherwise than with every family in the earth, how each, apart, how inconceivably lonely, sorrowful, and remote! Not one other on earth, nor in any dream, that can care so much what comes to them, so that even as they sit at the lamp and eat their supper, the joke they are laughing at could not be so funny to anyone else; and the littlest child who stands on the bench solemnly, with food glittering all over his cheeks in the lamplight, this littlest child I speak of is not there, he is of another family, and it is a different woman who wipes the food from his cheeks and takes his weight upon her thighs and against her body and who feeds him, and lets his weight slacken against her in his heavying sleep; and the man who puts another soaked cloth to the skin cancer on his shoulder; it is his wife who is looking on, and his child who lies sunken along the floor with his soft mouth broad open and his nakedness up like a rolling dog, asleep: and the people next up the road cannot care in the same way, not for any of it: for they are absorbed upon themselves: and the negroes down beyond the spring have drawn their shutters tight, the lamplight pulses like wounded honey through the seams into the soft night, and there is laughter: but nobody else cares. All over the whole round earth and in the settlements, the towns, and the great iron

stones of cities, people are drawn inward within their little shells of
rooms, and are to be seen in their wondrous and pitiful actions
through the surfaces of their lighted windows by thousands, by
millions, little golden aquariums, in chairs, reading, setting tables,
sewing, playing cards, not talking, talking, laughing inaudibly,
mixing drinks, at radio dials, eating, in shirt-sleeves, carefully
dressed, courting, teasing, loving, seducing, undressing, leaving the
room empty in its empty light, alone and writing a letter urgently,
in couples married, in separate chairs, in family parties, in gay
parties, preparing for bed, preparing for sleep: and none can care,
beyond that room; and none can be cared for, by any beyond that
room: and it is small wonder they are drawn together so cowardly
close, and small wonder in what dry agony of despair a mother may
fasten her talons and her vampire mouth upon the soul of her
struggling son and drain him empty, light as a locust shell: and
wonder only that an age that has borne its children and must lose
and has lost them, and lost life, can bear further living; but so it is.[7]

Self is circumstantial through and through and is utterly lost
if it does not learn to save circumstance in the expression of its needs
and knowing. Communicative sociology cannot trick the relation between self and circumstance by making of self or of circumstance a
thing, an organization, or a contract. The corporeal composition of
self and circumstance involves us in a daily metaphysics of contingency, relation, caprice, and corruption in which culture is not an
abstract and universal organ but a concrete and circumstantial practice without any other resort than the great natural orders of our
daily living.[8] Communicative sociology embraces the common dilemma of making sense together that it must share with all other lay
practitioners of the art. It exercises a limited reflexivity that attaches
us to the conversable particulars of use, limit, and value, which en-
gender the immense perspectives of the world, of family, class, gender,
truth, and rationality. Communicative sociology refrains from the ecstasy of conventional sociology in the presence of hieratic values,
rather to celebrate the integrity of everyday conduct and its own artful
accomplishment of concrete destinies. It is to be expected that such
a sociology of everyday life will involve a certain outrage as well as
systematic misunderstanding when viewed from the perspective of
establishment sociology. There is a certain irony in the terms of this
antagonism, for it is precisely communicative sociology that is a sociology of convention and establishment because of its patient ap-
prenticeship to the anonymous labor of social institution and of the
great natural orders of our communal life.

PART TWO: COMMUNICATIVE SOCIOLOGY

In practice communicative sociology achieves a return to things that is the direction of poetry. All of modern thought addresses nature's body, bringing reason to its sense through the recollection of the primacy of perceptual knowledge. In speaking of the poetics of everyday thought and emotion, I have in mind the connections between the seemingly hopeless condition of circumstance—the condition of no one in particular and yet of everyone—and the massive presumptions and uses of order in our sentimental and political lives. Moreover, this poetry is in keeping with the viewpoint of modern science, provided that in both cases we properly understand that the very notion of viewpoint in no way involves a fall into subjectivism and relativism. This must be said for the sake not only of critics but also of many who believe they are the new poets of relativity.

We deal in knowledge, perception, and values that are neither the universal acquisition of a disembodied and unsituated ego nor merely a local and willful imposition of sensory limits. Rather, the fact that the world has a different face for a fifth-century Athenian and a twentieth-century Torontonian, so far from making objective knowledge impossible, is the very organizing element of truth and its historical acquisition. Truth is never the achievement of once and for all agreements, any more than it is merely a temporary pact. These simple alternatives leave out of account the strength and appeal of local arrangement whose fame spreads upon the stream of generations, linking neighbors and posterity in the general labor of culture. "Culture for the dark-eyed men who meditate, argue, sing, preach, and dream in Ionia, Attica, Sicily, and Magna Graecia, means what is firm as opposed to what is unstable, what is fixed as opposed to what is fleeting, what is clear as opposed to what is obscure. Culture is not the whole of life, but only the moment of security, of certainty, of clarity. And the Greeks invent the concept as an instrument, not for replacing the spontaneity of life, but for making it secure."[9]

Today, of course, we are not much given to the patience of circumstance. We are sophisticated relativists, anthropologists, vulgar Freudians and Marxists, forever seeing through the candor of primitive use, weighing motive in the scales of class injustice, invoking that universal truth that is the trick of university, newspaper, and tourist culture. Modern culture assumes relativism so strongly that it will seem prescientific to deny it. We may grant this relativism and yet still reject its conclusion. For the relativity of science is a conclusion of classical mechanics rather than the sense of Einstein's relativity theory. Galileo and Newton regarded our empirical judgments of time, space, and motion as relative because they themselves postulated observers' absolute space, time, and movement. Einstein's mechanics rejects the absolutism of Euclidean space with the result that the relativity of space-time observations no longer yields mere appearances but a relative reality that is absolute because it is all we can know. The new relativity differs in its absolutism from that of the rationalist mechanics of Galileo and Newton inasmuch as it treats perspective as a constituent feature of reality. Thus viewpoint is an absolute ingredient of modern science and not at all a source of prescientific provincialism.

Yet in the social sciences we continue to treat knowledge as the product of an absolute observer who confounds subjective experience in the relativity of appearance and perspective. In this way, the social sciences alienate the daily labor of each one of us in bringing to bear our viewpoints, beliefs, attitudes, needs, and desires into the great stock and exchange of human culture and its shaping sensibility. *We are ourselves and our circumstances:* this is the natural light of a communicative sociology that has genuinely absorbed the convergence of science and poetry in the modern world.[10] It is from our circumstance that things and others have the ancestral shape of need, of friend and family, of instrument and advice. It is from circumstance that we have our moods like the changing light of day, our resignation, our hope, and our brooding memory. We and our circumstances are the material of metaphor and relevance as well as of plain talk, vice, and unfulfilled virtue. And we are these things day in and day out, and what we are in the midst of these things, small towns, trades, and landscapes, is their very light and our own reflection, their own offering and our own gift. The panorama of our beliefs, needs, and values is not given to the unsituated perspective of science; it is an everyday reality forged from the conversable uses and sufficiencies of our daily living:

> Are we, perhaps, here just for saying: House,
> Bridge, Fountain, Gate, Jug, Olive tree, Window,—
> possibly: Pillar, Tower? . . . but for saying, remember,
> oh, for such saying as never the things themselves
> hoped so intensely to be. Is not the secret purpose
> of this sly earth, in urging a pair of lovers,
> just to make everything leap with ecstasy in them?
> Threshold: how much it can mean
> to two lovers, that they should be wearing their own
> worn threshold a little, they too, after the many before,
> before the many to come, . . . as a matter of course!

Here is the time for the Tellable, *here* is its home.
Speak and proclaim. More than ever
the things we can live with are falling away, and their place
being oustingly taken up by an imageless act.
Act under crusts, that will readily split as soon
as the doing within outgrows them and takes a new outline.
Between the hammers lives on
our heart, as between the teeth
our tongue, which, nevertheless,
remains the bestower of praise.

Praise the world to the Angel, not the untellable: you
can't impress him with the splendour you've felt; in the cosmos
where he more feelingly feels you're only a tyro. So show him
some simple thing, remoulded by age after age,
till it lives in our hands and eyes as a part of ourselves.
Tell him *things*. He'll stand more astonished; as you did
beside the roper in Rome or the potter in Egypt.
Show him how happy a thing can be, how guileless and ours;
how even the moaning of grief purely determines on form,
serves as a thing, or dies into a thing,—to escape
to a bliss beyond the fiddle. These things that live on departure
understand when you praise them: fleeting, they look for
rescue through something in us, the most fleeting of all.
Want us to change them entirely, within our invisible hearts,
into—oh, endlessly—into ourselves! Whosoever we are.[11]

Communicative sociology is a species of intellectual love. For sociology cannot turn away from the consenting goods of human need and natural circumstance that bind us to the perfection of things as our own accomplishment and as the salvation of our souls. Sociology truly seeks a radical comprehension of human circumstance. But it has vulgarized its vocation in an impatient reduction of circumstance to environment, organization, class, and ethnicity. Sociology has reduced circumstance through its mathematical collection of motive as self, thing, and environment to nothing else than sociology's own possibilities of world making. To the extent that it is successful in this enterprise, sociology is an alien science and a hostile medium rather than the beneficent shell of human circumstance and need.

In its attachment to circumstance, communicative sociology saves the appearances of communal life from the normative ironies of the scientific attitude that abstracts from the horizonal truths and inscapes of daily living. Circumstance is not the instrument of reason, nor is it its bare material waiting upon the inspiration of science for its furnishing and interpretation. Circumstance is the inscape of sense and reason. It is the self's surround, the open sublation of inside and outside, of self and thing, of self and other. Circumstance is the reminiscence of sensibility and reason folding back upon the world's embrace of our daily living. Human circumstance is never a bare instrument but rather a loving care and inscription of those fantastic universals that are the poetry of time's body and Vico's first conception of wild sociology.

18

Communicative
Sociology
and Its
Circumstance

S cience always obliges us to forget what we know. In this way we learn much though we may still lack wisdom. In the case of the natural world, our power over things is compensation enough for the separations of knowledge. But in the social world we cannot start with any certain distance between what we know ordinarily and the reports of sociology. For the social world does not wait upon the constructions of scientific reasoning. It makes sense from the first day until the last in the all-day and everyday surroundings of others whose life we share. Nothing lies outside this circumstance, neither its ignorance nor its fears, neither its joys nor its injuries. The mystery of this circumstance measures the poverty of sociology.

Communicative sociology seeks to establish how it comes about that without any explicit appeal to rule or benefit of science, what we ordinarily know and value achieves the status of fact or, better, of *moral fact*.

We ordinarily experience the everyday social world as something that has preceded us and now faces us as an orderly scheme of things whose interpretation is handed on to us by parents, teachers, and almost anyone with whom we live and learn. On the basis of the general legacy of language and knowledge into which we are born, we use and enjoy the world in typical ways: we sit in the shade of trees, avoid barking dogs, drink milk, eat good things, and run to mother for protection. The way in which we speak and act in the world and among others is shaped by our immediate purposes and conventions, which furnish a schema of relavances regarding what features of the world are to be selected for generalization, rule of thumb, reminiscence, use, and avoidance. We commonly assume that things will continue to be as we have known them and that we can go about our business in a routine way, and so on, and so forth, so as to minimize doubt and decision. Or, when something goes wrong, we expect to be able to regularize it, to fix it without having to take apart the whole scheme of things on which we have relied so far.

In the natural attitude of our daily lives the world has for us certain and constant features. We assume that the objects, persons, and regions of the world with which we are familiar will continue to be as they are; similarly, we assume that the experiences and emotions we have relied upon hitherto will continue to work for us as before. We assume that the world is amenable to our purposes and needs and that we shall be able to realize our interests through action in and upon the world. Of course, each of these expectancies may fail to be realized, producing practical and emotional as well as theoretical problems. When this happens we do not entertain open and permanent doubts about our knowledge in general but only insofar as this enables us to restore what is questionable in our working knowledge, belief, and values.[1]

The world as we know it presents itself to us in a massive face, the faces of family and friends, of street and neighborhood, with receding contours of familiarity and reach that we expect to be able to penetrate without becoming entirely lost and without meeting others with totally incommunicable ways. Each of us has a certain amount of "expert knowledge" for his particular needs, or else available upon thorough inquiry and application. But the greater part of this knowledge will be merely what it is necessary to know for all practical purposes, as tricks of the trade, rules of thumb, proverbial and folk wisdom. Where our general knowledge suffices for the definition of our task and situation, that is to say, where it enables us to discover its theme and its elaboration in and by particulars of the situation so as to engage its normal values, likelihoods, and causal texture, then we are able to treat what is required of us as a routine matter. We may, of course, be frustrated in our expectations and activities. But any stoppage in our conduct is perceived in the frame of its overall temporal course, which allows for others to see what has gone wrong, give help where needed, and so get us on our way.

These commonsense presumptions of conduct are the basis, then, for our being open to the influence of others, to their advice and aid. It enables others to see what we are up to and where we are, and thus to sustain a common schema of here-and-now, here-and-there relevances, that is to say, to locate the *occasional* or *indexical* properties[2] of the other person's action or talk and thus to generalize its sense. Thus in the commonsense attitude our own presence in the world is regarded as directly relevant to our understanding of the world and others and in turn their understanding of us. For example, what I am saying now depends very much on how I have approached this work, on how I try to breathe into it the sense to be made of it by us together once you share in it as a reader and as one who can be called upon to have some general sense of the allusions, the references, and the overall question that I am addressing. I am aware, of course, that you will not see things exactly as I do, reading rather more or rather less into what I am saying than what I have in mind to say. By the same token, there is a chance that I am thinking along the very same lines as some of my readers, or that they are even ahead of me. But whatever the background differences among us, we assume as a matter of course, though not without art, that we can share viewpoints, sentiments, and beliefs without elaborate recourse to the disciplines of logic and science. This reasoning, however, is not established without general discussion, through which we always seek the resource of agreement.

> In exactly the way that persons are members to organized affairs, they are engaged in serious and practical work of detecting, demonstrating, persuading through displays in the ordinary occasions of their interactions the appearances of consistent, coherent, clear, chosen, planful arrangements. In exactly the ways in which a setting is organized, it *consists* of methods whereby its members are provided with accounts of the setting as countable, storyable, proverbial, comparable, picturable, representable—i.e., accountable events.[3]

The commonsense attitude of everyday life is not just a given. It is something that is evinced in our social conduct as part of our claim to a grasp of how things are, as our ability to handle our social surroundings, relevant others, and our own face. The attitude of everyday life is thus not simply a cognitive attitude but also an expressive or ethical attitude. It is a feature of everyday life that it supports our self-conceptions much of the time so that it is only when for some reason it leads us on to a disappointment or failure that we become aware of our self-investment in the way we see things. To withdraw such investments and to find new outlets for old selves can be painful indeed; these acts require the presence of others, even of the very persons who may have led us on, as they may later confess.

We are naturally surprised and shocked when things do not conform to our commonsense expectations of them. Every question of fact raises questions of moral identity as well as cognitive competence. We assume there is a world held in common that has certain constitutive features of sharedness that we manage in a self-patterned way, working back and forth, glossing meaning, taking particulars as evidence of an order of events yet to be established and, in turn, using this emerging order of events as "evidence" of the sense of its particulars. We regard the working of this scheme of things not just as an essay in knowledge but rather as the same thing as a moral claim to our grasp of reality, of our competence and responsibility in the working of an order of events to which we are partner, so that commonsense knowledge of social structures is for us the same thing as moral knowledge.

The scientist, it is said, breaks with the daily world of the natural attitude. He lays aside the common fabric of belief, habit, and custom in the service of a systematic doubt and his subscription to rationally constructed knowledge. In the pursuit of doubt the scientist aims at the overthrow of conventional knowledge, the destruction of routine, and the emancipation of choice and decision. To achieve this the scientist must disengage himself from the world of pragmatic interest and relevances and thereby reinterpret the world solely in keeping with his own scientific purpose, namely, to achieve the solution of a problem for its own sake.[4] Even with regard to his solution, the scientist is prepared to see it defeated, improved upon, or made more rigorous and free of contradiction. The scientist also suspends the spatiotemporal relevances motivated by his own presence in the world. He adopts a timeless and objective stance in which space-time coordinates function solely to state the conditions for repeating an experiment. Because the scientist has no "here" within the world and is immune to the reciprocity of viewpoint, with its horizons of intimacy and generality, he is obliged to construct a *model actor* to whom he imputes a *rational consciousness* interacting with others destined similarly to act like any-rational-man:

> The homunculus is invested with a system of relevances
> originating in the scientific problem of his constructor and not in

the particular biographically determined situation of an actor within the world. It is the scientist who defines what is to his puppet a Here and a There, what is within his reach, what is to him a We and a You or a They. The scientist determines the stock of knowledge his model has supposedly at hand. This stock of knowledge is not socially derived and, unless especially designed to be so, without reference to social approval. The relevance system pertinent to the scientific problem under scrutiny alone determines its intrinsic structure, namely, the elements "about" which the homunculus is supposed to have knowledge, those of which he has a mere knowledge of acquaintance and those others he just takes for granted. With this is determined what is supposed to be familiar and what anonymous to him and on what level the typification of the experiences of the world imputed to him takes place.[5]

Sociological accounts are beset by the pervasive problem of the encounter between the everyday world of the commonsense natural attitude and the problem-specific interests of scientific inquiry and explanation. There are a variety of ways to express this difficulty. The particular approach that I should like to develop starts from the problem of the *mutual accountability* of the commonsense and scientific attitudes. It is possible, for example, out of evolutionary and rationalist fervor, to dismiss the articulation of commonsense knowledge as an idol of the marketplace from which science delivers us. Such an attitude has the support of the philosophical tradition and serves to qualify the superior social status that men of knowledge claim for themselves by appealing to the asceticism of rational thought in its struggle with license and foolishness. But this tradition belies itself inasmuch as it also appeals to the sobriety of common sense to rescue us from the intoxications of speculative thought. For what is reasonable in human affairs is often found to be closer to common sense than is flattering for the scientists of conduct. Men are ordinarily aware that they are born much like any other men into a world whose ways and wisdom precede them. So far from inspiring subjectivity and disorder, common sense allies itself with that proper human folly that men find it necessary to acquire to live with themselves. True folly is alien to the corrosive fantasy of perfectly rational character and community.

It is in the interest of scientific sociology to destroy custom and to deride convention in order to make of human assembly a rule of reason. In this unseasonable aspiration sociology strives to be immune to the exigencies of conviviality and collective sentiment. If this were at all a possibility, then sociology would truly be a science of difference, that is, of egoism, interest, and violence collected in the division of labor, in contract, and in the republic of method. But it is precisely this aspiration that limits scientific sociology to the rule of appearances. This rule in turn saves the rational management of social life by hiding its antisocial foundations. It is in this fashion that Erving Goffman reveals to us the folly of descriptive social science. That is to say, his labor shows that there is nothing behind the surfaces of sociological description once sociology itself is no longer beholden to the grounds of collective life.[6] In such a situation sociological description merely glosses the practices of vanity, equality, and the fear of death. Once scientific sociology engages in the unseasonable folly of breaking with communal sense, its own appeal becomes problematic, or rather, it is reduced to an uncertain voice crying against an uncommon society. For the assembly of society and sociology is not a power of science:

> But suppose, right here, some wise man who has dropped down from the sky should suddenly confront me and cry out that the person whom the world has accepted as a god and a master is not even a man, because he is driven sheeplike by his passions; that he is the lowest slave, because he willingly serves so many and such base masters. Or again, suppose the visitor should command some one mourning his father's death to laugh, because now his father has really begun to live—for in a sense our earthly life is but a kind of death. Suppose him to address another who is glorying in his ancestry, and to call him low and base-born because he is so far from virtue, the only true fount of nobility. Suppose him to speak of others in like vein. I ask you, what would he get by it, except to be considered by everyone as insane and raving? As nothing is more imprudent than unseasonable prudence. And he is unseasonable who does not accommodate himself to things as they are, who is "unwilling to follow the market," who does not keep in mind at least that rule of conviviality, "Either drink or get out"; who demands, in short, that the play should no longer be a play. The part of a truly prudent man, on the contrary, is (since we are mortal) not to aspire to wisdom beyond his station, and either, along with the rest of the crowd, pretend not to notice anything, or affably and companionably be deceived. But that, they tell us, is folly. Indeed, I shall not deny it; only let them, on their side, allow that it is also to play out the comedy of life.[7]

It belongs to scientific folly to reckon men more rational than they care to be. Such folly easily allies with political pride to make men the instruments of rational organization beyond their will. Sociology is soon conscripted to this task. Or rather, without self-knowledge sociology never comes to terms with the temptations of scientific folly. It is essential, therefore, that we investigate the nature of the conduct that is inquiry into the lives of others. We must ask what it is, faith or method, that supports us in decentering our own life among others in order to make of it a dedicated focus of concern with the otherness of others. How do we accomplish this, what motivates its concern, how is it to be fulfilled? We are not to presume that it is the work of alienation; for it is not practiced outside the umbilical ties between us and others who feed us, smile upon us, help, hurt, and puzzle us. Among men rationality is the incarnate pursuit of understanding that breeds in bodily presences. This is the sustaining bond of sociological inquiry. What would it mean to cut ourselves off from this union in order to make of sociology a science? If we could achieve such a distance, to what in the end should we apply sociology?

In the face of this question sociology attaches itself to scientific description. Yet in modern literature and science nothing is less certain than description. Or rather, there have been times and places where narrative was more of a settled attitude, or the very composition of a settled attitude. But today words come apart and leap from the sentences that try to hold them to literary conventions. Sense and nonsense are if anything rival sensibilities rather than the frame and limit of understanding. Thus nothing can be more passionate than the commitment to true social narrative, that is, to a narrative that is patient with the intimacies of ordered and disordered life, through which the body becomes flesh of the world and the world in turn is fleshed into the sense and nonsense of character and society.

Communicative sociology acknowledges that it is born into the desperate circumstance of having to earn its living. For sociology is preceded by the marvelous acquisitions of commonsense living and pragmatic reasoning that make it impossible for sociology to begin, as does science, with a lack of confidence in man. Communicative sociology has no other way than to assume its conventional debts to the great traditions of our senses, manners, and natural reason. Thus it has no other narrative allegiance than to the virtues and ways of daily living from which we build up the institutions of understanding and goodwill. Communicative sociology cannot suspend the intimacies of need, of hope and injury, of tools and engines, of family and first love, nor of hate and broken friendship. These are never virtual engagements of ours attendant upon the commitments of speculative reason and its contracts of utility and profit. For our social life is not convertible to a thing of use, nor to an image of itself. Let this stand in the surrounds of abuse, utility, fantasy, machination, and contract that we bear, much as life holds against all its afflictions:

> The plainness and iterativeness of work must be one of the things which make it so extraordinarily difficult to write of. The plain details of a task once represented, a stern enough effort in itself, how is it possibly to be made clear enough that this same set of leverages has been undertaken by this woman in nearly every day of the eleven or the twenty-five years since her marriage, and will be persisted in in nearly every day to come in all the rest of her life; and that it is only one among the many processes of wearying effort which make the shape of each one of her living days; how is it to be calculated, the number of times she has done these things, the number of times she is still to do them; how conceivably in words is it to be given as it is in actuality, the accumulated weight of these actions upon her; and what this cumulation has made of her body; and what it has made of her mind and of her heart and of her being. And how is this to be made so real to you who read of it, that it will stand and stay in you as the deepest and most iron anguish and guilt of your existence that you are what you are, and that she is what she is, and that you cannot for one moment exchange places with her, nor by any such hope make expiation for what she has suffered at your hands, and for what you have gained at hers: but only by consuming all that is in you into the never relaxed determination that this shall be made different and shall be made right, and that of what is "right" some, enough to die for, is clear already, and the vast darkness of the rest has still, and far more passionately and more skeptically than ever before, to be questioned into, defended, and learned toward. There is no way of taking the heart and the intelligence by the hair and of wresting it to its feet, and of making it look this terrific thing in the eyes: which are such gentle eyes: . . . and they are to be multiplied, not losing the knowledge that each is a single, unrepeatable, holy individual, by the two billion human creatures who are alive upon the planet today; of whom a few hundred thousands are drawn into complications of specialized anguish, but of whom the huge swarm and majority are made and acted upon as she is: and of all these individuals, contemplate, try to encompass, the one annihilating chord.[8]

Repetition is the ground of character and true narrative, and it is in our ways, and it is what sociology needs to settle in our daily living. But sociology is not obliged to know what it needs to know, and that is what is difficult in the narrative it undertakes. For it may forsake its task in generalities, failing to call upon the names of the things that are its poetic sources. Sociology enlightens us with talk of individualism, equality, progress, and environmental improvement. But character and place both have roots that hold against what scientific sociology has in store for us. Sociology lets self go free, without place, or past, or any injury of family. Yet these things return upon us. Sociology, to save itself, treats them as "problems."

Communicative sociology abides in the daily necessity of having every day to make of necessity a daily thing and not tomorrow's mother. We know this, and what we know of it is that it is repetition, the daily repetition of our lives, that is in our lives every day and in our talk and in all our senses, that is the conversable ground of sociology's way. For this reason communicative sociology hides its own name. It is neither outside nor above the holy places it seeks to enter. It has no commanding voice, for it shuns the prescriptions of method and the forced entries of science. Communicative sociology seeks therefore to persuade and to charm; yet not irresponsibly, for it is faithful to the poetry and prayers of mankind. Method presumes upon its own practice, and in this it is careless and indifferent toward the particulars that fall under its rule. Communicative sociology rejects the rudeness of method that lacks any respect for the community that suffers its practices. By the same token, it is not simply conservative; rather it imposes upon its actions and speech the obligation to bring our lives together.

Communicative sociology is beholden to its community. For the sociologist needs other men, just as men make a family out of their happiness and their sorrows and do not bear these alone. No man really seeks privilege and exception but as gifts to be shared in the celebration of family and community in remembering our victories and defeats, welcoming our arrivals, and mourning our departures. Such community is rarely granted to us and is not to be usurped by the privilege of science intolerant of the ways of welcome. Thus communicative sociology defends the community it chooses to inhabit as the place of its deeds. In this it solicits the community's own reminiscence and powers of repetition, which furnish the commonplaces of its reflection and self-appraisal. In this way communicative sociology is obliged to observe and to listen for the bottom nature of things, where they are not ruled by passivity but rather launched upon the resolution to bring life together in work, in speech, in faith, and in understanding. Such a sociology is therefore without any method of its own beyond this very celebration that counts upon the labors of others to bring together our thoughts and speech, to offer us a chance of love and understanding. Thus in making sense together we appeal to the world as flesh, as an omnipresence that is never the material of science, for it lacks distance and indifference from us:

> Many things then come out in the repeating that make a history of each one for any one who always listens to them. Many things come out of each one and as one listens to them listens to all the repeating in them, always this comes to be clear about them, the history of them of the bottom nature in them, the nature or natures mixed up in them to make the whole of them anyway it mixes up in them. Sometime then there will be a history of every one.
>
> When you come to feel the whole of anyone from the beginning to the ending, all the kind of repeating there is in them, the different ways at different times repeating comes out of them, all the kinds of things and mixtures in each one, anyone can see then by looking hard at any one living near them that a history of every one must be a long one. A history of any one must be a long one, slowly it comes out from them from their beginning to their ending, slowly you can see it in them the nature and the mixtures in them, slowly everything comes out from each one in the kind of repeating each one does in the different parts and kinds of living they have in them, slowly then the history of them comes out from them, slowly then any one who looks well at any one will have the history of the whole of that one. Slowly the history of each one comes out of each one. Sometime then there will be a history of every one. Mostly every history will be a long one. Slowly it comes out of each one, slowly any one who looks at them gets the history of each part of the living of any one in the history of the whole of each one that sometime there will be of every one.[9]

The physicalism of scientific observation and reflection, by which I mean the presumption of distance, seems to me to lead sociology into an imperialism of method and rationality that undermines the ritual wholeness of the daily particulars that constitute the fabric of individual integrity and communal endurance. Every individual and community stands to us as a monument of human possibility expressed in the faces, the hands, the music, the food, the dwellings, and the tools that men endure against the earth and the twistings of man's own arrangements. The cycle of these things is born in an expansion of hope and possibility that is gradually simplified toward death. It is the burden of communicative sociology and its imaginative power to cultivate this cycle, to follow its seasons, its shaping, and its bearings of life. Scientific sociology cannot be faithful to this task so long as it is the instrument of the willfulness within modern society to deny the cycle of life, to subvert its repetitions by externalizing them into mechanical organs of production and reproduction.

Sociology's pride lies in its method of scientific analysis and unification, the aim of which is to make of the world a thing of construction through and through. We should not accept without reflection the physics built into the very notion of reflection's distance. What is the distance between men? How should thinking stand outside greetings, comings, and goings? In short, is not everything *between* men; is not everything nurtured in the fold of their *presence?* Sociology's face is toward the world though it does not love the world in its nature, its houses, its food and furniture, its music and dance, its prayers and terrors. Sociology is outward-looking, for it seeks to reshape destinies in the mold of environment. It shrugs off the weight of birth and family, the connections of blood, and the inevitability of death, in favor of reform and revolution. Sociology is democratic and progressive. Its method is the future via men's souls. It espouses the contingencies of love in order to write freedom into the chances of birth, family, class, and neighborhood. Sociology is convinced that what is difficult in its task is corrigible through the efforts of education, science, and politics to reduce all human arrangements to matters of rule.

Communicative sociology needs time, for it deals with surfaces beneath which there lies the silent, wild being that is our lives made from the legacy of this body and family of ours and from the work of our senses and intellect where they have touched others and taken from them some kind of knowing that can never be refused and must always venture itself again. Such a sociology is governed by a profound respect for the particulars of place, time, and conduct from which men build their associations and the institutions of trust that sustain their communal lives. Its narrative keeps faith with this trust through a self-conscious artfulness, in knowing that things are not as they are in order to facilitate a superficial realism or to indulge in idle aestheticism. These are species of contemplative thought that fail to attach us to the awesome work of particular and local deeds that are the connections of social life. For true sociological narrative is not the empty iteration of how things are, apart from how it is we know them to be as they are. That is to say, true narrative is the soul's conversation with its senses through which we are engaged in where we live and live as we know we do. This is the real ground of sociological description and inquiry, and thus communicative sociology is irredeemably a folk art. To keep its word it requires of us a holy vigil.

The Holy Watch:
A Meditation
upon Method
in the
Human Sciences

Communicative sociology opens in the reversal of the look, in the seer who is seen in that moment of prayer that joins us despite our daily trespasses. For the trespass of hands and eyes, of warmth and rejection, is the bread of our lives together. Sociological distance is not an empty space between us: it is the reach for what we have in common through our mundane needs and their natural orders of commerce and ritual. To stand outside these ancestral bonds, as does the observer, is to risk home and loss of faith.

Sociology is the study of man. How strange! For how does man become an object of study? What are the motives for such a practice, and how does it coexist with the forms of daily life that come under the optic of sociological observation? What is the faith that supports the sociologist in his life? How does he live with the conscience of seeing men other than how they see themselves? To whom does he attribute the folly of difference: to the vanity of those whom he observes or to the vanity of the community of rational men that guides his own comparisons? Such questions are likely to be regarded as mere rhetorical flourishes, as disingenuous attempts to arouse interest

213

in the long-solved practicalities of sociological work. Worse still, they might restore apathy, inasmuch as the difficulty of sustaining the direction of the inquiry they raise convinces us of the strength of the old ways to which we inevitably return.

And yet there is something uncanny in the sociological vision. It is not to be entered into lightly, nor, once acquired, should it be allowed to harden so that the care for what we see is no longer embracing. We cannot assume that our ideological, political, professional, or aesthetic faith will always be lively to *the collective focus of seeing and being seen* that is the ground of social life. Indeed, our politics may harden the original openness through which our concern for others irrupted into our lives and determined us never again to live outside the mutual regard that shapes our joys, our sorrows, and our hopes for every human undertaking, whether it is the building of a bridge or the birth of a child. Sociological vision is in reality more a structure of care and concern than any literal vision. It is the care that orders the wild commerce of our daily talk, looking, helping, hurt, and anger. By the same token, it is the display of our shared lives, of our own growth, and of the place others have in our lives without which we should be diminished and lonely:

> It is becoming apparent that concern is a normal dimension of everybody, including scholars and that for scholars in particular it is the corrective to detachment, and prevents detachment from degenerating into indifference.... It seems obvious that concern has nothing directly to do with the content of knowledge, but that it establishes the human context into which the knowledge fits, and to that extent informs it. The language of concern is the language of myth, the total vision of the human situation, human destiny, human aspirations and fears.[1]

Sociological concern is not averse to scientific method. Indeed, much of what is called the scientific attitude turns out to be a moral attitude that most of us practice in our daily lives. For few men act without a certain detachment and objectivity, and most are unwilling to fly in the face of contradiction and failure. In this regard, the social sciences are no weaker than the physical sciences because the concern that infects them is not at all a subjective impulse but rather a general respect of natures and mutual regard that is a large part of our civic culture. No one will deny that even in the arts the direction has been toward detachment and objectivity properly understood as human concern.[2] Thus the tendency in the arts and literature is to shape subjective concern in the objective labor of a *craft*.[3] And this is a necessary direction, despite the ruin of things and language, so long as men refuse to alienate the labor of culture and its representative sensibility. Sociological concern is not the easy expression of political demands or of immediate social reforms. These may equally express the fall of sociological concern into indifference, that is to say, into a neglect of the integrity of sociological concern and individual care. For there is a tension of responsibility in genuine sociological concern. This is ingrained in our double commitment to the value of the individual and to the value of the society that enhances and yet unavoidably obstructs these values.

The communicative sociologist needs heart, ideas, and ideology. He needs faith in the tissue of human time and the weave of human place in which he is caught more subtly than any notion of community can convey. Conventionality is the pulse of his life, stretching back into times and over distances he no longer recollects, resisting the ravages of his method, recalcitrant to organization. Communicative sociology labors on behalf of an infinity of mankind bonded against everything that threatens, distorts, cripples, and injures the human family. The concerns of scientific sociology are irredeemably tied to the daily institutions of politics, ideology, and professional practice. For this reason the language of sociology is at times an orchestration of human love and at times a distortion or a characterization of average values that stylizes sociological concern without any surrender to the particulars of its practice. Today more than ever, sociology is bewitched by its own language, its imperious generalizations, its ambitions of control, its usurpation of relevance. Sociology seduces us because its subject, like the pool of Narcissus, reflects the shadow of man even in its least concerns, while at its best it rejoices the connoisseurs of humanity in their comfortable and learned distance from its everyday hopes and injuries.

In *Let Us Now Praise Famous Men* James Agee introduces us to one of the deepest meditations upon the nature of communicative sociology that I know, and I want now to follow the path that it opens for us. The immediate concern of Agee's work is a documentary study of three families engaged in tenant farming and picking cotton. However, from the very outset Agee is concerned to guard against the sentimental and ideological distortions of sociological concern that are so often invited by the topics of sociological investigation. At the same time, he is deeply conscious of the set of relationships, the fraternal bonds, he is about to weave between himself and his readers, between his concerned public and the subjects of his study—and,

most agonizingly of all, between himself and the families among whom
he lives and whose lives he observes, very possibly to their harm or
merely for the peculiar enjoyment of a chorus of humanitarian readers and do-gooders. Under the weight of these considerations Agee
turns at times to the eye of the camera but also for the same reasons
to the compassionate icon of crucified humanity. And this is the way
of communicative sociology.

The risk involved in sociological work is that it will service
ideologies far removed from the particulars of human purpose or
else be received as an art to service the vague humanitarian aesthetics
of its consumers, its lay readers and middle-class students. In the first
case, the ideological reception of sociological work hardly begins to
fathom the depths of human injury and comes far too soon to conclusions regarding the tissue of human connections and the viruses
of relation, contract, and organization. In the second, the aesthetic
perception of sociological work is disembodied from the intersensory
and ancestral connections of mankind, whose infinitude defies dis-
section into science or art to such an extent that any observation risks
obscenity and distortion. Moreover, the very aesthetic sensibility for
which such risks might be undertaken has an awesome public ability
to absorb injustice, beauty, rage, horror, and frivolity. Thus anyone
who is tempted to succeed in appealing to such a monster as the
public must ask himself what has become of his first wonder at the
lives of those human beings whose innocence of such "twistings" was
his opening to the mystery of collective life. There is a certain obscenity about watching any human being, standing outside his life
when really the only place to be is at his side, sharing the same life.
We cannot all do the same work. We are born at different times and
under different circumstances. Yet the basic human desire to be in
roughly the same condition and way of life has over time been built
up in the institutions of the law and the church, of the Enlightenment,
and of the liberal and social democratic philosophies of equality, to
an extent that even when we find ourselves in the most different
circumstances we nevertheless feel that we share or are working toward a common humanity. There are a variety of ways of reinforcing
this bond with our fellow man. We can do it by simply sending money
to the African missions. We may join a left-wing or right-wing party
or become urban planners. All these activities are motivated by the
assumption that we know what others need, want, and are all about.
Yet in working on a common project or trying to produce a common
humanity, we find ourselves engaged in different ways of life. We are
as much cut off from one another through the division of labor in-

volved in working together as we are brought together. We find ourselves living possibly more intense but certainly more and more narrow lives. It thus becomes all the more important to establish ideological, political, and moral bonds with our fellow man.

Sociology contributes to the cement of these relations. Indeed, it is part of a whole range of urban man's vicarious experience. The more we separate from rural settings and move into industrial settings, the more we recreate the rural as nostalgia, in folk song and folk art. Thus we are conscious that there are people out there on the farms, or down in the slums, or out in the colonies. And we persuade ourselves that we are not entirely cut off from these people because we read newspapers, watch television reports, and drink orange juice or coffee to keep them in jobs. Or else we rationalize our charitable sentiments in the hope that our money will find its way into every crack and cranny of needful society. When we listen to folk and country music, when we pick up a book about the Cuban revolution, or when we read about the mill hands in the nineteenth century, what makes this a reasonable thing to do is not just that we happen to be music fans or students of revolution or of economic history but that we believe there is a common humanity that is made over, preserved, and advanced through just such activities, through our concern with other ways of life and their bearing upon our own living.

Such humanitarian concerns would be impossible if we were to hold on to solipsistic conceptions of mind or if we were to separate the mind and the heart in our understanding of sociological care. The care and concern that establish our social life are *institutions* of sentiment and science that are manifested as much in schoolchildren's donating gifts to the missions as in reading the pre-Socratic philosophers or manipulating Keynesian variables to stabilize the modern economy. Sociological work belongs to this pattern of civilized sentiment and knowledge. Nevertheless, we encounter a paradox of sociological concern, namely, that its own activity adds to the differences among men another alienation that is simultaneously the basis for its search for communality and care. This is not the simple observation that reflection presupposes leisure and is therefore ultimately tied to social exploitation. It is the existential predicament of the thinker, the artist, the priest, and the visionary that their otherworldliness is strange to the only world for which they have any care. They therefore have to instruct the world in the very things they have learned from the world. But if sociologists are at all successful in this, they acquire a style of life and appeal to an audience whose way of life in turn aggravates the injury and injustice suffered by our common humanity. Yet there is no escape from this commonplace. It is the bread of our fellow men and we cannot refuse it. The questions we raise about the reasons for sociological concern, about its rights and its motives, must be shared in the common talk of the sociologist or the artist and his public. Ultimately, these are questions of mutual trust to which we must lend ourselves as the sole means of discovering our own motives as well as the public response to them.

Agee asked himself whether his own sociological report was anything more than the expression of the impotency he experienced when he went out to help some people whose lives he found much richer, much more mysterious, than his own, but whom he had supposed in some way to be simpler, more comprehensible, more subject to alteration, and thus to justify the reasons he had assumed to be his purpose as a writer or social reformer. Thus he is concerned with the possibilities of obscenity, voyeurism, and betrayal as the real motives of sociological work. If this is at all true, then he fears he himself is more misshapen than the people among whom he moves, "all thus left open and defenseless to a reverent and cold-laboring spy." A good part of what we call social science is the study of individuals who are miserable enough to be the object of sociological inquiry. The wealthy, for the most part, escape sociological investigation, or when they fail to, the reason is evidently the alien designs of Marxists and muck-rakers. They are generally allowed to pass through life altogether before any inquiry is made about their way of life. Or else they are kind enough to leave us memoirs. But the poor and primitive do not write memoirs. Their lives have to be documented; therefore, their lives are the subject of ethnographies, questionnaires, and films. Thus the practice of sociology is entirely dependent upon the different forms of access to other individuals' lives, at the same time that sociology pretends to be a remedy for such inequality.

But communicative sociology is not merely a fascination with the lives of others. It is a kind of *vigil* we maintain as much in our talk and shared experience as in the look and watchful concern for our neighbors and their children. The vigilance I have in mind is not simply watching lest certain things happen. It is the vigil in which things are encouraged in their form, in which, so to speak, things and the people around us seem to grow in us and we in them. Such vigilance is not easily assumed, and it is for this reason that we see Agee's struggling with the scruples of cameralike realism or else with the image of the Cross in his search for a redemptive mediation of the holy particulars of human life:

For one who sets himself to look at all earnestly, at all in purpose
toward truth, into the living eyes of a human life: what is it he
there beholds that so freezes and abashes his ambitious heart? What
is it, profound behind the outward windows of each one of you,
beneath touch even of your own suspecting, drawing tightly back at
bay against the backward wall and blackness of its prison cave, so
that the eyes alone shine of their own angry glory, but the eyes of a
trapped wild animal, or of a furious angel nailed to the ground by
his wings, or however else one may faintly designate the human
"soul," that which is angry, that which is wild, that which is
untamable, that which is healthful and holy, that which is competent
of all advantaging within hope of human dream, that which most
marvelous and most precious to our knowledge and most extremely
advanced upon futurity of all flowerings within the scope of
creation is of all these the least destructible, the least corruptible,
the most defenseless, the most easily and multitudinously wounded,
frustrated, prisoned, and nailed into a cheating of itself; so situated
in the universe that those three hours upon the cross are but a
noble and too trivial an emblem how in each individual among most
of the two billion now alive and in each successive instant of the
existence of each existence not only human being but in him the
tallest and most sanguine hope of godhead is in a billionate choiring
and drone of pain of generations upon generations unceasingly
crucified and is bringing forth crucifixions into their necessities and
is each in the most casual of his life so measurelessly discredited,
harmed, insulted, poisoned, cheated, as not all the wrath,
compassion, intelligence, power of rectification in all the reach of
the future shall in the least expiate or make one ounce more light:
how, looking thus into your eyes and seeing thus, how each of you
is a creature which has never in all time existed before and which
shall never in all time exist again and which is not quite like any
other and which has the grand stature and natural warmth of every
other and whose existence is all measured upon a still mad and
incurable time; how am I to speak of you as "tenant" "farmers," as
"representatives" of your "class," as social integers in a criminal
economy, or as individuals, fathers, wives, sons, daughters, and as
my friends and as I "know" you? Granted—more, insisted upon—
that it is in all these particularities that each of you is that which he
is; that particularities, and matters ordinary and obvious, are exactly
themselves beyond designation of words, are the members of your
sum total most obligatory to human searching of perception:
nevertheless to name these things and fail to yield their stature,
meaning, power of hurt, seems impious, seems criminal, seems
impudent, seems traitorous in the deepest: and to do less badly

seems impossible: yet in withholdings of specification I could but
betray you still worse.[4]

Sociological vigilance is the care of things in their wholeness
and integrity. It is neither an averaging nor an irony. It is a way of
seeing things round, of celebrating time and place and the endurance
of their human bonds. The saving of particulars and the frail connections of the human family is work that rests upon a variety of
faiths. It may be the work of the ideologist, the political reformer, the
social planner. But these perspectives easily lose sight of the particulars of ordinary life. It is for this reason that the images of the
camera and of the Crucifixion are the instruments of Agee's concern
with the epiphany of human events. The problem is how to see the
eye seeing and not the recorded eye: how to see the eye and how to
listen to what we hear in the sounding of human care. This comes
from our openness to the belonging together of our senses and the
community of being that is the possibility we have of learning togetherness and watchfulness. There is an obvious sense in which we may
be counted among the community of mankind. But our humanity is
properly our orientation to the community of being as our destiny or
allotment. This community, our nature, approaches us in the involvements of care, not as a lacking but as a presencing of our situation.

Care, then, is the domicile of our being together.[5] But our
being together is easily subject to sociological rule. The division of
labor and technology that subordinates human identity and difference to the confrontation of man and nature represents the reduction
of care to need and domination. Thus, despite the intricate calcula-
tions and exchanges involved in sociological rule, it proceeds by chal-
lenging the framework or *institution* of human concern and solicitude
for our corporate membership.

Agee remarks, as we have already seen, that he is writing about
human beings who are not in any way concerned with the problems
of the artist, or the musician, or even the priest or social worker. The
problems of writers, artists, priests, and sociologists are entirely alien
to the concerns of the people. Those who have such concerns are
strange beings. They are monsters of concern. They want to do good,
they want to save, they want to express, they want to celebrate. They
experience themselves as above or outside the lives of those for whom
they care. Their efforts are infected with a kind of superfluity, with
doubts concerning truth and reality that have no counterpart in the
lives of those for whom they intend help. And further, if the sociologist or artist is at all successful in resolving his problem of concern

and alienation, his work will be taken up by others in the reading public whose lives make their concern with it a matter of good taste, education, liberal consciousness, Christian concern, so that the writer's work becomes a double alienation of the original suffering and beauty or whatever it was he saw in the lives of his fellow men.

These problems surround Agee's approach to the subjects of his study. The Mass is the canopy of the approach, entrance, worship, and return to the world celebrated through its own offerings of the fruits of its labors. The Mass is therefore the natural framework of Agee's report. Nor is this a mere literary device. It is the resonance of the *Introibo*, which is the approach to the holy interior of another life with whom we communicate through the efficacy of the Crucifixion. We are not, of course, dealing here with matters of religious certainty. What is at stake is the openness of human life to the approach of the other whose need is irresistible, even though its intent or consequences may lie far beyond our understanding. The approach makes us aware that human life is huddled about its own purposes, in its belongings, families, farms, towns, and villages. To enter a town or to approach people is to encroach upon their welcome, to seek a kindness whose offer must bridge the first strangeness, the searching eyes, and the beginnings of talk that make the human bond.

Agee relates three encounters in which he approaches first a group of blacks enjoying themselves, a white family, and then a young black couple out walking. In the first instance, Agee and Walker Evans are introduced to a Sunday morning family gathering of visitors and children all obliged to assemble and sing for the landlord's intruders. Agee is agonized by the privilege that forces an intrusion into the lives of these people who nevertheless maintain an inner calm and dignity despite the injury they feel at having to treat what is of absorbing concern to them as something that must give pride of place to the curiosity and indulgence of others:

> Meanwhile, and during all this singing, I had been sick in the knowledge that they felt they were here at our demand, mine and Walker's, and I could communicate nothing otherwise; and now, in a perversion of self-torture, I played my part through. I gave their leader fifty cents, trying at the same time, through my eyes, to communicate much more, and said I was sorry we had held them up and that I hoped they would not be late; and he thanked me for them in a dead voice, not looking me in the eye, and they went away, putting their white hats on their heads as they walked into the sunlight.[6]

On another occasion Agee and Evans come to a fork in the road where Agee asks directions from a family sitting on their porch: a young man, a young woman, their children, and an older man. The family is silent, all the while watching the approach of the two strangers. But it is not an empty silence that hangs between them. Agee and Evans are already caught in the conversation of eyes that sustains and marks their approach. Already much has been said within the silently knit family, drawn together by the daily necessity of preservation against the invasions of injustice, cruelty, and misunderstanding, and the chance relief of these in good times and by occasional kindnesses:

> None of them relieved me for an instant of their eyes; at the intersection of those three tones of force I was transfixed as between spearheads as I talked. As I asked my questions, and told my purposes, and what I was looking for, it seemed to me they relaxed a little toward me, and at length a good deal more, almost as if into trust and liking; yet even at its best this remained so suspended, so conditional, that in any save the most hopeful and rationalized sense it was non-existent. The qualities of their eyes did not in the least alter, nor anything visible or audible about them, and their speaking was as if I was almost certainly a spy sent to betray them through trust, whom they would show they had neither trust nor fear of.[7]

Thus a passing inquiry may smell of danger and is not to be lightly made of local people whose security rests in a natural knowledge of place and for whom the stranger opens the huge ambivalence toward him of fear and help. This is a visceral exchange. As the stranger approaches he is able to see more of the people on whom he imposes and they in turn read from his dress and bearing something of his intentions toward them. Between them there mounts the necessity of exchange long before any word is spoken. To tell all this would take too long. Thus Agee chooses to resolve the statement of their mutual relations and his relation to them through presenting them as statuesque figures, as though monumental in their sorrow and in their silence, molded by the pain of their labor, by the sparseness of their language, and above all in the way they stand over against the little part of the world and of human experience that belongs to them.

The third encounter that I want to describe arises out of Agee and Evans' coming upon a closed church that they want to enter. Again, the interest of this encounter is that it symbolizes the mystery of integrity and approach that throws back upon its spectator the look by which he seeks to inspect the secrets of persons and things:

It was a good enough church from the moment the curve opened and we saw it that I slowed a little and we kept our eyes on it. But as we came even with it the light so held it that it shocked us with its goodness straight through the body, so that at the same instant we said *Jesus*. I put on the brakes and backed the car slowly, watching the light on the building, until we were at the same apex, and we sat still for a couple of minutes at least before getting out, studying in arrest what had hit us so hard as we slowed past its perpendicular.

It lost nothing at all in stasis, but even more powerfully strove in through the eyes its paralyzing classicism: stood from scoured clay, a light lift above us, no trees near, and few weeds; every grain each nailhead, distinct; the subtle almost strangling strong asymmetries of that which had been hand wrought toward symmetry (as if it were an earnest description, better than the intended object): so intensely sprung against so scarcely eccentric a balance that my hands of themselves spread out their bones, trying to regiment on air between their strengths its tensions and their mutual structures as they stood subject to the only scarcely eccentric, almost annihilating stress, of the serene, wild, rigorous light: empty, shut, bolted, of all that was withdrawn from it upon the fields the utter statement, God's mask and wooden skull and home stood empty in the mediation of the sun: and this light upon it was strengthening still further its imposal and embrace, and in about a quarter of an hour would have trained itself ready, and there would be a triple convergence in the keen historic spasm of the shutter.[8]

The sociological eye is caught in that which it sees because it is beholden to the community of the body's senses and its labors that stand out against time and the sky as the monuments of mankind. Thus every perception of ours belongs to the labor of man, fashioning himself and the legacy he leaves in his children. The church that stands against the sky is a symbol of the body's architecture and the shaping elements in the lives of the community that built it. The eyes that follow the contours of the church and upon entering take inventory of its furnishings cast the visitor's whole body into a reverent and mindful posture and thereby join him to the community in which he is at first a visitor or stranger. This is an experience that is repeated whenever we regard things with sociological concern: the disintegration or harmony we sense around us enters into us and determines our mood and purpose in the community. Thus the community shapes sociological concern at least as much as it is in turn molded by the ambitions of sociology. But we are forgetful of this in method, while proclaiming our factualism of realism. The truth is, however, that every object, like the church or the families encountered by Agee, is never a mere surface any more than the eye is the naked instrument of vision. We are caught in what we see and what we feel, and the path to the things and persons around us is paved with the story of our own lives, without which there would be no bridges in the moment.

The communicative sociologist is obsessed with trespass; for this is his access to the lives of others. In their third encounter Agee and Evans, still trying to break into the closed church, notice a young black couple walking by. They decide to ask them whether the minister can be found to let them in. Since the young couple are fifty yards or so ahead, Agee follows after them, his eyes taking advantage of their beautiful and buoyant bodies in a way that at a closer distance would be improper. For a brief moment, Agee is filled with the vision of the young woman, her young man—the sway of their bodies, the way they are together—yet afraid all the time that his presence will startle them. Worse, still, Agee is agonized lest his admiration be read as malicious intent through the young couple's misunderstanding of why he is coming up behind them. Suddenly, they startle, he calls after them, and they set off in a frightened run, more terrified as Agee in great anguish runs after them to plead that he meant no harm. The whole incident is a passing one, and yet it is central to the consideration of the nature of trust implicit in the intrusions of social life. Every day we must penetrate the lives of others, interrupting their thoughts, or getting them to pause on their way or to set aside their work for a moment. We do this from a thousand needs and not because we presume upon their help or mean to encroach upon others without consideration for them. For these reasons we need to trust to the rituals of approach even where, as sometimes happens, they do not quite succeed. At such times, I think we have to rely upon one another's experience to mend things. Agee fails to allow for this deeper trust in the young couple, perhaps a while later, to recover themselves and decide he meant them no harm. Thus, although he has the highest respect for the dignity of those whom he intrudes upon, Agee on this occasion in some sense denies them the judgment that experience brings in handling the inevitable misunderstandings that arise in human encounters. If Agee sins at all against the couple, it is because he does not allow for forgiveness from them. He insists upon being the greater victim of the misunderstanding, whereas the young couple, despite all the times they have been chased and beaten, might on this occasion have realized they had been startled and that it was their fear that set the other man after them because of his own anxiety not to be thought ill of by them. In short, there are some human encounters that can never be brought to account even though they are remembered by us and shape our conscience.

Communicative sociology is not a solo effort. One might even say that it is not especially an affair of the heart, however it may seem to involve the emotions. Indeed, it is precisely because of the emotions involved that wild sociology is not properly alive in us unless it begins in the deepest trust toward others to understand and reciprocate the care we intend. Sociological care is not paternalism. It does not righteously diminish the responsible growth and variety of opinion that it will surely meet. It is not parasitic. Yet it is nurtured only in belonging to others. It seeks community without wanting to dominate the community. Sociological care is mutual; it remains active only in giving and being given life. Sociological care is not simpering. It is not exercised from empty need, or from loneliness. It is a musical response, a dance. Sociological care is not burdened. It does not work from obligation, nor from guilt or any self-abasement. Communicative sociology sings the world. Yet it always has a particular task, a local need, a definite work to do, not wasted in vain generality or empty intentions. Communicative sociology never ceases to learn from what it believes it knows.

Communicative sociology shoulders a common task. For this it is beholden to the world of everyday use, of custom, of trust, of invention, of hope and memory, and of the countless and immemorial repetitions of the human family, which has tilled and irrigated the fields, sailed seas, built towns and villages and cities; which has woven wool and cloth, carved wood and stone, written books, made music and song and dance, and all in so fine a tapestry that none of us can ever find the first thread. Communicative sociology faces the seamless web of human activity in need of its own place and without any magisterial claim upon men's time. By contrast, scientific sociology is impatient for success. It seeks identity through domination. Thus it is tempted to usurp the unfinished task of community as the proper work of sociology, to manage it and divide it into the spoils of science. For this reason method and role are the idols of sociology's usurpation. They make of work an assured thing and of persons a transparent collective. In this way much is lost in favor of saving the possibility of sociology.

Sociology, as I see it, assumes the secularization of the redemptive tasks of humanity given in our care for one another, in our talk and listening, in the exchange of our labors. We have nothing that cannot be taken from us; everything we give must be received. We cannot live without welcome. This is the work of our frail divinity, which belongs neither to science nor to religion. It rests in the eye of God, which is the eye of love and the light of a compassionate world. Thus the family is the shelter of our concern and deserves more than anything the care of sociology. To accomplish this, sociology has to set aside its noisy individualism and daytime ambitions, just as the family itself must gather into itself everything that separates and isolates it upon this earth.

This family must take care of itself; it has no mother or father: there is no other shelter, nor resource, nor any love, interest, sustaining strength or comfort, so near, nor can anything happy or sorrowful that comes to anyone in this family possibly mean to those outside it what it means to those within it: but it is, as I have told, inconceivably lonely, drawn upon itself as tramps are drawn round a fire in the cruelest weather; and thus and in such loneliness it exists among other families, each of which is no less lonely, nor any less without help or comfort, and is likewise drawn in upon itself:

Such a family lasts, for a while: the children are held to a magnetic center:

Then in time the magnetism weakens, both of itself in its tiredness of aging and sorrow, and against the strength of the growth of each child, and against the strength of pulls from outside, and one by one the children are drawn away:

Of those that are drawn away, each is drawn elsewhere toward another: once more a man and a woman, in a loneliness they are not liable at that time to notice, are tightened together upon a bed: and another family has begun:

Moreover, these flexions are taking place every where, like a simultaneous motion of all the waves of the water of the world: and these are the classic patterns, and this is the weaving, of human living: of whose fabric each individual is a part: and of all parts of this fabric let this be borne in mind:

Each is intimately connected with the bottom and the extremest reach of time:

Each is composed of substance identical with the substance of all that surrounds him, both the common objects of his disregard, and the hot centers of stars:

All that each person is, and experiences, and shall never experience, in body and in mind, all these things are differing expressions of himself and of one root, and are identical: and not one of these things nor one of these persons is ever quite to be duplicated, nor replaced, nor has it ever quite had precedent; but each is a new and incommunicably tender life, wounded in every breath, and almost as hardly killed as easily wounded: sustaining, for a while, without defense, the enormous assaults of the universe:

So that how it can be that a stone, a plant, a star, can take on the burden of being; and how it is that a child can take on the burden of breathing; and how through so long a continuation and cumulation of the burden of each moment one on another, does any creature bear to exist, and not break utterly to fragments of nothing: these are matters too dreadful and fortitudes too gigantic to meditate long and not forever to worship.[9]

Like all creative thought, sociological thinking needs the rhythm of night and day. This is because the communicative sociologist is caught in the everyday involvements of his fellow men, using them without thought, presuming upon their mixed kindness, cruelty, and indifference. Every day he is witness to the differences of wealth, strength, intelligence, compassion, and beauty that mark the parade of his fellow men, shaping their homes, their children and the news they have of one another. The communicative sociologist breathes these differences, making them into the pulse and rhythm of his own life and family. At the same time, he longs for the unity and embrace of mankind, for the sheltering care that harbors the particulars, faults, and injuries of human life. For this reason the night thoughts of the sociologist swarm around the windows of the little houses men have set like stars in the earth.

Every thought of ours seeks shelter from the journey it begins and in its course remembers how life began well, enclosed and protected in the embrace of home. All our adventures, imaginations, and dreams are nurtured in the bosom of home, and however far they lead us they remain in the circle of the homeward return. And somehow every observation of ours bears this same caress and is not an aimless looking nor an empty stare. We see things and others in the shaping circle of our intrusion and embrace; the weight of bodies, the paper on the walls, the lamps and chairs, the sounds of mealtimes, are never bare particulars but warm animal signs that attract us even though we stand off because they are not our home but half remind us. Thus in his heart the communicative sociologist pays the price of knowledge in the truancy of childhood memories and moves among men in search of his right home and his true family, to which he has no title but the price of love and sorrow.

Concluding Sociological Prayer

How should sociology keep its place? After all, sociology is powerful, men are in need of it, and the world is increasingly the instrument of organization. Why should anything keep its place; what, after all, is *place* in a world that is "going places"? We are now so accustomed to change and growth that we scarcely stop to consider the sources that feed the stream of our life. Indeed, the modern world gives us our lives in such comfortable surroundings that the question of self and its circumstance is likely to remain a residual anxiety, aggravated perhaps by our political responsibility toward those on the margins of modern ease. Surely, sociology is a permanent institution. We have built it up beyond anything that need remind it of its poverty. Where sociology holds the mirror to nature how should it see itself?

The commonplace nature of communicative sociology will not be easily understood. Thus many will read what I am saying and not find in it anything like sociology. My concerns will seem to answer to no concrete sense of the conduct of professional sociology. The lack here does not lie in what I fail to say of that sort but in the reader's lack of any need to inspect what authorizes his or her own concrete version of sociology as something to be found or to be missed in his reading. Sociology is not a literal fact to be discovered apart from the circumstance of its approach or the way we are alerted to what we have to reckon with in looking for sociology. The task is to find our sociological bearings. This is not a problem of method. It is a question of concentrating upon sociology the salvation of self and circumstances as a connection of love as well as of knowledge.

We sense who we are and where we are mostly as a result of local habit. Let us say we are sociologists; let them say we are philosophers. The philosophers will only smile. It is enough, in any case, that we have found a path along which we can think. For we must know where we are at home if ever we are to be able to look elsewhere. We cannot distinguish other ways or see other places unless we know our own. We must bear in ourselves the tension between our own spot and the places that are distant and strange. In this, our knowledge of good and evil is like the difference between home and away, between where we can be ourselves and where we cannot abide or dwell:

> Anything is one of a million paths [*un camino entre cantidades de caminos*]. Therefore you must always keep in mind that a path is only a path; if you feel you should not follow it, you must not stay with it under any conditions. To have such clarity you must lead a disciplined life. Only then will you know that any path is only a path, and there is no affront, to oneself or to others, in dropping it if that is what your heart tells you to do. But your decision to keep on the path or to leave it must be free of fear or ambition. I warn you. Look at every path closely and deliberately. Try it as many times as you think necessary. Then ask yourself, and yourself alone, one question. This question is one that only a very old man asks. My benefactor told me about it once when I was young, and my blood was too vigorous for me to understand it. Now I do understand it. I will tell you what it is: Does this path have a heart? All paths are the same: they lead nowhere. They are paths going through the bush, or into the bush. In my own life I could say I have traversed long, long paths, but I am not anywhere. My benefactor's question has meaning now. Does this path have a heart? If it does, the path is good; if it doesn't, it is of no use. Both paths lead nowhere; but one has a heart, the other doesn't. One makes for a joyful journey; as long as you follow it, you are one with it. The other will make you curse your life. One makes you strong; the other weakens you.[1]

Circumstance, reason, and love, joined in bringing each of the particulars of our lives to their communal and historical fullness, accomplish the salvation of sociology. Yet in making sociology an extension of our love of circumstance we do not mean that it may not be nourished on a rough and harsh ground. For there is no love that does not till the ground of circumstance. Thus circumstantial love is not moved by things to our own perfection but is rather a love toward the perfecting of things and others that saves our first need of them in their universal connection and plentitude. It is a love to be found as much in our own gatherings as in the gatherings of things, and in both of these what are saved are the opening and light of the world in which we are reflected and multiplied like Adam in Paradise, or any man anywhere beholden to the life around him. Circumstantial love is the perfection of common need and its uses. This is not a matter of proving oneself but of belonging and beginning again, which is the commonplace of daily living. This ancestral place does not yield to those who hunt it; it does not lie in achievement or status. The commonplace is approached only in the widening circle of care. In his doctrine of the commonplaces Aristotle treats dialectic and rhetoric as separable modes of intellectual and moral persuasion.[2] But such a separation is precisely what made sophistic dialect the intellectual pride and danger of Greek political life. For dialectic may persuade at the expense of the moral community to which it appeals, thereby undermining the true place of rhetoric. For these reasons Isocrates sought to make rhetoric service the ideals of *paideia,* that is, to correct the alternatives of intellectual arrogance and Platonic spiritualism with the commonplaces of community and nation.[3] In this manner Isocrates understood that rhetoric's own seat is its place within the life of the community whose discourse it strengthens in order, in turn, to draw upon it for its own special eloquence. Thus the commonplaces of rhetoric strengthen the communal art of memory and the associations of civic knowledge. For rhetorical style is the embellishment of the way of life that it reinforces and not simply a matter either of the speaker's character or of his topic.

Thus, to address sociology is not to deal in the personifications of a backward art. It is simply to suit our speech to its topic, which is the place of our communal life. What we seek to diminish or to embellish in the practice of sociology is addressed in terms of extreme alternatives in order to gather its tensions. For our aim is not the victory of a virtuous sociology any more than it is the avoidance of temptations in the ordinary practice and institutions of sociology.

It may be asked, then, whether a sociology of the commonplace can be radical. I shall answer that in the face of the bureaucratic and corporate rationality of the professional sciences nothing can be more radical than a sociology inspired by the love of human circumstance and its great conventions. Communicative sociology rejects the ambition of the professional social sciences to assimilate themselves to the structure of domination that teaches the oppressed to see themselves through the eyes of their oppressors, to sift the oppressor's language for some word the people can understand, to accept as charity the return of their own gifts. This is not to deny that the social sciences may intend help, justice, and betterment. But these expectations have been promoted long enough now to leave the poor cynical toward those whose own lives are all that has benefited from our subscription to the social sciences. The danger in this is that practitioners of the sciences will find the lay community ignorant of the complexity of reform and thus rationalize lay hostility toward its practice even where the people's anger is reasonably grounded in the experience of disappointment and failure. For social reformers prefer to judge themselves by their own intentions rather than by the results of the institutions they bequeath to the poor.

Communicative sociology encourages a way of looking at things and saying things that matures with its own practice. It presumes upon no hierarchy of men; it does not command the first word, nor does it insist upon the last word. It is found in a dialogue that is entirely rooted in the aspirations of human development and political community. Such a sociology cannot thrive where some have the right to speak and others only the obligation to listen. For in such a situation no one truly speaks and no one truly listens:

> Human existence cannot be silent, nor can it be nourished by false words, but only by true words, with which men transform it. Once named, the world in turn reappears to the namers as a problem and requires of them a new *naming*. Men are not built in silence, but in word, in work, in action-reflection.[4]

Without community, sociology has no duty to listen for itself, to seek address, and to respond to those whose listening addresses their own self-inquiry and mutual need. True dialogue makes men and it is only men who are partners to dialogue. But such speech is impossible where there is no love of man and of the world he is called to think and say. Nor is this a sentimental love, for it is the bond of freedom and humanity against injustice, darkness, and oppression. Such a love therefore must know its enemies as well as its own weaknesses in order to fight oppression.

Communicative sociology will encourage radicalism. Yet it will be hard on its own radicalism, suspecting further evils from its own activity should it presume upon its relation to the lay community. It may well be that the daily practice of sociology encourages arrogance among its members, undermining the very resources of humanism with a numb professionalism or the shrill cry of ideology. If this is not to happen our sociology must make a place for itself, and to accomplish this it must engage hope and utopia. Hope is the time it takes to make the place in which men think and talk and work together. Thus communicative sociology is essentially engaged in the education of the oppressed.

Sociology is nothing apart from its attachment to the world. It is for this reason that communicative sociology must be mindful of its own spectacle. It cannot stand outside the collective focus of seeing and being seen that is the natural light of man. In this light the world is our circumstance, the surround of things and others, the time they take, the places they inhabit, so that we are obliged to know their ways by living among them, shaping our own lives, our talk, and all our senses to their community. The task of communicative sociology is not to organize the world for sociology. Communicative sociology gathers only out and about in the world, in the epiphany of city, family, work, path, way, manner, face, child. It is a craft with nothing in hand but its own willingness to become a shape of community, a house of being.

Society is the great body of sociology. In this body the sociological eye is not the eye of the scientific observer but the eye of human divinity, the mystery of the care in the human look, its holy watch. Prior to synthesis or analysis the sociologist's look dwells upon the particularity and universality of each human being: of his moods, his places, and his works. This indwelling is a connection of the eye, the ear, the heart, and the mind of the sociologist in the great body of mankind that heals its own wounds in the strength of its time. The vision of communicative sociology is a celebration, a responsibility, and a humble task no greater than a mother's care for her children and no more than a father's labor, and it is entirely unredeemed if it fails them in their patience, in their hope, and in their endurance. Its vision is beholden to its sense of mystery, its anger, its thirst for justice. In this, communicative sociology is ambivalently suspended between self-purification and social reform, between revolution and unending predicament, between betrayal and forgiveness. For sociology is bewitched by a power of order, by the hope of some plan or design in which the lives of men and women will not seem fleeting occasions of the failure of humanity. And this expectation arises above all from the warm presence of human beings, from their ideas, hopes, and fears, which admit the sociologist without the cover of strangeness and alienation, however much these seize upon him in his watchful hours.

The communicative sociologist means to keep faith with the great commonplaces of human life, birth, marriage, work, and death, and to be faithful to what is strange and varied, brave and defeated, in them. He must therefore learn to understand his own curiosity and not place it above its proper human concerns. For in the great body of mankind, in all its times and places, in all its beliefs and visions, the sociologist's own activity risks monstrosity in its pretended freedom and in its rootless possibility. Sociology is the poorest of the sciences, because it is not always sure of its own work and is thus tempted by other enterprises as models of power and accumulation. These possibilities consume much of the energy of sociology in the effort to force its bread in the unseasonable factories of method. The way of ordinary men is infinitely more patient; it is repeated upon their lives in countless labors, monumental in the movement of fingers, eyes, and hands; in bending, lifting, folding, sowing, and cutting; in hauling, shipping, mining, flying, weaving, and baking; in watching, digging, planting, selling, and buying; in eating, drinking, sleeping, and living; in reading, writing, praying, and singing; in burying, marrying, mothering, and learning. And each of these is so finely wrought upon the bodies of men and women and of their children and families—in their homes, fields, factories, schools, and churches; in their markets, streets, and parks—that they are all so much music to the shaping circle of our being, our joy, and our sorrow, all in their endless epiphany.

It is in the midst of these things that are the world's blessing and instrument that we assume the parochial cares of sociology. For the concern of communicative sociology is not just the encouragement of order in others but the very shape of our own life. It is for this reason that the commonplaces of social life are the occasions of our thanksgiving.

Notes

Part 1: Preface

[1]John O'Neill, "The Disciplinary Society: From Weber to Foucault," *The British Journal of Sociology* 37, no. 1 (March 1986): 42–60.

[2]Maurice Merleau-Ponty, *Phenomenology of Perception,* trans. Colin Smith (London: Routledge and Kegan Paul, 1962), 355.

[3]John O'Neill, *Five Bodies: The Human Shape of Modern Society* (Ithaca, N.Y.: Cornell University Press, 1985).

Chapter 1

[1]Maurice Merleau-Ponty, *Phenomenology of Perception,* trans. Colin Smith (London: Routledge and Kegan Paul, 1962), 179.

[2]Ibid., 180.

[3]Ibid., 182.

[4]Ibid., 171.

[5]Ibid., 187.

[6]Ibid., 197.

[7]For an excellent analysis of the issues here see Calvin O. Schrag, *Communicative Praxis and the Space of Subjectivity* (Bloomington: Indiana University Press, 1986).

[8]Jacques Derrida, *Speech and Phenomena,* trans. David B. Allison and Newton Garver (Evanston, Ill.: Northwestern University Press, 1973).

[9]See Schrag, *Communicative Praxis,* passim.

[10]Merleau-Ponty, *Phenomenology of Perception,* 229.

[11]Ibid., 236–37.

[12]Ibid., 297–98.

[13]Ibid., 235; Alphonso Lingis, "Intentionality and Corporeity," vol. 1 of *Annalecta Husserliana,* ed. Anna-Teresa Tymienecka (Dordrecht: D. Reidel Publishing Company, 1970), 75–90.

[14]Merleau-Ponty, *Phenomenology of Perception,* 157–58.

[15]Ibid., 163–64.

[16]Ibid., 166.

[17]Ibid., 91.

¹⁸Ibid., 92.

¹⁹Ibid., 58–59.

²⁰Ibid., 96.

²¹Maurice Merleau-Ponty, *The Visible and the Invisible, Followed by Working Notes*, ed. Claude Lefort, trans. Alphonso Lingis (Evanston, Ill.: Northwestern University Press, 1968), 179.

²²Ibid., 130.

Chapter 2

¹Maurice Merleau-Ponty, *Phenomenology of Perception*, trans. Colin Smith (London: Routledge and Kegan Paul, 1962), 63.

²Ibid., 212, my insertion in brackets.

³Maurice Merleau-Ponty, *The Visible and the Invisible, Followed by Working Notes*, ed. Claude LeFort, trans. Alphonso Lingis (Evanston, Ill.: Northwestern University Press, 1968), 131.

⁴Part Two, passim.

⁵Merleau-Ponty, *The Visible and the Invisible*, vol. 6, 144.

⁶Ibid., 213.

⁷Ibid., 259.

⁸Ibid., 267.

⁹See Chapters 7 and 8.

¹⁰James Schmidt, *Maurice Merleau-Ponty: Between Phenomenology and Structuralism* (London: Macmillan, 1985).

¹¹Merleau-Ponty, *The Visible and the Invisible*, 266.

¹²See Chapters 7 and 8; John O'Neill, "The Mother-Tongue: The Infant Search for Meaning," *University of Ottawa Quarterly* 55, no. 4 (October/December 1985): 59–71.

Chapter 3

¹Maurice Merleau-Ponty, *Phenomenology of Perception*, trans. Colin Smith (London: Routledge and Kegan Paul, 1962), 428.

²Ibid., viii.

³The problem of the relation of Merleau-Ponty's thought to his sources calls for a separate essay on his conception of philosophy as interrogation. "Between an 'objective' history of philosophy (which would rob the great philosophers of what they have given others to think about) and a meditation disguised as a dialogue (in which we would ask the questions and give the answers) there must be a middle-ground on which the philosopher we are speaking about and the philosopher who is speaking are present together, although it is not possible even in principle to decide at any given moment just what belongs to each" (Maurice Merleau-Ponty, *Signs*, trans. Richard C. McCleary [Evanston, Ill.: Northwestern University Press, 1964], 159). With this in mind, the documentary study of Merleau-Ponty's reading of Husserl is enormously aided by the essay of H. L.

Van Breda, "Maurice Merleau-Ponty et les Archives-Husserl à Louvain," *Revue de métaphysique et de Morale* no. 4 (1962): 410–30.

[4]Merleau-Ponty, *Phenomenology of Perception,* xiv.

[5]"In our opinion Husserl's originality lies beyond the notion of intentionality: it is to be found in the elaboration of this notion and in the discovery, beneath the intentionality of representations, of a deeper intentionality, which others have called existence" (ibid., 121, n. 5).

[6]We are paraphrasing Merleau-Ponty's remarks in the discussion that follows the paper by A. de Waelhens, "L'Idée de la phénoménologie," *Husserl,* Cahiers de Royaumont, Philosophie No. III (Paris: Minuit, 1959), 157–69.

[7]Merleau-Ponty, *Phenomenology of Perception,* xv.

[8]Ibid., ix.

[9]Ibid., xiv.

[10]Ibid., 5.

[11]Ibid., 11.

[12]Ibid., 28.

[13]Ibid., 31.

[14]Ibid., 48, emphasis on *motive* added.

[15]Ibid., 49–50, final emphasis added.

[16]Maurice Merleau-Ponty, *The Structure of Behavior,* trans. A. L. Fisher (Boston: Beacon Press, 1963), 145–60.

[17]Merleau-Ponty, *Phenomenology of Perception,* 61.

[18]Ibid., xvii, emphasis added.

Chapter 4

[1]Merleau-Ponty's method is the result of his reflections upon Husserl's critique of psychologism and his own interpretation of Gestalt psychology. "Husserl was really seeking, largely unknown to himself, a notion like that of the Gestaltists—the notion of an order of meaning that does not result from the application of spiritual activity to an external matter." Cf. "Phenomenology and the Sciences of Man," in Maurice Merleau-Ponty, *The Primacy of Perception, and Other Essays,* ed. James M. Edie (Evanston, Ill.: Northwestern University Press, 1964), 72.

[2]"The attack of the constancy-hypothesis carried to its logical conclusion assumes the value of a genuine phenomenological reduction" (Maurice Merleau-Ponty, *Phenomenology of Perception,* trans. Colin Smith [London: Routledge and Kegan Paul, 1962], 47); but Aron Gurwitsch, *The Field of Consciousness* (Pittsburgh: Duquesne University Press, 1964), pt. 3, § 4, "The Phenomenological Interpretation of the Dismissal of the Constancy-Hypothesis," considers that this leads only to an *incipient* phenomenological reduction.

[3]Kurt Goldstein, *Human Nature in the Light of Psychopathology* (New York: Schocken Books, 1963), chap. 5. Charles Taylor, *The Explanation of Behavior* (New York: Humanities Press, 1964), 270, concludes that "S-R theory is

rich in such question-begging special hypotheses, merely verbal solutions which leave the problem untouched—'conditional' cues, relative stimuli, sensory integration, acquired drives of all sorts—which are usually a symptom of a theory's ill-health."

[4]Maurice Merleau-Ponty, *The Structure of Behavior*, trans. A. L. Fisher (Boston: Beacon Press, 1963), 25.

[5]Ibid., 23.

[6]F.J.J. Buytendijk, "Über die akustische Wahrnehmung des Hundes," *Archives néerlandaise de psychologie*, 17 (1933): 267, quoted in Merleau-Ponty, *Structure of Behavior*, 61.

[7]Kurt Goldstein and Adhémar Gelb, "Analysis of a Case of Figural Blindness," in *A Source Book of Gestalt Psychology*, ed. Willis D. Ellis (London: Routledge and Kegan Paul, 1955), 315–25.

[8]Henry Head, *Aphasia and Kindred Disorders of Speech* (New York: Macmillan, 1926).

[9]Kurt Goldstein, *Language and Language Disturbances* (New York: Grune and Stratton, 1960), 63.

[10]Merleau-Ponty, *Structure of Behavior*, 90.

[11]W. Koehler, "Simple Structural Functions in the Chimpanzee and in the Chicken," in *A Source Book of Gestalt Psychology*, 217–27.

[12]Merleau-Ponty, *Structure of Behavior*, 118.

[13]Merleau-Ponty, *Phenomenology of Perception*, 145–46.

[14]Merleau-Ponty, *Structure of Behavior*, 125.

[15]Kurt Goldstein, *Human Nature in the Light of Psychopathology* (New York: Schocken Books, 1963), 174, emphasizes that the term *preferred behavior* "does not imply any conscious awareness or choice of a special way of performing; it is merely descriptive of the observable type of behavior."

Chapter 5

[1]Maurice Merleau-Ponty, *Phenomenology of Perception*, trans. Colin Smith (London: Routledge and Kegan Paul, 1962), 90.

[2]Ibid., 111.

[3]Maurice Merleau-Ponty, *The Structure of Behavior*, trans. A. L. Fisher (Boston: Beacon Press, 1963), 168.

[4]Ibid., 199.

[5]Merleau-Ponty, *Phenomenology of Perception*, 50, italics added.

[6]Ibid., 239.

[7]Ibid., 403.

Chapter 6

[1]Maurice Merleau-Ponty, *Phenomenology of Perception*, trans. Colin Smith (London: Routledge and Kegan Paul, 1962), xix.

[2]Ibid., xii–xiii.

[3]"Husserl et la notion de nature, notes prises au cours de Maurice Merleau-Ponty," *Revue de métaphysique et de morale,* no. 3 (1965): 257–69.

[4]"Husserl in his last period concedes that all reflection should in the first place return to the description of the world of living experience (*Lebenswelt*). But he adds that, by means of a second 'reduction,' the structures of the world of experience must be reinstated in the transcendental flow of a universal constitution in which all the world's obscurities are elucidated. It is clear, however, that we are faced with a dilemma: either the constitution makes the world transparent, in which case it is not obvious why reflection needs to pass through the world of experience, or else it retains something of that world, and never rids it of its opacity. Husserl's thought moves increasingly in this second direction, despite many throwbacks to the logicist period—as is seen when he makes a problem of rationality, when he allows significances which are in the last resort 'fluid' (*Erfahrung und Urteil,* 482), when he bases knowledge on a basic" (Merleau-Ponty, *Phenomenology of Perception,* 365, n. 1).

[5]"If that is what it is, it relapses into the Cartesian error of the *hypothesis of a Nichtigkeit of the world,* whose immediate consequence is the postulation of an indubitable *mens sive anima* (part of the world)——Every negation of the world *but equally* any neutrality with regard to the existence of the world, has the immediate consequence that it loses hold of the transcendental. The *epoché* is properly a neutral attitude only in regard to the world as effectively closed upon itself, as pure externality: it must allow the subsistence of this self-contained phenomenon, this externality.

"The transcendental field is a field of transcendencies. Inasmuch as it is the resolute surpassing of a *mens sive natura* and the realm of psychology, the transcendental is the transcendence of subjectivity in the sense of countertranscendence and immanence. Husserl is right to remark that the transition to intersubjectivity is only contradictory in an incomplete reduction. A complete reduction, on the other hand, leads beyond the pretended transcendental 'immanence'; it leads to the absolute spirit, understood as *Weltlichkeit,* to the *Geist* as an *Ineinander* of spontaneities, itself grounded upon an aesthesiological *Ineinander* and on the sphere of life as a sphere of Einfühlung and intercorporeality——the notion of the *species* = notion of interanimality. The interweaving of biology or psychology and philosophy = *Selbstheit* of the *world*" (Maurice Merleau-Ponty, *The Visible and the Invisible, Followed by Working Notes,* ed. Claude Lefort, trans. Alphonso Lingis (Evanston, Ill.: Northwestern University Press, 1968), 171–72, modified).

[6]Maurice Merleau-Ponty, "The Philosopher and His Shadow," in *Signs,* trans. with an introduction by Richard C. McCleary (Evanston, Ill.: Northwestern University Press, 1964), 163.

[7]Ibid., 178; the concluding phrase is my translation.

[8]To touch and to touch oneself (to touch oneself = the touching-touched) cannot coincide in the body: what touches is never quite what is

touched. That does not mean that they coincide "in the mind," or at the level of "consciousness." Something more than the body is needed to bring about this conjuncture: it occurs in the *untouchable*——that which in the other I can never touch. But what I can never touch, he, too cannot touch. So there is no privilege of oneself over the other in this case, and therefore it is not consciousness which is the untouchable——'Consciousness' would have to be something positive, and so it would or does recreate the duality of the reflecting-reflected upon in terms of that of the touching-touched. The untouchable is not something touchable which happens to be inaccessible——the unconscious is not a representation in practice inaccessible. The negative in this case is not a *positive which is elsewhere* (a transcendent)——It is a real negative, that is, an *Unverborgenheit* of the *Verborgenheit*, an *Urpräsentation* of the *Nichturpräsentierbar*. In other words, it is the originary source of the *elsewhere*, a *Selbst* which is an Other, a Fold——therefore there is no sense at all in saying that the junction between the touching-touched is effected by Thought or Consciousness: Thought or Consciousness is Offenheit of a corporeity to . . . World or Being" (Merleau-Ponty, *Visible and the Invisible*, 254, modified).

⁹Merleau-Ponty, *Phenomenology of Perception*, 363.

¹⁰Merleau-Ponty, *Signs*, 170.

¹¹"But although it is of the essence of consciousness to forget its own phenomena thus enabling 'things' to be constituted, this forgetfulness is not a mere absence, it is the absence of something which consciousness could bring into its presence: in other words consciousness can forget phenomena only because it can recall them, it neglects them only because they are the cradle of things" (Merleau-Ponty, *Phenomenology of Perception*, 59).

¹²Ibid., xxi.

Chapter 7

¹This is amply illustrated from the comprehensive survey of socialization theory and empirical research edited by John A. Clausen, *Socialization and Society* (Boston: Little, Brown and Company, 1968).

²These lectures are contained in the form of student notes published with Merleau-Ponty's approval in *Bulletin de Psychologie*, tome 18, no. 236 (November 1964): 3–6. Of these lectures "The Child's Relations with Others" has been translated by William Cobb in Maurice Merleau-Ponty, *The Primacy of Perception, and Other Essays*, ed. James M. Edie (Evanston, Ill.: Northwestern University Press, 1964), 96–155. See also Maurice Merleau-Ponty, *Consciousness and the Acquisition of Language*, trans. Hugh J. Silverman (Evanston, Ill.: Northwestern University Press, 1973).

³*Bulletin de Psychologie*, 112–15, 176–85, 199, 204–10, 216. See Richard M. Zaner, "Piaget and Merleau-Ponty: A Study in Convergence," *Review of Existential Psychology and Psychiatry* 6, no. 1 (Winter 1966): 7–23.

⁴See Chapters 5, 6, and 9.

[5]R. D. Laing, *The Politics of Experience* (New York: Ballantine Books, 1968).

[6]Here I think there is an obvious link between Merleau-Ponty's phenomenological psychology and the work of Lacan in psychoanalysis and Lévi-Strauss in anthropology.

[7]*Bulletin de Psychologie,* 111.

[8]Kurt Goldstein, *Human Nature in the Light of Psychology* (New York: Schocken Books, 1963), chap. 5; Charles Taylor, *The Explanation of Behavior* (New York: Humanities Press, 1964), 270.

[9]Maurice Merleau-Ponty, *The Structure of Behavior,* trans. A. L. Fisher (Boston: Beacon Press, 1963), 25.

[10]Kurt Goldstein and Adhémar Gelb, "Analysis of a Case of Figural Blindness," in *A Source Book of Gestalt Psychology,* ed. W. D. Ellis (London: Routledge and Kegan Paul, 1955), 315–25; Aron Gurwitsch, "Gelb-Goldstein's Concept of 'Concrete' and 'Categorial' Attitude and the Phenomenology of Ideation," in his *Studies in Phenomenology and Psychology* (Evanston, Ill.: Northwestern University Press, 1966).

[11]Henry Head, *Aphasia and Kindred Disorders of Speech* (New York: Macmillan, 1926).

[12]Maurice Merleau-Ponty, *Phenomenology of Perception,* trans. Colin Smith (London: Routledge and Kegan Paul, 1965), 239.

[13]*Bulletin de Psychologie,* 185–87.

[14]Ibid., 194–98.

[15]Ibid., 130–34, 187–94.

[16]Seymour Fisher and Sidney E. Cleveland, *Body Image and Personality* (New York: Dover Publications, 1968). Despite an extensive bibliography (415–38) on empirical research into the *body-image* this extremely influential work makes no mention of Merleau-Ponty or Jacques Lacan; cf. Gerald E. Myers, "Self and Body Image," in *Phenomenology in America: Studies in the Philosophy of Experience,* ed. with an intro. by James M. Edie (Chicago: Quadrangle Books, 1967), 147–60; Richard M. Zaner, "Merleau-Ponty's Theory of the Body-Proper as *Etre-au-monde,*" *Journal of Existentialism* 6, no. 21 (Fall 1965): 31–39.

[17]*Bulletin de Psychologie,* 133.

[18]Maurice Merleau-Ponty, *The Prose of the World,* ed. Claude Lefort, trans. with an intro. by John O'Neill (Evanston, Ill.: Northwestern University Press, 1972).

[19]"La Conscience et l'Acquisition du Language," *Bulletin de Psychologie,* 226–59.

[20]Merleau-Ponty, "Child's Relations with Others," 109.

[21]Ibid. Merleau-Ponty gives as his reference for the case François Rostand, "Grammaire et Affectivité," *Revue Française de Psychanalyse* 14 (April–June 1950), 299–310.

[22]Ibid., 110.

[23]John O'Neill, "How Is Society Possible?" in my *Sociology as a Skin Trade: Essays Towards a Reflexive Sociology* (London: Heinemann Educational Books, 1972).

[24]Merleau-Ponty, *Phenomenology of Perception*, 355. My stress in the first line.

[25]Merleau-Ponty, "Child's Relations with Others," 115.

[26]Frank A. Tillman, "On Perceiving Persons," in *Phenomenology in America*, 161–72.

[27]Merleau-Ponty, *Phenomenology of Perception*, 1, chaps. 1 and 2; "Phenomenology and the Sciences of Man," in Merleau-Ponty, *Primacy of Perception*, 43–95.

[28]Aron Gurwitsch, "A Non-egological Conception of Consciousness," 287–300.

[29]"Child's Relation with Others," 118.

[30]For these connections and in particular the affective bases of reciprocity, although he omits any mention of Merleau-Ponty (indeed, this is no fault), see Aaron V. Cicourel, "Basic and Normative Rules in the Negotiation of Status and Role," in *Recent Sociology No. 2: Patterns of Communicative Behavior*, ed. Hans Peter Dreitzel (New York: Macmillan, 1970), 4–45; and note 23.

[31]On this central problem of phenomenological psychology see the crucial discussion by Alfred Schütz, "The Problem of Transcendental Intersubjectivity in Husserl," in his *Collected Papers III: Studies in Phenomenological Philosophy*, ed. I. Schutz, with an intro. by Aron Gurwitsch (The Hague: Martinus Nijhoff, 1966), 51–91; as well as "Scheler's Theory of Intersubjectivity and the General Thesis of the Alter Ego," and "Sartre's Theory of the Alter Ego," in *Collected Papers I: The Problem of Social Reality*, ed. and intro. by Maurice Natanson (The Hague: Martinus Nijhoff, 1967), 150–79, 180–203.

[32]Erving Goffman, *Interaction Ritual: Essays on Face-to-Face Behavior* (New York: Doubleday and Co., 1967).

[33]*Bulletin de Psychologie*, 134–36, 300–302. Compare Cooley's notion of the looking-glass self in *Human Nature and the Social Order* (New York: Schocken Books, 1964), 183–85, 196–99; and Mead's conception of the "I" and "Me" relation in *Mind, Self and Society*, ed. with an intro. by Charles W. Morris (Chicago and London: University of Chicago Press, 1967) 173–78, 192–200.

[34]Merleau-Ponty, "Child's Relations with Others," 136–37; cf. Jacques Lacan, "Le Stade du miroir comme formateur du fonction du je," *Revue Française de Psychanalyse* 13, no. 4 (October–December 1949): 449–55.

[35]Lacan remarks that in treating the struggle between master and slave in which each seeks to be recognized without in turn recognizing the other as a symbol of the history of the world Hegel "has furnished once and for all the true function of aggression in human ontology, to the point almost of prophesying the iron law of our age." *Ecrits* (Paris: Editions du Seuil,

1966), 121; Paul Ricoeur, *De l' Interpretation: Essai sur Freud* (Paris: Editions du Seuil, 1965); John O'Neill, "History as Human History in Hegel and Marx" in Jean Hyppolite, *Studies on Marx and Hegel,* trans. with notes and bibliography by John O'Neill (New York: Basic Books, 1969); Alexandre Kojève, *Introduction to the Reading of Hegel,* ed. Allen Bloom, trans. James H. Nichols, Jr. (New York: Basic Books, 1969).

[36]Norman O. Brown, *Love's Body* (New York: Vintage Books, 1966); John O'Neill, "On Body-Politics," in *Recent Sociology No. 4: Family, Marriage and the Struggle of the Sexes,* ed. Hans Peter Dreitzel (New York: Macmillan, 1972).

Chapter 8

[1]Harold Bloom, *The Anxiety of Influence: A Theory of Poetry* (New York: Oxford University Press, 1973).

[2]Seymour Fisher, *Body Experience in Fantasy and Behavior* (New York: Appleton-Century-Crofts, 1970).

[3]Seymour Fisher and S. E. Cleveland, *Body Image and Personality* (New York: Dover Press, 1968).

[4]Warren Gorman, *Body Image and the Image of the Brain* (St. Louis: Warren H. Green, 1969).

[5]Franklin C. Shontz, *Perceptual and Cognitive Aspects of Body Appearance* (New York and London: Academic Press, 1969).

[6]Paul Schilder, *The Image and Appearance of the Human Body* (New York: International Universities Press, 1950).

[7]Maurice Merleau-Ponty, *Phenomenology of Perception* (London: Routledge and Kegan Paul), 1962.

[8]Jacques Lacan, "The Mirror Stage as Formative of the Function of the I," in *Ecrits: A Selection,* ed. Jacques Lacan, trans. Alan Sheridan (New York: W. W. Norton and Company, 1970), 1–7.

[9]J. Laplanche and J.-B. Pontalis, *The Language of Psycho-Analysis* (New York: W. W. Norton and Company, 1973).

[10]Maurice Merleau-Ponty, "Resumé des ses cours établi par des étudiants et approuvé par lui-meme," *Bulletin de Psychologie* 18 (1964): 3–6. Maurice Merleau-Ponty, "The Child's Relations with Others," in Maurice Merleau-Ponty, ed., *The Primacy of Perception, And Other Essays on Phenomenological Psychology: The Philosophy of Art, History and Politics,* ed. James M. Edie (Evanston, Ill.: Northwestern University Press, 1964).

[11]Henri Wallon, *Les origines du caractère chez l'enfant* (Paris: Presses universitaires de France, 1949).

[12]Martin C. Dillon, "Merleau-Ponty and the Psychogenesis of the Self," *Journal of Phenomenological Psychology* 9 (1978): 84–98.

[13]Henri Ey, *L'Inconscient* (Paris: Desclée de Bròuwer, 1966).

[14]Jacques Lacan, *Ecrits* (Paris: Editions du Seuil, 1966).

[15]D. W. Winnicott, "Mirror-Role of Mother and Family in Child Development," in *The Predicament of the Family: A Psycho-Analytical Symposium,* ed. Peter Lomas (London: Hogarth Press, 1967), 26–33.

[16]Richard M. Zaner, *The Problem of Embodiment: Some Contributions to a Phenomenology of the Body* (The Hague: Martinus Nijhoff, 1964). Richard M. Zaner, *The Context of Self: A Phenomenological Inquiry Using Medicine as a Clue* (Athens: Ohio University Press, 1981).

[17]Merleau-Ponty, *Primacy of Perception,* 115.

[18]Charles Cooley, *Human Nature and the Social Order* (New York: Schocken Books, 1964); George H. Mead, *Mind, Self, and Society,* ed. with an intro. by Charles W. Morris (Chicago and London: University of Chicago Press, 1967); Erving Goffman, *Interaction Ritual: Essays on Face-to-Face Behavior* (New York: Doubleday Anchor Books, 1967); John O'Neill, "On Simmel's 'Sociological Apriorities,' " in *Phenomenological Sociology: Issues and Applications,* ed. George Psathas (New York: John Wiley and Sons, 1973), 91–106.

[19]Merleau-Ponty, *Bulletin de Psychologie,* 137.

[20]J. Laplanche and J.-B. Pontalis, *Life and Death in Psychoanalysis,* trans. with an intro. by Jeffrey Mehlman (Baltimore and London: Johns Hopkins University Press, 1976).

[21]Charles Goodwin, *Conversational Organization: Interaction between Speakers and Hearers* (New York: Academic Press, 1981).

[22]For a subtle analysis of the body boundary as a communicative texture between self-disclosure (*Selbstdarstellung*) and self-centeredness (*Weltbeziehung durch Innerlichkeit*), see Mildred Bakan, "Alienation and the Interpretive Framework," in *The Crisis of Culture: Steps to Reopen the Phenomenological Investigation of Man,* ed. Anna-Teresa Tymieniecka (Dordrecht: D. Reidel Publishing Co., 1976), 219–26. Bakan argues, however, that since self-disclosure is linguistically mediated it is both thought-centered and feeling-centered. Moreover, since feeling-centered experience is shaped in the infant's early family environment, its communicative mode may never quite mesh with its later public communication and may need to be repressed or else released in special ritual techniques such as poetry, religion, and psychoanalysis. It is the task of critical social theory to bring together man's two bodies, respecting in public discourse what cannot be said in the feeling, embodied self. See John O'Neill, "Homotextuality: Barthes on Barthes, Fragments (RB), with a Footnote," in *Hermeneutics: Questions and Prospects,* ed. Gary Shapiro and Alan Sica (Amherst: University of Massachusetts Press, 1983), 165–82.

[23]Harry Stack Sullivan, *The Interpersonal Theory of Psychiatry,* ed. Helen Swick Perry and Mary Ladd Gawel (New York: W. W. Norton and Company, 1953), 100.

[24]D. W. Winnicott, *Playing and Reality* (New York: Basic Books, 1971), 12.

[25]Ibid., 107.

[26]Bruno Bettelheim, *The Empty Fortress: Infantile Autism and the Birth of the Self* (New York: Free Press, 1967).

[27]Sigmund Freud, "Beyond the Pleasure Principle," *The Standard Edition of the Complete Psychological Works of Sigmund Freud,* vol. 18 (London: Hogarth Press, 1920).

[28]Jacques Lacan, *Ecrits,* 2.

[29]Schilder, *The Image and Appearance of the Human Body,* 80.

[30]Beulah Kramer Amsterdam and Morton Levitt, "Consciousness of Self and Painful Self-Consciousness," in *The Psychoanalytic Study of the Child,* vol. 35 (New Haven: Yale University Press, 1980), 67–83.

[31]Erik H. Erikson, *Childhood and Society* (New York: W. W. Norton and Company, 1963).

[32]Melanie Klein, "Early Stages of the Oedipus Conflict and of Super-Ego Formation" in her *The Psycho-Analysis of Children* (London: Hogarth Press, 1932), 123–48.

[33]Paul Guillaume, *Imitation in Children* (Chicago and London: University of Chicago Press, 1969), 152–53; Henry Elkin, "Towards a Developmental Phenomenology: Transcendental-Ego and Body-Ego," in *The Late Husserl and the Idea of Phenomenology: Idealism-Realism, Historicity and Nature,* ed. Anna-Teresa Tymienecka and Lawrence Haworth (Dordrecht: D. Reidel, 1972), 258–66.

[34]Roland Barthes, *The Pleasure of the Text,* trans. Richard Miller (New York: Hill and Wang, 1975); O'Neill, "Homotextuality," 165–82.

Chapter 9

[1]Maurice Merleau-Ponty, "Institution in Personal and Public History," in *In Praise of Philosophy and Other Essays,* trans. John Wild, James Edie, and John O'Neill (Evanston, Ill.: Northwestern University Press, 1988).

[2]Ibid., 108–9.

[3]Maurice Merleau-Ponty, *Phenomenology of Perception,* trans. Colin Smith (London: Routledge and Kegan Paul, 1965), 412.

[4]"On the Phenomenology of Language," in Maurice Merleau-Ponty, *Signs,* trans. Richard C. McCleary (Evanston, Ill.: Northwestern University Press, 1964), 85.

[5]Merleau-Ponty's interpretation of Saussure must first of all be understood in terms of his reading of Husserl that determines his interest in the ontogenesis of speech and his interpolation of a psychology lacking in Saussure but complementary to the line of development that Merleau-Ponty introduces. Cf. Merleau-Ponty, "The Problem of Speech," *In Praise of Philosophy,* 87–94; and Maurice Lageux, "Merleau-Ponty et la linguistique de Saussure," *Dialogue* 4, no. 3 (1965): 351–64.

[6]Merleau-Ponty, *Signs,* 96.

[7]Ibid., 89.

[8]Merleau-Ponty, "Studies in the Literary Usage of Language," in *In Praise of Philosophy and Other Essays,* 80–86.

[9]Merleau-Ponty, *Signs,* 91.

[10]Ibid., 92.

[11]"Indirect Language and the Voices of Silence," in ibid., 69.

[12]"The Philosopher and His Shadow," in ibid., 165.

[13]Maurice Merleau-Ponty, *The Primacy of Perception, and Other Essays,* ed. James M. Edie (Evanston, Ill.: Northwestern University Press, 1964), 9.

[14]Merleau-Ponty, *Signs,* 59.

[15]"Husserl at the Limits of Phenomenology," in *In Praise of Philosophy and Other Essays,* 181–91. Merleau-Ponty's interpretation of the relation of constituting consciousness to the medium of language is disputed in Jacques Derrida's masterful introduction and translation of Edmund Husserl's *L'Origine de la géometrie* (Paris: Presses Universitaires de France, 1962); cf. pp. 71 ff. and 122 ff.

[16]Merleau-Ponty, *Signs,* 96–97.

[17]"Materials for a Theory of History," in Merleau-Ponty, *In Praise of Philosophy and Other Essays,* 95–106.

[18]Merleau-Ponty, *Signs,* 75.

[19]"We have here a rationality in contingency, a livid logic, an autoconstitution which is precisely what we need to understand the union of contingency and meaning in history, and Saussure may well have outlined a new philosophy of history" (Maurice Merleau-Ponty, *Éloge de la philosophie et autres essais* [Paris: Gallimard, 1960], 64).

[20]Thomas Langan, *Merleau-Ponty's Critique of Reason* (New Haven and London: Yale University Press, 1966), 42–59.

[21]"The Crisis of the Understanding," in Merleau-Ponty, *The Primacy of Perception,* 204.

[22]Merleau-Ponty, *Phenomenology of Perception,* 172.

[23]Merleau-Ponty, *Signs,* 97.

[24]John O'Neill, *Essaying Montaigne: The Renaissance Institution of Writing and Reading* (London: Routledge and Kegan Paul, 1982).

Chapter 10

[1]For a phenomenology of the notion of "catch" and the related experience and concept of "surrender," see Kurt H. Wolff, *Surrender and Catch: A Palimpsest Story,* Sorokin Memorial Lecture, no. 3 (Saskatoon: University of Saskatchewan Press, 1972).

[2]James M. Edie, "Was Merleau-Ponty a Structuralist?" *Semio-tica* (1972): 297–323; Maurice Lagueux, "Merleau-Ponty et la linguistique de Saussure," *Dialogue* 4, no. 3 (1965): 351–64. Edie's article, in particular, furnishes the basic data as well as raising the fundamental questions that may guide further research in Merleau-Ponty's phenomenology of language. My own approach is determined by an interest in the way the phenomenology of language furnishes a key to similar analysis of cultural institutions in general.

[3]Edmund Husserl, *The Crisis of European Sciences and Transcendental Phenomenology: An Introduction to Phenomenological Philosophy,* trans. David Carr (Evanston, Ill.: Northwestern University Press, 1970), 9.

[4]Maurice Merleau-Ponty, *The Prose of the World,* ed. Claude Lefort, trans. John O'Neill (Evanston, Ill.: Northwestern University Press, 1973).

[5]Maurice Merleau-Ponty, *Phenomenology of Perception,* trans. Colin Smith (London: Routledge and Kegan Paul, New York: Humanities Press, 1965), xiv–xv. The internal quotation is from Husserl, *Meditations Cartesiennes,* trans. Gabrielle Peiffer and Emmanual Levinas (Paris: Colin, 1931), 33.

[6]Merleau-Ponty, *Phenomenology of Perception,* xviii.

[7]Ibid., xix–xx.

[8]On the relations among language, logic, linguistics, and semantics, see Mikel Dufrenne, *Language and Philosophy,* trans. Henry B. Veatch (Bloomington: Indiana University Press, 1963).

[9]Frank Budgen, *James Joyce and the Making of Ulysses* (Bloomington: Indiana University Press, 1960), 21.

[10]Husserl, *Crisis,* 351.

[11]See Chapter 7.

[12]Maurice Merleau-Ponty, "Philosophy as Interrogation," in *In Praise of Philosophy and Other Essays,* trans. John Wild, James Edie, and John O'Neill (Evanston, Ill.: Northwestern University Press, 1988), 167–80.

[13]Husserl, *Crisis,* 394–95.

[14]See Chapter 13.

[15]Maurice Merleau-Ponty, *Signs,* trans. Richard C. McCleary (Evanston, Ill.: Northwestern University Press, 1964), 69.

[16]The argument upon which I have drawn here is developed more fully in Chapter 15.

[17]"We have also become aware in the most general way that human philosophizing and its results in the whole of man's existence mean anything but merely private or otherwise limited cultural goals. In *our* philosophizing, then—how can we avoid it?—we are *functionaries of mankind.* The quite personal responsibility of our own true being as philosophers, our inner personal vocation, bears within itself at the same time the responsibility for the true being of mankind; the latter is, necessarily, being toward a *telos* and can only come to realization, *if at all,* through philosophy—through *us, if* we are philosophers in all seriousness. Is there, in this existential 'if,' a way out? If not, what should we, who *believe,* do in order to *be able* to believe? We cannot seriously continue our previous philosophizing; it lets us hope only for philosophies, never for philosophy" (Husserl, *Crisis,* 17).

[18]Maurice Merleau-Ponty, *Humanism and Terror: An Essay on the Communist Problem,* trans. John O'Neill (Boston: Beacon Press, 1969).

[19]Merleau-Ponty, *Prose of the World,* 73.

[20]"Was Merleau-Ponty a Structuralist?," 317–18. Edie's argument should be consulted in detail as well as for some marvelous passages from Merleau-Ponty on language and "singing" the world.

[21]Merleau-Ponty, *Prose of the World,* 82–83.

[22]Ibid., 86–87.

[23]Ibid., 86.

²⁴Paul Ricoeur, "Husserl and the Sense of History," in his *Husserl: An Analysis of His Phenomenology* (Evanston, Ill.: Northwestern University Press, 1967).

²⁵Merleau-Ponty, *Prose of the World*, 85–86.

²⁶John O'Neill, "Hegel and Marx on History as Human History," in Jean Hyppolite, *Studies on Marx and Hegel*, trans. John O'Neill (New York: Basic Books, 1969).

²⁷Aron Gurwitsch, "The Last Work of Edmund Husserl," in his *Studies in Phenomenology and Psychology* (Evanston, Ill.: Northwestern University Press, 1966), 445–47.

Chapter 11

¹Maurice Merleau-Ponty, *Phenomenology of Perception*, trans. Colin Smith (London: Routledge and Kegan Paul, 1962), 369.

²John O'Neill, *Essaying Montaigne: A Study of the Renaissance Institution of Writing and Reading* (London: Routledge and Kegan Paul, 1982).

³René Descartes, *Discourse on Method* and *The Meditations*, trans. F. E. Sutcliffe (Harmondsworth: Penguin Books, 1968), 113.

⁴Ibid., 96.

⁵Walter Benn Michaels, "The Interpreter's Self: Pierce on the Cartesian 'Subject,'" in *Reader-Response Criticism: From Formalism to Post-Structuralism*, ed. Jane P. Tomkins (Baltimore: Johns Hopkins University Press, 1980), 185–200.

⁶Michel Foucault, *Madness and Civilization: A History of Insanity in the Age of Reason* (New York: Vintage Books, 1961); Jacques Derrida, "Cogito and the History of Madness," in his *Writing and Difference* (Chicago: University of Chicago Press, 1978), 31–63.

⁷Merleau-Ponty, *Phenomenology of Perception*, 401.

⁸Robert Champigny, "The Theatrical Aspect of the Cogito," *Review of Metaphysics* 12 (1959): 370–77; Ralph Flores, "Cartesian Striptease," *Substance* 39 (1983): 75–88.

⁹Jean-Luc Nancy, "Larvatus Pro Deo," *Glyph 2* (1977): 14–36; and his *Ego Sum* (Paris: Flammarion, 1979).

¹⁰Merleau-Ponty, *Phenomenology of Perception*, 383.

¹¹Maurice Merleau-Ponty, "The Concept of Nature, I," in *In Praise of Philosophy and Other Essays*, 130–55.

¹²Maurice Merleau-Ponty, *The Visible and the Invisible, Followed by Working Notes*, trans. Alphonso Lingis (Evanston, Ill.: Northwestern University Press, 1968), 131.

¹³Jacques Taminiaùx, "La Phénoménologie dans le dernier ouvrage de Merleau-Ponty," in his *Le regard et l'excédent* (The Hague: Martinus Nijhoff, 1977), 72–89. J. T. Barry, "The Textual Body: Incorporating Writing and Flesh," *Philosophy Today* (Spring 1986): 16–31.

¹⁴Merleau-Ponty, *Visible and the Invisible*, 139.

¹⁵Chapter 10.

[16]John O'Neill, "A Realist Model of Knowledge: With a Phenomenological Deconstruction of Its Model of Man," *Philosophy of the Social Sciences* 16, no. 1 (March 1986): 1–19.

[17]Jacques Derrida, *Edmund Husserl's Origin of Geometry: An Introduction,* trans. with a preface by John P. Leavey, Jr. (Stony Brook, N.Y.: Nicolas Hays, Ltd., 1978).

[18]Edmund Husserl, *The Crisis of European Sciences and Transcendental Phenomenology: An Introduction to Phenomenological Philosophy,* trans. David Carr (Evanston, Ill.: Northwestern University Press, 1970), 395.

[19]Merleau-Ponty, *Visible and the Invisible,* 188. Bernard Charles Flynn, "Textuality and the Flesh: Derrida and Merleau-Ponty," *Journal of the British Society for Phenomenology* 15, no. 2 (May 1984): 164–79.

[20]John O'Neill, "Homotextuality: Barthes on Barthes, Fragments (RB), with a Footnote," in *Hermeneutics: Questions and Prospects,* ed. Gary Shapiro and Alan Sica (Amherst: University of Massachusetts Press, 1984), 165–82.

[21]Maurice Merleau-Ponty, "The Philosopher and His Shadow," in his *Signs,* trans. Richard C. McCleary (Evanston, Ill.: Northwestern University Press, 1964), 159.

[22]Ibid., 402.

[23]John O'Neill, "*Mecum meditari:* Demolishing Doubt, Building Prayer," in *Practical Reasoning in Human Affairs,* ed. J. L. Golden and J. J. Pilotta (Dordrecht: D. Reidel Publishing Company, 1986), 105–17.

[24]See Chapter 12.

[25]Maurice Merleau-Ponty, "Cézanne's Doubt," in his *Sense and Non-Sense* (Evanston, Ill.: Northwestern University Press, 1964), 9–25; "Eye and Mind," in his *The Primary of Perception, And Other Essays on Phenomenological Psychology: The Philosophy of Art, History and Politics,* ed. James M. Edie (Evanston, Ill.: Northwestern University Press, 1964), 159–90.

[26]Anna-Teresa Tymienecka (ed.), *Maurice Merleau-Ponty, le psychique et le corporel* (Paris: Aubier, 1988).

[27]John O'Neill, *Essaying Montaigne: The Renaissance Institution of Writing and Reading* (London: Routledge and Kegan Paul, 1982).

Chapter 12

[1]Georg Lukács touches the issue most closely in his criticisms of the inadequacy of Merleau-Ponty's existentialist concept of opinion and its dialectical relation to objective social and historical processes. Lukács's conclusion is that Merleau-Ponty's existentialism, despite its more concrete approach to politics, ultimately falls into eclecticism and nihilism. Cf. *Existentialisme ou Marxisme?* (Paris: Nagel, 1948), pt. 3, chap. 5. My remarks, though not directed at Lukács's criticism, would, I think, answer it as well as give some idea of the rather special sense that Merleau-Ponty gives to the existentialist perspective.

[2]Maurice Merleau-Ponty, *Humanism and Terror: An Essay on the Communist Problem,* trans. with notes by John O'Neill (Boston: Beacon Press, 1969).

[3]"Reading Montaigne," in Maurice Merleau-Ponty, *Signs,* trans. Richard C. McCleary (Evanston, Ill.: Northwestern University Press, 1964), 198–210.

[4]"A Note on Machiavelli," in ibid., 211–23.

[5]The italicized quotations are cited by Merleau-Ponty from Montaigne's *Essays,* Book III: 13, "Of Physiognomy." The standard English translation—no French edition is referred to by Merleau-Ponty—is *The Complete Essays of Montaigne,* trans. Donald M. Frame (Stanford, Ca.: Stanford University Press, 1958).

[6]Merleau-Ponty, *Signs,* 203.

[7]Ibid., 205.

[8]Ibid., 207.

[9]The following comment upon Arthur Koestler's *Darkness at Noon,* to which *Humanism and Terror* is also a response, seems to be true for both works: "I fancy that this novel has fallen under a temporary cloud. That is partly because it is political, and because it was inspired by the Moscow Trials the butterflies of criticism imagine that it can be tucked away in the file marked 'Topical.' It was topical, is topical and always will be topical for in no foreseeable future will the circumstance that gave rise to it be eliminated. It will remain topical just as *Gulliver's Travels* has remained topical for those who have discovered it is not just a children's book" (John Atkins, *Arthur Koestler* [New York: Roy Publishers, 1956], 177–78).

[10]Merleau-Ponty, *Humanism and Terror,* 2.

[11]Ibid., 11.

[12]Ibid., 5.

[13]Ibid., 27.

[14]"There is no serious humanism except the one which looks for man's effective recognition by his fellow man throughout the world. Consequently, it could not possibly precede the moment when humanity gives itself its means of communication and communion" (Merleau-Ponty, *Signs,* 222).

[15]Merleau-Ponty, *Humanism and Terror,* 37.

[16]Ibid., 95.

[17]Ibid.

[18]Ibid., 96.

[19]"Here we are not speaking in favor of an anarchical liberty: if I wish freedom for another person it is inevitable that even this wish will be seen by him as an alien law; and so liberalism turns into violence. One can only blind oneself to this outcome by refusing to reflect upon the relation between the self and others. The anarchist who closes his eyes to this dialectic is nonetheless exposed to its consequences. It is the basic fact on which we have to build freedom. We are not accusing liberalism of being a system of violence, we reproach it with not seeing its own face in violence, with veiling the pact upon which it rests while rejecting as barbarous that other source of freedom—revolutionary freedom—which is the origin of

all social pacts. With the assumptions of impersonal Reason and rational Man, and by regarding itself as a natural rather than an historical fact, liberalism assumes universality as a datum whereas the problem is its realization in the dialectic of concrete intersubjectivity" (ibid., 35, n. 11).

[20]Merleau-Ponty, *Signs,* 211.

[21]Ibid., 211–12.

[22]Ibid., 213.

[23]Ibid., 216.

[24]*Éloge de la philosophie* (Paris: Gallimard, 1953), 41.

[25]Ibid., 47.

Chapter 13

[1]*Situations I–III* (Paris: Gallimard, 1947–1949). Essays from *Situations I and III* translated by Annette Michelson have been published as *Literary Essays* (New York: Philosophical Library, 1957), and most of *Situations II* translated by Bernard Frechtman as *What Is Literature?* (New York: Philosophical Library, 1949). Quotations are from the English translations.

[2]*Situations IV,* trans. Benita Eisler (Paris: Gallimard, 1964); *Situations* (New York: George Braziller, 1965). There is a fascinating history of an alternating conception of environment as a deterministic force (milieu) and as a beneficent shell or field (ambiance) to which the thought of Heidegger, Sartre, Marcel, and Jaspers might be related. I refer to the essays of Leo Spitzer, "Milieu and Ambiance: An Essay in Historical Semantics," *Philosophy and Phenomenological Research* 3 (1942–1943): 1–42, 169–218.

[3]Iris Murdoch, *Sartre, Romantic Rationalist* (New Haven: Yale University Press, 1959).

[4]*Being and Nothingness,* trans. Hazel E. Barnes (New York: Philosophical Library, 1956), 142.

[5]F. Jameson, *Sartre, The Origins of a Style* (New Haven: Yale University Press, 1961).

[6]Sartre, *Literary Essays,* 7.

[7]Ibid., 19.

[8]Ibid., 23.

[9]Sartre, *Situations,* 195.

[10]Sartre, *Situations,* 336.

[11]Ibid., 345.

[12]Sartre, *Being and Nothingness,* 487–88.

[13]Ibid., 509. See also Samuel B. Mallin, *Merleau-Ponty's Philosophy* (New Haven: Yale University Press, 1979), Ch. 1 and 2.

[14]Sartre, *Literature and Existentialism,* 57–58; in the original *Situations II,* 106–7.

[15]"The Artist and His Conscience," *Situations,* 205–24.

[16]Ibid., 296.

[17]Maurice Merleau-Ponty, *Phenomenology of Perception,* trans. Colin Smith (London: Routledge and Kegan Paul, 1962), 433.

[18]Ibid., 455.

[19]James Schmidt, "Lordship and a Bondage in Merleau-Ponty and Sartre," *Political Theory* 7, no. 2 (May 1979): 201–28.

[20]For a more detailed account see Barry Cooper, *Merleau-Ponty and Marxism: From Terror to Reform* (Toronto: University of Toronto Press, 1979).

[21]Maurice Merleau-Ponty, *Humanism and Terror: An Essay on the Communist Problem,* trans. with notes by John O'Neill (Boston: Beacon Press, 1969), 109.

Chapter 14

[1]The critique of Marxist scientism was first advanced for English readers (if we leave aside the earlier and then untranslated work of Karl Korsch, *Marxism and Philosophy,* and Georg Lukács, *History and Class Consciousness*) by Karl Popper in his *The Open Society and Its Enemies* and *The Poverty of Historicism.* I have examined this debate in John O'Neill, ed., *Modes of Individualism and Collectivism* (London: Heinemann, New York: St. Martin's Press, 1973).

[2]In a number of essays I have argued for the unity of Marxist humanism and science. See John O'Neill, *For Marx against Althuser, and Other Essays* (Washington: University Press of America, 1982).

[3]George Lichtheim, *From Marx to Hegel, and Other Essays* (London: Orbach and Chambers, 1971).

[4]George Lichtheim, *Marxism in Modern France* (New York and London: Columbia University Press, 1966) and *From Marx to Hegel* (London: Orbach and Chambers, 1971).

[5]Alfred Schmidt, *The Concept of Nature in Marx* (London: NLB, 1971).

[6]Jean Hyppolite, *Studies on Marx and Hegel,* ed. and trans. John O'Neill (New York: Basic Books, London: Heinemann, 1969).

[7]Alexandre Kojève, *Introduction to the Reading of Hegel* (New York: Basic Books, 1969).

[8]Richard Crossman, ed., *The God That Failed* (New York: Harper and Row, 1949); Michel-Antoine Burnier, *Choice of Action,* trans. Bernard Murchland (New York: Random House, 1968).

[9]Maurice Merleau-Ponty, *Humanism and Terror: An Essay on the Communist Problem,* trans. and with an intro. by John O'Neill (Boston: Beacon Press, 1969).

[10]Maurice Merleau-Ponty, *Phenomenology, Language and Sociology: Selected Essays,* ed. John O'Neill (London: Heinemann, 1974).

[11]Maurice Merleau-Ponty, *Adventures of the Dialectic,* trans. Joseph Bien (Evanston, Ill.: Northwestern University Press, 1973), 6, my emphasis.

[12]Alphonse de Waelhens, *Une philosophie de l'ambiguité: L'existentialisme de Maurice Merleau-Ponty* (Louvain: Publications Universitaires de Louvain, 1967).

[13]Merleau-Ponty, *Humanism and Terror,* 109–10, my emphasis.

[14]Maurice Merleau-Ponty, "Reading Montaigne," *Signs,* trans. Richard C. McCleary (Evanston, Ill.: Northwestern University Press, 1964).

[15]See Chapter 13.

[16]Merleau-Ponty, *Humanism and Terror,* 100–101.

[17]*Report of Court Proceedings in the Case of the Anti-Soviet "Bloc of Rights and Trotskyites,"* Moscow, 2–13 March 1938 (Moscow: People's Commissariat of Justice of the USSR, 1938).

[18]Nathan Leites and Elsa Bernaut, *Ritual of Liquidation: The Case of the Moscow Trials* (Glencoe, Ill.: Free Press, 1954).

[19]Maurice Merleau-Ponty, *Themes from the Lectures at the Collège de France, 1952–1960,* in his *In Praise of Philosophy and Other Essays,* trans. John Wild, James Edie, and John O'Neill (Evanston, Ill.: Northwestern University Press, 1988).

[20]John O'Neill, "Le Langage et la décolonisation: Fanon et Freire," *Sociologie et Societés* 6, no. 2 (November 1974): 53–65.

[21]See Part II.

[22]Maurice Merleau-Ponty, *Phenomenology of Perception,* trans. Colin Smith (London: Routledge and Kegan Paul, 1962), 171–73.

[23]Merleau-Ponty, "The U.S.S.R. and the Camps," *Signs,* 263–73.

[24]"There is indeed a Sartrean violence, and it is more highly strung and less durable than Marx's violence." *Adventures of the Dialectic,* 159.

[25]Merleau-Ponty, *Humanism and Terror,* 129.

[26]Merleau-Ponty, *Adventures of the Dialectic,* 30–31.

[27]Georg Lukács, *History and Class Consciousness: Studies in Marxist Dialectics,* trans. Rodney Livingstone (London: Merlin Press, 1971).

[28]See Chapter 13.

[29]Merleau-Ponty, *Adventures of the Dialectic,* 37–38.

[30]Jean-Paul Sartre, *Being and Nothingness,* trans. and with an intro. by Hazel E. Barnes (New York: Washington Square Press, 1969), pt. 3.

[31]Sartre, *Being and Nothingness,* 544–45.

[32]Merleau-Ponty, *Adventures of the Dialectic,* 142.

[33]"In his empirical analyses Marx comprehends the history of the species under the categories of material activity *and* the critical abolition of ideologies, of instrumental action *and* revolutionary practice, of labour *and* reflection at once. But Marx interprets what he does in the more restricted conception of the species' self-reflection through work alone. The materialist concept of synthesis is not conceived broadly enough in order to explicate the way in which Marx contributes to realizing the intention of a really radicalized critique of knowledge. In fact, it even prevented Marx from understanding his own mode of procedure from this point of view." Jürgen Habermas, *Knowledge and Human Interests,* trans. Jeremy J. Shapiro (Boston: Beacon Press, 1971), 42. Cf. Jürgen Habermas, *Theory and Practice,* trans. John Viertel (Boston: Beacon Press, 1973), chap. 4, "Labor and Interaction: Remarks on Hegel's Jena *Philosophy of Mind.*"

[34]Merleau-Ponty, *Adventures of the Dialectic,* 52.

[35]Georg Lukács, *Lenin: A Study on the Unity of His Thought* (London: NLB, 1970).

[36]Lukács, *Lenin,* 79.

[37]This much has been established in the academic debate over the early and later writings of Marx. One would have thought that it is no longer arguable that Marxism can be separated from its Hegelian sources. Yet, recently this argument has reappeared in the influential contributions to critical theory developed by Habermas and by the structuralist readings of Marx fostered by Althusser. I have considered these arguments in my "On Theory and Criticism in Marx," in *For Marx against Althuser,* 19–42.

[38]John O'Neill, "Authority, Knowledge and the Body Politic," in *Sociology as a Skin Trade,* 68–80.

[39]Merleau-Ponty, *Adventures of the Dialectic,* 200.

[40]Maurice Merleau-Ponty, *The Prose of the World,* trans. and with an intro. by John O'Neill (Evanston, Ill.: Northwestern University Press, 1973), 86.

[41]Merleau-Ponty, *Humanism and Terror,* 188–89.

Chapter 15

[1]Jürgen Habermas, "Knowledge and Interests: A General Prospective," appendix to his *Knowledge and Human Interests,* trans. Jeremy J. Shapiro (London: Heinemann Educational Books, 1971).

[2]Ibid., 305–6.

[3]Hannah Arendt, *Between Past and Future: Six Exercises in Political Thought* (Cleveland and New York: Meridian Books, 1963), 112–15.

[4]Herbert Marcuse, "Industrialization and Capitalism in Max Weber," in *Negations, Essays in Critical Theory* (Boston: Beacon Press, 1968).

[5]John O'Neill, *Five Bodies: The Human Shape of Modern Society* (Ithaca, NY: Cornell University Press, 1985).

[6]Ludwig Landgrebe, *Major Problems in Contemporary European Philosophy: From Dilthey to Heidegger,* trans. Kurt F. Reinhardt (New York: Frederick Ungar Publishing Co., 1966), 11.

[7]Edmund Husserl, *The Crisis of European Sciences and Transcendental Phenomenology: An Introduction to Phenomenological Philosophy,* trans. David Carr (Evanston, Ill.: Northwestern University Press, 1970).

[8]Max Weber, "Science as a Vocation," in *From Max Weber: Essays in Sociology,* trans., ed., and with an intro. by H. Gerth and C. Wright Mills (New York: Oxford University Press, 1958), 138.

[9]Ibid., 140.

[10]Talcott Parsons, *The Structure of Social Action: A Study in Social Theory with Special Reference to a Group of Recent European Writers* (New York: Free Press of Glencoe, 1964).

[11]Husserl, *Crisis of European Sciences and Transcendental Phenomenology,* 394–95.

[12]Maurice Merleau-Ponty, *Signs,* trans. Richard C. McCleary (Evanston, Ill.: Northwestern University Press, 1964), 59.

[13]Ibid., 96–97.

[14]Maurice Merleau-Ponty, *Themes from the Lectures at the Collège de France 1952–1960,* in *In Praise of Philosophy and Other Essays,* trans. John Wild, James Edie, and John O'Neill (Evanston, Ill.: Northwestern University Press, 1988), 108–9.

[15]Merleau-Ponty, *Signs,* trans. Richard C. McCleary (Evanston, Ill.: Northwestern University Press, 1964), 69.

[16]"Materials for a Theory of History," in Merleau-Ponty, *In Praise of Philosophy and Other Essays,* trans. John Wild, James Edie, and John O'Neill (Evanston, Ill.: Northwestern University Press, 1988), 95–106.

[17]Merleau-Ponty, *Signs,* 75.

[18]Albert Camus, *The Rebel: An Essay on Man in Revolt,* trans. Anthony Bower (New York: Vintage Books, 1956), 306.

Part 2: Preface

[1]John O'Neill, "From Phenomenology to Ethnomethodology: Some Radical 'Misreadings,' " in Scott G. McNall and Gary N. Howe, eds., *Current Perspectives in Sociological Theory* (Greenwich, Conn.: JAI Press, 1980), 7–20.

[2]Maurice Merleau-Ponty, "The Philosopher and Sociology," *Signs,* trans. Richard C. McCleary (Evanston, Ill.: Northwestern University Press, 1964), 110.

Chapter 16

[1]James Agee, *A Death in the Family* (New York: Bantam Books, 1969), 11, 14.

[2]M. C. D'Arcy, S.J., *The Mind and Heart of Love: Lion and Unicorn: A Study in Eros and Agape* (Cleveland and New York: World Publishing Company, Meridian Books, 1956).

[3]Soren Kierkegaard, *Concluding Unscientific Postscript,* trans. David F. Swenson and Walter Lowrie (Princeton, N.J.: Princeton University Press, 1941), bk. 2, chap. 3, sec. 4, "The Subjective Thinker: His Task, His Form, His Style."

[4]José Ortega y Gasset, *Meditations on Quixote,* trans. Evelyn Rugg and Diego Marin (New York: W. W. Norton & Co., 1961), 45.

[5]"The essential is to describe the vertical or *wild Being* as that pre-Spiritual milieu without which nothing is thinkable, not even the spirit, and by which we pass into one another, and ourselves into ourselves in order to have *our own* time." Maurice Merleau-Ponty, *The Visible and the Invisible,* ed. Claude Lefort, trans. Alphonse Lingis (Evanston, Ill.: Northwestern University Press, 1968), 204, my emphasis.

Chapter 17

[1]Cassiodorus Senator, *An Introduction to Divine and Human Readings,* trans. Leslie Webber Jones (New York: Octagon Books, 1966), 133.

[2]Maurice Merleau-Ponty, *The Prose of the World,* ed. Claude Lefort, trans. John O'Neill (Evanston, Ill.: Northwestern University Press, 1973); *The New Science of Giambattista Vico,* trans. from the 3d ed. (1744) by Thomas Goddard Bergin and Max Harold Fisch, revised and abridged (Ithaca, N.Y., and London: Cornell University Press, 1970).

[3]Elizabeth Sewell, *The Orphic Voice: Poetry and Natural History* (New Haven, Conn.: Yale University Press, 1960); Michael Polyani, *Personal Knowledge: Towards a Post-Critical Philosophy* (Chicago: University of Chicago Press, 1958); *Intellect and Hope: Essays in the Thought of Michael Polyani,* ed. Thomas A. Langford and William H. Poteat (Durham, N.C.: Duke University Press, 1968); Hans Jonas, *The Phenomenon of Life: Toward a Philosophical Biology* (New York: Dell Publishing Co., 1966); Erwin Strauss, *The Primary World of the Senses: A Vindication of Sensory Experience,* trans. Jacob Needleman (New York: Free Press of Glencoe, 1963); Maurice Merleau-Ponty, *Phenomenology of Perception,* trans. Colin Smith (London: Routledge and Kegan Paul; New York: Humanities Press, 1962).

[4]Michael Oakeshott, "The Voice of Poetry in the Conversation of Mankind," in his *Rationalism in Politics and Other Essays* (London: Methuen & Co., 1962), 199.

[5]*King Lear,* act V, scene III.

[6]Gertrude Stein, *Lectures in America* (Boston: Beacon Press, 1957), 11.

[7]James Agee and Walker Evans, *Let Us Now Praise Famous Men* (New York: Ballantine Books, 1966), 51–52.

[8]John O'Neill, "On Simmel's 'Sociological Apriorities,' " in *Phenomenological Sociology: Issues and Applications,* ed. George Psathas (New York: John Wiley & Sons, 1973), 91–106.

[9]José Ortega y Gasset, *Meditations on Quixote,* trans. Evelyn Rugg and Diego Marin (New York: W. W. Norton & Co., 1961), 96.

[10]"I am myself plus my circumstance, and if I do not save it, I cannot save myself. *Benefac loco illi quo natus es,* as we read in the Bible. And in the Platonic school the task of all culture is given as 'to save the appearances,' the phenomena, that is to say, to look for the meaning of what surrounds us" (Ortega y Gasset, *Meditations on Quixote,* 45–46). Cf. Julian Marias, *José Ortega y Gasset: Circumstance and Vocation,* trans. Frances M. Lòpez-Morillas (Norman: University of Oklahoma Press, 1970); and Owen Barfield, *Saving the Appearances: A Study in Idolatry* (New York: Harcourt, Brace & World, Harbinger Books, 1965).

[11]Rainer Maria Rilke, *The Duino Elegies,* trans. J. B. Leishman and Stephen Spender (New York: W. W. Norton and Company, 1939), The Ninth Elegy, 75–77.

Chapter 18

[1]Alfred Schutz, *Collected Papers,* vol. 3, *Studies in Phenomenological Philosophy,* ed. Ilse Schutz (The Hague: Martinus Nijhoff, 1966); Alfred Schutz, *Reflections on the Problems of Relevance,* ed. Richard M. Zaner (New Haven, Conn.: Yale University Press, 1970); José Ortega y Gasset, *Man and*

People, trans. Willard R. Trask (New York: W. W. Norton & Co., 1957). John O'Neill, "Mutual Knowledge," in *Changing Social Science: Critical Theory and Other Critical Perspectives,* ed. Daniel R. Sabia, Jr., and Jerald T. Wallulis (Albany: State University of New York Press, 1983), 53–70.

[2]Harold Garfinkel, *Studies in Ethnomethodology* (Englewood Cliffs, N.J.: Prentice-Hall, 1967), chap. 1, "What is Ethnomethodology?" 1–34; and Edmund Husserl, *The Crisis of European Sciences and Transcendental Phenomenology: An Introduction to Phenomenological Philosophy,* trans. David Carr (Evanston, Ill.: Northwestern University Press, 1970), 122.

[3]Garfinkel, *Studies in Ethnomethodology,* 34. John O'Neill, "The Mutuality of Accounts: An Essay on Trust," in *Theoretical Perspectives on Sociology,* ed. Scott G. McNall (New York: St. Martin's Press, 1979), 369–80.

[4]Max Weber, "Science as a Vocation," in *From Max Weber: Essays in Sociology,* trans. and ed. Hans Gerth and C. Wright Mills (New York: Oxford University Press, 1958), 129–56. Cf. Herminio Martins, "The Kuhnian 'Revolution' and Its Implications for Sociology," in *Imagination and Precision in the Social Sciences,* ed. T. J. Nossiter, A. H. Hanson, and Stein Rokkan (London: Faber and Faber, 1972), 13–58; Robert W. Friedrichs, *A Sociology of Sociology* (New York: Free Press, 1970).

[5]Alfred Schutz, *Collected Papers,* vol. 1, *The Problem of Social Reality,* ed. Maurice Natanson (The Hague: Martinus Nijhoff, 1964), 41–42. John O'Neill, "A Realist Model of Knowledge: With a Phenomenological Deconstruction of Its Model of Man," *Philosophy of the Social Sciences* 16, no. 1 (March 1986): 1–20.

[6]Erving Goffman, *The Presentation of the Self in Everyday Life* (Garden City, N.Y.: Doubleday & Co., Anchor Books, 1959); *Relations in Public: Microstudies of the Public Order* (New York: Harper & Row, Harper Colophon Books, 1973); Daniel C. Foss, "Self and the Revolt against Method," *Philosophy of the Social Sciences 2,* no. 4 (December 1972): 291–307.

[7]Desiderius Erasmus, *The Praise of Folly,* trans. Hoyt Hopewell Hudson (Princeton, N.J.: Princeton University Press, 1941), 37–38. Reprinted by permission of Princeton University Press.

[8]James Agee and Walker Evans, *Let Us Now Praise Famous Men* (New York: Ballantine Books, 1966), 290–91.

[9]Gertrude Stein, *The Making of Americans* (New York: Harcourt, Brace & Co., 1934), 128. Reprinted by permission of Harcourt Brace Jovanovich, Inc.

[10]For a remarkable work in this spirit, see John Forester, *Planning in the Face of Power* (Berkeley: University of California Press, 1989).

Chapter 19

[1]Northrop Frye, "The Knowledge of Good and Evil," in *The Morality of Scholarship,* by Northrop Frye, Stuart Hampshire, and Conor Cruise O'Brien, ed. Max Black (Ithaca, N.Y., and London: Cornell University Press, 1967), 16.

[2]Leo Steinberg, *Other Criteria: Confrontations with Twentieth-Century Art* (New York: Oxford University Press, 1972).

[3]John O'Neill, *Sociology as a Skin Trade: Essays towards a Reflexive Sociology* (London: Heinemann; and New York: Harper & Row, 1972).

[4]James Agee and Walker Evans, *Let Us Now Praise Famous Men* (New York: Ballantine Books, 1966), 91–92.

[5]Martin Heidegger, *Essays in Metaphysics: Identity and Difference,* trans. Kurt F. Leidecker (New York: Philosophical Library, 1960).

[6]Agee and Evans, *Let Us Now Praise Famous Men,* 30.

[7]Ibid., 33.

[8]Ibid., 37.

[9]Ibid., 53–54.

Chapter 20

[1]Carlos Castaneda, *The Teachings of Don Juan: A Yaqui Way of Knowledge* (New York: Ballantine Books, 1970), 105–6.

[2]Aristotle, *Rhetoric and Poetics,* trans. W. Rhys Roberts and Ingram Bywater (New York: Random House/Modern Library, 1954); *Aristotle on Dialectic, The Topics: Proceedings of the Third Symposium Aristotelicum,* ed. G. E. L. Owen (Oxford: Clarendon Press, 1968).

[3]W. W. Jaeger, *Paideia: The Ideals of Greek Culture,* trans. Gilbert Highet, 3 vols. (New York: Oxford University Press, 1939–1946).

[4]Paulo Freire, *Pedagogy of the Oppressed,* trans. Myra Bergman Ramos (New York: Herder and Herder, 1970), 76. John O'Neill, "Decolonization and the Ideal Speech Community: Some Issues in the Theory and Practice of Communicative Competence," in *Critical Theory and Public Life,* ed. John Forester (Cambridge: The MIT Press, 1985), 57–76.